A WISEWOMAN'S GUIDE

TO SPELLS, RITUALS AND GODDESS LORE

BY

ELISABETH BROOKE

THE CROSSING PRESS, FREEDOM, CA

Also by Elizabeth Brooke:
An Astrological Herbal for Women
Women Healers Through History

First published in Great Britain by The Women's Press Ltd, 1993
Copyright © Elisabeth Brooke 1993
Published in the U.S.A. in 1995 by The Crossing Press
2nd Printing 1996

Cover design by Amy Sibiga
Cover art by Pamela Moore
Printed in the U.S.A.

For information on bulk purchases or group discounts for this and other Crossing Press titles, please contact our **Special Sales Manager at 800-777-1048.**

Library of Congress Cataloging-in-Publication Data

Brooke, Elisabeth.
    A wisewoman's guide to spells, rituals and goddess lore / Elisabeth Brooke.
        p. cm.
    Includes bibliographical references and index.
    ISBN 0-89594-779-X
    1. Witchcraft. 2. Magic. 3. Goddesses. 4. Goddess religion.
    5. Rites and ceremonies. I. Title.
    BF1566.B745 1995
    133.4'3'082--dc20   95-20304
                                             CIP

The author would like to thank the following:

Associated University Presses, for extracts from *The Planets Within* by Thomas Moore, 1982.

Cornell University Press, for extracts from *Witchcraft in the Middle Ages* by Jeffrey Barton Russell, 1972.

Farrar, Straus & Giroux, Inc, for an excerpt from 'Words Spoken By a Mother to Her Newborn Son As She Cuts the Umbilical Cord' from *In the Trail of the Wind* edited and translated by John Bierhorst. Copyright © 1971 by John Bierhorst. Reprinted by permission of Farrar, Straus & Giroux, Inc.

Peters Fraser & Dunlop for permission to quote from Hugh Trevor-Roper's *The European Witchcraze of the Sixteenth Century*, Penguin, Harmondsworth, 1969.

Princeton University Press, for extracts from *Myth, Religion, and Mother Right* by J J Bachofen, 1967, and *Essays on the Science of Mythology*, by C G Jung, translated by R F C Hull, 1950.

Quest Books for an extract from *The Royal Road* by Stephen Hoeller, 1975.

Reed International Books, for extracts from *The Prophet* by Kahlil Gibran, William Heinemann Ltd, 1966.

Routledge & Kegan Paul, for extracts from *The Science of Mythology* by C G Jung and C Kerenyi, 1985.

Shambhala Publications, for an extract from *Woman as Healer* by Jeanne Achterberg, © 1990 by Jeanne Achterberg. Reprinted by arrangement with Shambhala Publications, 300 Massachusetts Avenue, Boston, MA 02115.

Virago, for an extract from *Of Woman Born* by Adrienne Rich, 1977.

A P Watt Ltd on behalf of The Trustees of the Robert Graves Copyright Trust, for extracts from *The White Goddess* by Robert Graves.

Samuel Weiser, Inc, for extracts from *Aradia: Gospel of the Witches* by Charles Godfrey Leland, 1899.

The Women's Press Ltd, for an extract from *The Moon and the Virgin* by Nor Hall, first published by The Women's Press Ltd, 1980.

Every effort has been made to trace the original copyright holders, but in some instances this has not been possible. It is hoped that any such omission from this list will be excused.

Contents

Dedicated to troublesome hags, crones and harpies
wherever you might be.

1

INTRODUCTION

A book of shadows is a record of spells, rituals, recipes and Goddess-lore which was handed down from mother to daughter in the wisewoman tradition. No one has seen one. Perhaps they were burned, along with their owners in the burning times, or maybe they are a wishful myth created by latter-day witches cut off from their roots. We will never know. The Inquisitors did their job well and only hearsay and whispers of dreams remain of the witch culture prior to the Witchcraze.

This book is about my relationship with the Goddess, as I express it through the practice of witchcraft. I have brought together my learnings and experiences, with history and traditional practice (as far as they are known), to present a personal account of witchcraft as it is practised in the West in the late twentieth century.

The Goddess is everywhere, immanent. She is the creatrix of the universe and is found at the beginning of all life, and at its close. The Great Mother gives birth to all living things, and they return to her as they die. From the Goddess radiates all the power and beauty of the natural world. And it is this power and this beauty that witches embody.

The Goddess empowers women and for this reason many modern witches are feminists. Witchcraft gives us a vision of ourselves which is whole and encompasses both the darkness and the light. A wholeness which is denied by Fathergod (the male god of the Christians, Jews and Muslims). In patriarchal religion, Fathergod embodies only what is good, while woman holds all that is evil. In contrast, the Goddess promises both wisdom and clarity, power and compassion, joy and sorrow. She speaks to us of a balanced world.

In Chapter 3 on the Goddess, I discuss how she was usurped by Fathergod. In telling two versions of the myth of Persephone I aim to show how the shift from woman as Goddess to woman as slave and rape victim was accomplished. Myths were and are used to teach us values, and rules to live by. The Greeks were no exception. The myth of Persephone was changed from the matriarchal myth of a woman's journey deep into herself to the patriarchal story of rape and abduction. It clearly shows us how the peaceful values of the Goddess worshipping people were replaced by the violence and force of the Fathergod.

The book reflects my interest in history (herstory) and the value I place on it. Women need to re-write our history not once or twice, but a thousand times and in a thousand different ways for it to survive and counter the negative images Fathergod promotes.

Our foremothers come from all over the world, particularly from the great continent of Africa, but our ancestry is a common one. The Egyptian Goddess Isis who found her way to these shores was carried by ancient seafarers through Greece, Spain and France. The Celts of Britain and Ireland were strongly influenced by the mystery traditions of the Egyptians and Chaldeans.

The peoples of Europe, the Middle East and India exchanged their mystery traditions, through traders and scholars. When the burning times came to Europe, this knowledge went underground and was kept alive by country folk and wandering tribes of gypsies.

Witchcraft is almost universally regarded as harmful. This reflects not only the misogynist culture which knows no boundaries (most witches are still women), but often a very realistic fear of those who play with occult forces. The accusations made against witches are the same made against any minority, whether racial, religious or ethnic: infanticide, sexual perversion and conspiracy to shatter the status quo. The latter, although often lost in the hysteria surrounding the two former changes, is the bedrock of persecution of any minority. For clearly and logically, any persecuted minority would want things to be different. When force makes decision, subversion has to be the order of the day. In this respect, witches are no different from any other persecuted people (see Chapter 4).

It has to be stated clearly that witchcraft has nothing whatever to do with Satanism or any of the perversions which come under that name. Satanism is a corruption of the Roman Catholic faith, the Black Mass is the centre of its practice. Its rituals centre around blood sacrifice, sexual exploitation and sadomasochism and are a distortion of Christian teachings. *Witchcraft has nothing to do with these practices.* The Craft abhors them.

Witchcraft pre-dates all of the patriarchal religions by millennia and is completely separate and independent of them. Many of the Christian festivals were lifted wholesale from pagan/Wiccan traditions in a conscious campaign to replace the Goddess with the Christian God. (see Chapter 5.) Part of this campaign to dethrone the Goddess was to remove any power, spiritual or temporal, from women. To do that women were accused of being anti-life, evil, dirty, devilish. From this, the witchcraze grew into a world-wide belief in the evil of women. Misogyny can be traced directly back to the appearance of the patriarchal religions. These beliefs are now so firmly enshrined in our culture that it is extremely difficult to imagine a time when they were not so. Unconsciously the fear of witches remains a potent and disabling force. Witches are seen as the epitome of evil, the embodiment of the dark, devouring Mother and, much more importantly, the forces of chaos. 'The crime of magic is the crime of rebellion.' (The Book of Samuel.)

The green women and men of these islands took to the hills to escape the religious persecution of the Christians, but they did not die. The body of the earth soaked up their blood. The north wind blew the ashes of their funeral pyres into the Cairns and Holy Wells. The screams of tortured women were lifted high above the clouds into the noonday sun. The sweat of the brow of the abused and downtrodden peasant mingled with the rich, red earth, and the oak tree grew.

Witches did not die; they went underground until such time as the stranglehold of the Christians loosened a little. They waited for a time when it would be safe to worship the Mother, when they might again celebrate the wheel of the year and the moon's passage through the night sky, and dance through the midsummer meadows.

Magic is power. As we begin to work with occult forces

the vexed question of how we use that power arises. We are accustomed to being – or perceiving ourselves as – powerless. Feminist witches are defining a new ethic which allows us personal and collective power, without oppressing anyone else. Our magical behaviour must be constantly appraised in the light of this ethic. Our spells, our rituals and thoughtforms must be harmless.

Patriarchal religion has a common theme of woman hatred and the bondage and exploitation of nature and all those who are vulnerable. This has led us to the rape and poisoning of the very earth we walk on and the air we breathe. Witchcraft and Goddess-lore offer an alternative to the slow, inexorable slide into perdition. Rebuilding our tradition is one of the greatest contributions we, as individuals, can make to saving our planet. The values of witchcraft are life enhancing, nature-celebrating, peaceful and tolerant. These values are needed urgently in the culture of death that is the legacy of Fathergod.

The witches I have associated with are feminist witches, whose practice for the most part came about through the second wave of feminism in the 1960s and 1970s. As we researched into our common history we uncovered a genocide of women, starting when patriarchal belief systems replaced the Goddess worship. The horror of our findings prompted many of us to go back into pre-his-story to find a time when equality and respect were our birthright.

We were searching for the time before. Before the life denying rule of Fathergod. Over the years evidence has accumulated to prove that there was a time when women were worshipped, when we were respected, when we had both spiritual and worldly power.

Feminism, therefore, colours witchcraft. But so does a revulsion against the materialistic culture Fathergod has created. People, surfeited and often sickened by excesses of materialism, or denied access to its fruits, are becoming increasingly aware of the opposite pole, the spiritual.

Religion and spiritual practice make sense of, and provide an antidote to, the glamours of the material world. When times are hard people look for explanations of their suffering and search for a meaning to their lives.

Witches are a polymorphic body, loosely constructed of like-minded folk who share certain beliefs and practices. For the most part, they celebrate the eight festivals, and the thirteen full moons. Most will be involved in some kinds of divination, and have a knowledge of astrology. They will have some understanding of plant lore and may be gardeners. Many keep cats.

There is no one form of witchcraft, and not all witches worship the Goddess in the ways I have described; some, for instance, worship the God as the masculine polarity of the Goddess. But our spiritual practices are not designed to replace Fathergod with Mothergod as a hierarchical system. Instead we believe in immanence, the Goddess within. This belief sees everything as sacred and no one act as being of more value than another.

In Chapter 3 on the triple Goddess, I talk about the witch's concept of the spiritual. Through the myth of Demeter and Persephone the three faces of the Goddess, maiden, mother and crone, emerge. Visible, her three faces show in the moon's phases, and in the waxing and waning of the solar year.

Witchcraft is closely related to the natural world, and wise-women use the cycles of both sun and moon as touchstones and reference points for their own cyclic development. The moon is close to the life of woman, and her cycles reflect those of this most mysterious planet. Through the waxing and waning of the moon we come to understand the fluid nature of our bodies, and we can learn to use those changes in the most creative ways. Chapter 6 on starcraft and the moon discusses the full moon in each sign of the zodiac and how to fit magical work in with the astrological year.

Witchcraft is a celebration of life, and the yearly festivals (Chapter 8) mark the changing seasons and different stages in our lives. The rituals at the eight main festivals as well as the new and full moons help to anchor our spiritual practice. The ebb and flow of life as described by the sun's journey around the zodiacal year mirrors the death-rebirth cycle of all life.

In Chapter 7 on ritual I show how the changing face of the moon reflects both the monthly menstrual cycle and the life cycle of maiden, mother and crone. Plants and all natural life are integral parts of that great round and the yearly festivals mark the changing seasons and the mystery teachings which they reveal. The celebration of the witch's year gives a structure to our lives and yet leaves room for individual creativity and preferences.

Witchcraft can be as simple or as complex as you choose. The rituals I have written about will give an idea of what is possible and can be used as a template for readers who wish to develop their own rituals.

Creating new and vivid ritual is vital. As a culture we are undergoing the profoundest of changes and many people feel deeply alienated and powerless in the face of this upheaval. The traditional ways have, for the most part, long since gone, and have been replaced by an ersatz TV culture of consumerism and greed.

Witches value nature as having worth in itself and not as goods which can be translated into money. We favour ecologically sound practices in agriculture, in industry, and responsibility in the way we share this beautiful planet of ours. Feminist witches align themselves with the peace movements, with ecology and human rights campaigns.

Herbal lore is another magical practice kept alive despite the concerted efforts of the ruling classes to stamp it out. Plants can reveal the innermost workings of the Earth Mother and are integral to any practice of witchcraft (see Chapter 13).

Witchcraft is about empowering the individual not solely for her own sake, but so that she might then be a useful and valued member of society. The concept of service is discussed in Chapter 9 about ethics. Any work on self-development is undertaken so that we might participate fully in life, not as an end in itself.

I have tried only to write about things I have had personal experience of or which I have studied. For this reason, people-centred skills are fully represented. Many witches choose to do personal one-to-one work as a way of re-cycling spiritual energy. Chapters 11 and 12 on psychic skills and Tarot give a taste of these two fields of service. The images of the Tarot hold the key to the Western mystery tradition. Disguised in picture form to prevent profane eyes understanding them, these cards are deeply esoteric. Together with astrology, the

Tarot is the cornerstone of our magical tradition, and their study has been preserved despite 500 years of persecution by the patriarchs. The chapter on the Tarot discusses the history of the cards as well as my own interpretations for all the cards of the major and minor arcana.

Witches need to understand the nature of the subtle bodies so they might use their energy wisely. The chakras and the etheric and astral planes teach us about our own inner workings as well as the ways we interact with others. The chakras show us how we exchange energy with our environment. Chapter 11 on healing and psychic skills discusses the etheric body and the chakra system and gives some practical exercises to develop psychic skills.

On saying I am a witch, people often jokingly ask if I can do a spell for them; sometimes they are not joking. Spells are acts of will which can transform reality. In Chapter 10 on spellcraft I discuss how spells can change lives. I have included some ordinary spells which can be done to find work, a lover or protect yourself. Women need to develop such skills and to find creative ways to deal with our violent, materialist culture. In this respect, witchcraft encourages self-determination and responsibility rather than passivity and the acceptance of being a helpless victim.

This book is written in dedication to the Goddess, the immanent divinity of the roses in my fire place, the healing herbs a friend grew and brought me, the scent of sandalwood, and the soft aroma of cooking apples. All these things remind me of her presence in my life. The biting Siberian wind and the egg-blue sky speak of the darkness of this past winter and promise spring and new beginnings. The wheel of the year moves on carrying our lives with it. This is her mystery.

> Conjure, with your dreaming
> moonlight shadows.
> Dance in solemn steps
> This mystery.

Elisabeth Brooke
Beltane, 1993

2
HERSTORY

In the beginning, there was no time. People wandered the earth searching for food, warmth and shelter. Ice covered the land. Slowly the ice began to melt and the long winter gave way to a fertile spring. As the sheets of ice retreated further and further northwards, the earth which they uncovered unfurled its green shoots. In the wide grasslands the first plants grew, followed by bushes and finally trees. The land became covered with grasslands and forests. Animals, birds, insects and flowers flourished. Eating berries and ripe fruits, the wanderers trapped animals and noticed the changing seasons, times of plenty and times of darkness. Travelling across the land they were guided by the sun during the day and by the moon and stars by night.

Afraid, and very small in so vast a land, the people looked to the sun and moon as their guides, as spirits which protected them. The sun always moved in the same direction and remained constant, but the moon, mysterious light of the darkness, changed her shape. Like the women in the tribe, she sometimes swelled as if full of spirit and at other times she was not there. The darkest of nights. People within the tribes, older women, young girls before their first bleed, began to take the light of the moon, who had become Mother, into their bodies, and young men took in the male god of the hunt, dressed in skins and horns. These sacred workers travelled into the Otherworld of shadows, spirit realms, where the moon kissed them and the sun warmed their bones and they were taught all mysteries. They knew how to fly with the dead ones and take their spirit home to the Mother. In the Otherworld they learned how to make the sacred drinks to heal the sick and to read omens for the hunt.

The people began to settle, at first in caves and later, as more families gathered together, they built huts of wood and stone and moved down on to the plains. As the communities grew, laws were made from tribal customs and the clan elders formed councils. Sacred potters made images of the Goddess, the Great Mother of All whose ample breasts and belly brought health and fertility to the tribe. Drawings were made in caves of the hunt, the gods of the chase, and the Old Ones who carried the sun and moon.

Millennia passed; the Old Ones became the Great Ones, their civilisations flourished: in Sumer, Egypt, Atlantis. They watched the passage of the stars, charted them and the divine science of astrology was born. They counted, and saw and recorded the sacred symmetry of numbers. Watching the souls of the dying and the incoming of the new-born, they followed the soul's passage through the many heavens. Studying sickness and health they theorised on the body and its relationship to the soul, and made healing plasters and elixirs. They looked for omens and auguries to make sense of the vicissitudes of their lives; the plagues, the floods, the curses and blessings. They named their gods and built shrines to them, and the shrines grew into temples and then whole cities were dedicated to the Goddess.

Great in their glory, the power of the Great Ones was awesome and terrible, and behind the lesser gods was the Cosmic Mother of All, whose breasts poured milk into the firmament and who birthed new stars, whose curved and luscious body was the very earth they trod on. Her undulations were the forest, grove, copse and spring. Immanent, she was everywhere. In each rock, each leaf, in the lowliest animal and in the greatest. She nursed them all, brought them to life, held them as they grew, fed and protected them, and when their time was over, she took them back to her.

Burrows were made and stone circles, temples and high towers; she was worshipped in fields and groves, in towns and on the wildest shore. The land grew rich with grains, all manner of fruits and sweet wine, and with the beasts of the field and the birds of the air.

The temples flourished. Priestesses of the Goddess, who had many names, presided over birth and death, the blessing of fields and the building of cities. They became rich, their rites

more complex, their caste more separate. This was a golden
time when peace reigned. But as ripened fruit soon rots these
idylls perished by fire and flood and bloodshed. Atlantis, the
sacred island, was subsumed by a great wave, all its glory
washed away like so much shingle. The primeval waters of
the Mother washed away the greedy and corrupt priestesses,
who, forgetting her, imagined her power was their own and
used the sacred Kundalini[1] fire for temporal things.

Tilted dangerously in the soft blue waters of the Mother,
the world shifted on its axis, madly tumbling its helpless
people into the fire of blood and iron.

Men came, hordes of them from the southern deserts, in
wave upon wave, from the northeastern wastes. At first they
fell under the spell of the Goddess, but as more and more
poured in, wielding swords, raping and burning their way
across the land, the rule of the fathers smashed the Mother's
paradise. Everywhere the world went mad. The invaders
moved downwards, and the tide of rape, pillage and bloodshed was unstoppable. Omens did not help, neither did sacrifices. Once begun, the hordes who knew no gods but war
and no beauty but blood and iron, raped and pillaged and
enslaved all women. Priestesses were hung by their hair in
sacred groves, temples and shrines were burned, desecrated,
defiled.

With fear and hatred they took over, and with an iron glove
they ruled. There was no end to their audacity; they usurped
the Mother Goddess and put a father in her place. The people
were afraid. They gathered in fields, in market places, in
shrines and caves, frightened at what the Mother might do,
what terrible vengeance she might wreak.

Plagues came, wave upon wave of terrible sickness. People
died screaming in agony in the streets; there was no god.
Thousands upon thousands were choking on their own blood,
with swelling, blackened limbs, deadly boils. The Black Death
swept with the Reaper's cloak across the land. Crows picked
the eyes off corpses and the Morrigan stalked the land. Hecate
in her nighttime places urged rebellion. The pustule of the
Father, which the people called love, burst open, spewing
forth all manner of demons. People died in agony, crops failed,

wars raged. Godthefather in his death-head mask replaced life. All hope was gone.

He had, they said, sent his only son, the Prince of Peace, avatar of love, but the men of the Father killed him too, like Odin, nailed to a cross. The Prince of Peace, who overturned the money-lenders' sordid trade, and had his sacred whore, the Magdalene, closest to him. His words fell like raindrops on a parched desert; priests of the Father quickly kicked over the traces and carried on as before. Embodying the mirror image of love, their darkness knew no end, no depth too low for them to sink.

With force and fear they conquered and spread a putrid stain across the world. No corner was safe, they sailed to the farthest lands, the fairest people, and butchered them.

The Old Ones took to the hills, when persuasion and discourse failed. They moved away from the new cities of pomp and gilt, to the Mother's sacred groves and mountainsides. They hid and kept their counsel.

Fear kept them from writing. The Old Ones moved, roamed around, nomads again, telling their tales, curing and counselling. Speaking of ancient myths of sacred lineages they carried news from sacred groves to every hearth and orchard where a welcome waited for them and the Old Ways were kept alive. They still watched the stars and kept to the eight sacred festivals. Watching the moon move from dark to full, they calculated poetic meters, the names of the Goddess and the centuries that might pass before peace prevailed. They hexed and healed with incandescent verse and watched over their healing sisters as they laid out the dead, birthed new life and mothered the clans.

The darkness grew. The father's men grew more afraid that the common people would not swallow the lie and did not set much store by empty rituals. Neither did the fine monuments or churches, nor the bones of saints move the heart of commoners. They looked for their Goddess and found a sterile Mary, a pale replica of the fecund thighs and belly and the wild, deep mysteries of the Mother. In small wells and shrines they worshipped. The priests danced alongside them at festivals, whose names they changed, in the hope the people might forget their origins. But the spirit had gone. Where was this love of God they preached? They listened to sermons of hell-fire and damnation, of their wickedness, their filthiness, their sin. But the people saw other things, the whorehouses the priests ran, and the wine shops. They saw the priests' wealth while they themselves starved. They saw how their greed was like a canker, how they wore robes of the finest silks and satins, huge jewelled rings and crucifixes, and how they carried golden goblets and filigree salvers while the people shivered outside in coarse robes, shoeless in the snow, with the tithes to be paid even if there was no food for the table.

War was declared against all unbelievers. Great armies, men, women, clerics, walked and rode to Jerusalem, the Holy City. They left behind a land starved and parched. These soldiers of Christ were promised blessings in the after-life while their families starved and anarchy followed in their wake. The sacred world of the Goddess splintered further and further. The rich grew richer and brought untold wealth from far lands. They brought disease and famine.

As the Holy Wars were fought, plague after plague deci-mated the people. They became angrier, more desperate and some planned rebellion, revenge against the All Powerful Mother brought low.

The people gathered in mountain groves, in secret caves, on beaches in the moonlight. They were afraid. This was the Mother's curse, the land laid bare. Nothing prospered, no green shoots or chinks of light were seen. In despair they called to Her and other avenging gods: Hern the hunter, Hecate the revenger, Themis the wise. The Fathergod gave them no hope, offered only more pain and suffering in a dark place called Hell. Groups formed, societies, sororities of seekers after truth, who wished for peace, for a return to order and an ending to all the bloodshed.

The father's men responded in kind, declared another war, a break between crusades and the conquering of Paradise. They declared all witches should be burned, tortured to the very limits of human endurance. Their money would fill the coffers of the church, and they would denounce their friends and family. Law after law was passed; there was no hiding place. Europe was aflame with the pyres of burning women. Children, pregnant women, the old were burned by the purifying fires of the Father. Half a millennium later nine million women were dead and society was rent from bottom to top. No woman was safe, not one.

Witch, witch, witch. An icy fear ran through the veins of each woman. It meant rape, torture and death by hanging or burning. But not before she had named twelve accomplices and watched her children tortured or burned before her eyes, screaming. The inquisitors grew fat, protected by their henchmen and armour beneath their robes. They went about in fear of revenge. Some few were indeed strung up by outraged families – but not enough. The inquisitors carried their evil into the New World, and tortured and killed their way across the continent.

The Wise retreated further, although the hills offered precious little protection. Family clans turned in among themselves, exchange stopped, no one talked or even looked the other in the eye. There was silence.

You cannot kill a people, a culture. It lives on, after the last person has been slaughtered. In the rocks, the trees, the rivers, in the very winds which moisten the land. The spirits wait in sacred hollows, in springs and rock pools until the bloodletting has finished.

3

THE TRIPLE GODDESS

... below the surface of sensory experience and beyond
the generalisations based upon its phenomena, there lies an
area in which the sources of a culture can be found. These
sources, since they are below the surface, cannot be directly
observed, but their character can be inferred from their
expression in art and religion. Frank Boas[1]

Where do we go to look for our roots? Where can we find
them? Writers such as Johann Bachofen and Jane Harrison[2]
sensed there was something that was not being said. Writing
in the middle of the last century Bachofen suggested that the
fact the Roman patriarchal system was so suppressive implies
it was actively engaged in crushing an earlier, matriarchal
system. The same was true of the ancient Greeks[3] who put
motherless Athena at the top of the female pantheon and set
her against the Amazonian warriors who were seeking to
defend the rights of women. The Greeks' emphasis on purity
suggests a whitewash.

Myth, Bachofen contests, ' . . . must form the starting point
for any serious investigation of ancient history. Myth contains
the origins, and myth alone can reveal them.'[4]

There are many myths I could have looked at which would
have told the same story – Innana, Isis, the Celtic round – but
I have chosen the Greek myth of Demeter and Persephone for
several reasons. First because the work that has already been
done on this story makes it fairly easily accessible, but more
importantly, because the ancient Greeks themselves both
assimilated and reworked the myth. The rape of Persephone
mirrored the actual rape of the matriarchal culture, as the
northern invaders swept through southern Europe. The rape-
myth buried the real meaning, a woman's descent into herself

to find her own buried treasure. The culture of Mother Right, as Bachofen calls it,

> . . . belongs to a cultural period preceding that of the patri-archal system; it began to decline only with the victorious development of the paternal system. The matriarchal forms are observed chiefly among the pre-Hellenic peoples and are an essential component of this archaic culture, upon which they set their imprint as much as do patriarchal forms upon Greek culture.[5]

The union of immortal mothers with mortal fathers, the empha-sis on maternal property and maternal kinship, gave rise to the terms 'mother country' and 'motherland'. The maternal principle produces a sense of unity, which dies once the idea of paternity dominates. Mothers connect and fathers divide. Matriarchal states were famous for their freedom from conflict[6] and it was from them that the notion of family derived, cele-brated in their great festivals. They regarded injury to their fellow humans and to animals as serious crimes. (Women were the first judges; Hannibal in his pact with the Gauls stipulated all disputes were to be settled by Gallic matrons.[7]) Where the Great Mother was worshipped, women's stature was high, as the relationship between Demeter and Persephone (Kore) shows. Their high status gave them priestly functions, which is in accordance with the mystery of woman: ' . . . mystery is inherent in the law of Demetrian motherhood, manifested to woman in the transformations of the seed grain and in the reciprocal relation between perishing and coming into being.'[8]

In this culture it is the womb as nurturer of the seed which has primacy, and leads to night being valued more highly than day. Time was counted by nights; it was the time for taking counsel, for meting out justice, for ritual. Matriarchy gave preference to the moon over the sun, the dark aspect of death over the luminous aspect of life, the dead over the living, of mourning over rejoicing. The feminine names for devotion and justice show their roots to be in matriarchal culture, as do the qualities of rectitude, piety and culture.

There are numerous examples of women who wished to settle while men, who preferred the nomadic life, resisted them. Civilisation and culture grow around a woman and her family.[9] Children need stability, a constant food source and education. A society which values women prioritises these areas and culture flourishes. Conversely, a patriarchal society values fighting and conquest above domestic life.

Strabo (63 BCE-24 CE) writes about the culture-bringing, benign power of women as follows:

> ... the fear of God, which first dwelled in woman and which she implanted in the men. It was believed that woman was closer than man to the godhead and endowed with a superior understanding of the divine will. She embodies the law of matter. She manifests justice unconsciously but with full certainty, she is the human conscience ... That is why women were held sacred, regarded as the repositories of justice, the source of prophecy. That is why the battle lines parted at their bidding, the priestess was an arbiter who could compose quarrels among nations. And this was the religious foundation of matriarchy. Woman was the source of the first civilisation.[10]

I tell the myth of Demeter and Persephone twice, to illustrate my point. The first, patriarchal, account is the generally accepted version. Here it is the male which awaits Persephone underground (in the mother's terrain?) and it is he who impregnates her, giving her the sacred child. In the second version, it is Persephone herself who elects to go underground as she cannot bear the cries of the dead. One is forced, the other voluntary. We might see the myth as the great round of nature reflected in the waxings and wanings of our own lives. And most importantly, it teaches of the fecund, transcendental nature of darkness.

PERSEPHONE'S REALM

THE PATRIARCHAL MYTH OF PERSEPHONE

First the common post-matriarchal myth. Persephone, the daughter of Demeter, the Greek Earth-Grain goddess, was out

persephone, queen of the underworld

picking flowers one day with two of her girl friends, Artemis and Athena. Leaving her companions in a nearby meadow, she saw a beautiful flower with a rich, narcotic scent and leant forward to pick it. As she did, the earth split open and she fell into the abyss. Her screams were heard by Demeter, her mother, and Hecate, who was in a nearby cave. For nine days, Demeter, without eating or bathing, bore two burning torches as she sought for Persephone. On the tenth day she encountered Hecate, also bearing a torch (making three) and together they went to Helios, the sun, who was the only witness, to ask what had happened to Persephone. The sun told them that Persephone had been abducted by Hades, Lord of the Underworld.

Demeter let out a howl that chilled the whole world, and from that moment on nothing grew; the earth became barren. Her daughter, who was a part of herself, a maiden, had been abducted and raped by an alien force, man.

All mothers watch this happen to their daughters, who are, in a sense, torn from them and initiated into the world of men. Men rape them and keep them in bondage, but give them the gift of life. For Persephone returns with the divine child, which is not hers but is born of her body. She has been initiated into a great mystery.

The Demeter–Persephone myth reflects the pre-patriarchal myths of the Triple Goddess, the Great Mother. The trinity comprises Persephone the maiden, Demeter the mother and

Hecate the crone. Hecate was in a cave as befits the crone or Dark Mother of the Shadows; she saw the rape and met Demeter carrying a torch. Three torches, two goddesses, looking for the innocent Persephone, who will never be the same again. Mother, maiden and crone, the ancient three faces of the Great Goddess, which becomes a quadruplet when the son is born.

But Persephone has to die to inherit her kingdom (for she becomes Queen of that realm, not slave), she has to die to separate from her mother, to grow up. Is the rape a symbol of the psychological death, intrusion of the unconscious, which erupts like earthquakes, often when we feel at our most sublime, into the innocence of ignorance?

Like Hades/Pluto bubbling up from the darkness to shatter old forms, liberating, demanding recognition and payment for the riches which myth tells us are hidden deep within the earth. So what is hidden there in the underworld? The kingdom Persephone inherits? We learn she has eaten the pomegranate, the fruit sacred to the Goddess, given her by Hades/Pluto to bind her to him. Once she has eaten the seeds she must return for one third of the year – lest she forget? Or no longer practices what she has been taught? And she emerges with the gift of life, a child, but a male child, another alien being.

While searching for Persephone, Demeter comes to the land of the king of Eleusis. Inconsolable, she sits by the well outside the palace gates, known as the Well of Beautiful Dances. The king's daughters find her as they come to draw water. Recognising Demeter as a noble woman, they give her water and feed her and offer her work tending the child of the king.

Demeter is offered wine by the king's wife but she refuses it and instead has a mixed drink made from barley, water and mint, prepared in a special vessel to break her fast. As a goddess, and by way of thanks, Demeter decides to make the king's child immortal, by putting him into the fire every night. She is caught by them and tells them that they are wrong. Good appears evil, and evil good, in the twisted world of men. She was giving the greatest gift there is to the king's son, a treasure beyond price, immortality. And the blind and ignorant mortals think she was killing him. This is her mystery.

Demeter is goddess of the grain, and grain needs to be cooked with fire; cooking the child with fire makes him immortal. Fire burns, fire purifies, from the ashes of the funeral pyre the phoenix rises.

Demeter reveals herself as a goddess and demands a temple should be built to her above the Well of Beautiful Dances. It is built. She withdraws and continues her mourning. Demeter fasts, Demeter rages and the world is laid waste. Then Persephone reappears (in some myths Hecate goes to find her, in others, Hermes). She reappears but she is no longer child to the mother, rather she is mother to the child. Mothers and their daughters are a continuum.

Persephone returns to the world and is greeted by Hecate, and the two are from that time on inseparable. She sees the crone, who before had been in the cave, in the shadows. Persephone acknowledges the crone, embraces her and from that time forth shares her life with her. The maiden who has become the mother greets the crone and they are united.

So Persephone has had an experience which has enabled her to see the ugly, hag-face of the Goddess, for Hecate, too, is a goddess. She has been transformed. She, too, has been in the fire.

Who lives in the underworld? Hecate was Queen of the Underworld until the patriarchal pantheon usurped her. It was her realm. Now she lives in a cave, still in the darkness, but not underground. But it is Hecate who with her torch seeks out Persephone, descends into the land of the dead to find her. In the underworld a nightmare awaits the maiden, the Gorgon, the real nightmare woman, whose head is alive with slithering, hissing serpents, whose hideous face and deadly eyes petrify men. She is the devouring mother belching blood, the great leveller; king and commoner alike are turned to stone. No one escapes her gaze. And she, of course, is Persephone: 'a monstrosity that has usurped the place of the unimaginably beautiful, the nocturnal aspect of what by day is the most desirable of things.'[11]

Persephone has seen herself. In the darkest, most desolate of places, away from all comforts and support, she confronts the nightmare. Abduction, rape, the horror of the Gorgon's head. And yet she emerges from this nightmare impregnated.

Full of life, but transformed. And she embraces not only her mother, but Hecate, the usurped queen of her realm. And Persephone does not come back only as a mother, eating the seed (of immortality?). She is forever bound to the Gorgon's head and will never forget her experience in the underworld. Whenever she is mentioned in the Iliad she is awful, this goddess of the underworld, and she will hear curses and enact them. When the earth is beaten with hands, this terrible goddess is summoned. Lady of death. She has seen the Gorgon's face and has embraced it, and carries it with her as she carries the monster's gift of life.

She has seen the blood of the mother, and blood is woman's mystery:

> 'A woman's life is close to the blood. Every month she is reminded of this, and birth indeed is a bloody business, destructive and creative. A woman is only permitted to give birth, but the new life is not her creation. In her heart of hearts she knows this and rejoices in the grace that has fallen to her. She is a little mother, not the Great Mother. But her little pattern is like a great pattern. If she understands this she is blessed by nature, because she has submitted in the right way and can thus partake in the nourishment of the Great Mother . . . [12]

She is not Perseus who needs to cut the head of the Gorgon (Medusa) with a moon-shaped sickle; she takes the hideous mother inside herself, and the serpent sheds its skin and becomes a child.

And she emerges into the sunlight. She does not become petrified; she embraces life. But she never forgets. And if she tries, the seed (which has taken root) reminds her. The seed of the pomegranate will, in turn, give birth to the fruit. Nature and life are cyclical and immortality comes through fire. There is no going back. We may choose to step forward into the black hole, the unknown, or, lacking faith, we can stay petrified on the edge of the abyss, preserved for all time in a pathetic sterility. In the unreal mists of the nether world, neither dead nor alive, just breathing. But Persephone leaps into the blackness and is born again in fire. 'Brimo has given birth to

Brimos, the Strong One to the Strong One. [Brimos is Queen of the dead, Brimo the wanderer by night, the subterranean goddess of the underworld.] The Queen of the dead has given birth in fire!'[13]

Eleusis

For two thousand years the mystery of Eleusis was the most sacred and secret rite of classical civilisation. It was never acted on stage and only open to initiates who had previously undergone a long purification.

It is said that after Demeter and Persephone were reunited, Demeter returned to her temple at Eleusis and initiated the Kings into the Mystery. The rites were inaugurated somewhere between 1400 and 1100 BCE and were considered vital for the spiritual life of the ancient Greeks. The rites were *bios* (life) to the people of Athens who could not live life (*abiotos*) without them. Initiates of Eleusis were blessed (*olbios*). ' . . . the psychology of the Demeter cult has all the features of a matriarchal order of society where the man is indispensable but on the whole a disturbing factor.'[14] Kerenyi[15] estimates around 30,000 people took part in the rite, probably most of the population of Athens – women as well as men. But no one who had spilt blood could be initiated into the mysteries of Eleusis, the dark rites of the triple goddess were no place for the crudities of warriors. This ritual was celebrated every year and was steeped in power and mystery.

The dream-nightmare of Persephone (*arrhetos koura* – the ineffable maiden) and Demeter (she who bears fruits) was re-enacted each year at the seed-sowing season in Attica which fell in the month of Boedromion – Jane Harrison, an English anthropologist working at the beginning of the century, calls it Pyanepsion – (October–November – our Samhain). The rite was celebrated in the last third of the month, days 11 to 13, where: '[the] moon is robbed of itself and goes wandering in search of the ravished portion until it at last reached total darkness.'[16]

In common with all Goddess rites, the ritual began at night. Holding aloft burning brands, the initiates, dressed in mourn-ing and wreathed in myrtle, snaked their way along the long road to Eleusis. Some women carried the sacred wicker baskets or *cista* on their heads. Willow, from which the baskets were woven, was sacred to the Goddess, a snake curled around the big basket, *cista mystica*, which contained a replica of the womb.[17] Pigs, sacred to the Goddess, were sacrificed in her honour, by throwing them into rock clefts. (A swine herd and his pigs were said to have fallen into the underworld with Persephone.) The following year they were drawn up and laid on the altar and the blessed remains were then mixed with the seed before it was sown.

Initiates of the lesser mysteries of Agrai, a suburb of Athens, proceeded in the night, lit by similar torches to the ones Demeter and Hecate had lit to find Persephone Queen of the Dead. Shrouded, they became the brides of death, surrendering to the forces of darkness. Fasting, like Demeter, they wandered as if searching in the darkness.

On the first night the initiates were called for a secret rite. On the second, the women fasted sitting on the ground, like Demeter on the Smileless Stone by the Well of Beautiful Dances. They were silent and pensive. The cry rang out: 'Keep solemn silence. Keep solemn silence. Pray to the two Thesmophoroi, to Demeter and to Kore'.[18]

Then the celebrants plunged into the sea connecting with the watery Great Mother, baptising and replenishing themselves. The initiates then proceeded to the temple of Demeter at Eleusis where the rite began. Led into the deepest recesses of the sacred building the initiates were shown the three faces or sides of the mystery: the doing, the saying and the showing. The initiate confession has been found: 'I have fasted; I have drunk the mixed drink; I have taken out of the *cista* [little chest], worked with it, and then laid it in the basket and out of the basket into the *cista*.'[19] Mother to the child and child to the mother, from chest to basket and back again, but giving homage to the dark, barren fasting mother, who gives the mixed drink, water and wine, or blood and milk.

'Initiate' means to close, to close the eyes and ears and mouth and open the other sense, the esoteric sense, to this the greatest of mysteries. To watch the sacred dance of Eleusis, to be beguiled by its beauty and then to see or not see, as all lights were extinguished.

As the torches were doused, the priest and priestess enacted the sacred marriage, the rape, not of Persephone but of her mother, Demeter, who is forced into marriage with Zeus. The rape of the mourning mother heals. 'Amid total darkness the gong is struck, summoning Kore from the underworld; the realm of the dead bursts open . . . Suddenly the torches create a sea of light and fire, and the cry is heard. "The noble goddess has borne a sacred child".[20] Wrought in fire, fashioned in darkness, life bursts upward. These cries echoed around the bay of Eleusis, which means place of happy arrival. The cries echoed and the light could be seen by all Athens as it flashed across the water. Even the profane could share in the mystery.

Who is who in this story? Two raped women? Two sacred children? Or just the age-old myth repeating itself. In silence, the grain of corn is shown to the initiates, the 'perfect great light that comes from the ineffable'.[21] The abduction and rape, the penetration by an alien force and the birth of the sacred child, do not imply it is the masculine which forces a re-birth or reconnection with the mother, but the woman who 'fecunds herself'.[22]

Only then has the Feminine undergone a central transform-ation, not so much by becoming a woman and a mother, and thus guaranteeing earthly fertility and the survival of life, as by achieving union on a higher plane with the spiritual aspect of the Feminine, the Sophia aspect of the Great Mother, and thus becoming a moon goddess.[23]

Because Persephone becomes a Goddess, she becomes im-mortal. A light-bearer, mother of the divine child, she can no longer be abducted by Hades because she is immortal and beyond his reach.

In a fifth-century BCE relief, found at Eleusis, the Goddess Demeter (Kore) and a boy, Triptolemus, were depicted. Tripto-lemus is the primordial man (son of the Goddess) who must come to Demeter for the gift of grain. He is converted from a violent, warlike way of life, to a peaceful, agrarian existence. He is supposed to have disseminated three commandments: honour your parents, spare the animals, and honour the gods with fruits. Demeter's son is invested with the grain of wheat to distribute throughout the world. He cannot, a man, construct or locate the chthonic (relating to the underworld) and fecundating female, but he can be given the gift of it by woman. He is given a chariot drawn by dragons. The golden grain is the priceless teaching of the Mystery. Men who were initiated at Eleusis were forever marked:

> Happy is he among men upon earth who has seen these mysteries; but he who is uninitiate and who has no part in them, never has like good things once he is dead, down in the darkness and gloom.[24]

On the last day of the mystery (day 13) two unstable, circular vases were set up. Called the *Plemochoai*, the pourings of plenty, one sat facing east, the other west. As the contents of these vases were poured on to the ground the priestess said: 'Flow! Conceive!'[25] The milk and the blood, two precious fluids, the stuff of life, water and earth, the mother and the maiden. Women's Mystery.

> A woman lives earlier as a mother, later as a daughter. The conscious experience of these ties produces the feeling that her life is spread out over generations – the first step towards the immediate experience and conviction of being outside time, which brings with it a feeling of immortality . . . An experience of this kind gives the individual a place and a meaning in the life of generations, so that all unnecessary obstacles are cleared out of the way of the life stream that is to flow through her. At the same time the individual is rescued from her isolation and restored to wholeness. All ritual preoccupation with archetypes ultimately has this aim and result.[26]

The sanctuary was destroyed, after 2,000 years, by the northern barbarians; the Goths under Alaric invaded Greece in 396 CE. This fulfilled the prophecy which claimed that when Eleusis fell, so would Greece.[27]

But not all men faced with the terrible mother embrace her. Perseus killed her with a sickle, its moon-shaped blade used to harvest crops, cutting her head from her body, a patriarchal act, and 'de-powered' her. Or so he hoped. She just went further underground. The labyrinths were even more tortuous, the obstacles far greater. But she did not die. Her head gloats above every battlefield and she laughs her manic laugh that funeral pyres try to destroy. A friend to fascists, murderers, rapists, bigots, inquisitors alike, the maggot-headed Gorgon still lives in the shadowy in-between worlds, her death rattle audible in the spaces between worlds.

The Triple Goddess, Great Cosmic Mother of All, forms the basis for my beliefs and those of many witches. Her three faces reflect the three stages we go through in our lives, Maiden, Mother and Crone, as the new, crescent moon, the full moon and the dark of the moon (see Chapter 6, p. 61).

THE MOTHER

When in the presence of something overwhelming one is silenced by the magnitude of the experience. It is mysterious because it is ineffable – there are simply no words to explain. Experience that cannot be articulated is generally under-valued in a world ignorant of the mysteries. Such a world creates psychic havoc for people whose mode of existence is feminine, for people who have given the greater part of their lives to woman's work – bearing children, caring for the living, and tending the dying. They are made to question their intrinsic worth because they haven't any words to convey the essence of primary experience.[28]

Mother, the Great Mother, is our first relationship on which all subsequent relationships are based. She is the face we see as we die. Holder of the ineffable mysteries of life, woman in whose arms we nestle, knowing our very survival depends upon her. No wonder we are deeply ambivalent, why worship-pers of godthefather quake at the thought of their dependence on her. Burping, shitting, fractious infants, they did not spring out of any head fully grown, washed and dressed. Rather, they were birthed, along with blood, shit and mu-cus, as their mothers strained and sweated, panting and cursing the awesome pain of it. Some men never recover from the trauma of seeing their women give birth, some women never recover from it themselves.

Followers of Fathergod contort themselves to control this first, last and greatest female mystery. In some places it is illegal for women to minister to a woman in labour. The fathers and their henchmen elbow women aside, women who know, who have given birth themselves, and push and bully and demean virtually the last sacred rite a woman has. The sacred becomes the profane and women are encouraged to become unconscious before they give birth, lest they become privy to the mystery. This is the curse of Eve, but Lilith is Eve's handmaiden and midwife. The walker in shadows and dweller on the threshold, she knows death's chill breath. With a foot in each camp she holds Eve's hand during this most perilous of journeys. For it is the closest the living come to dying. Africans say a woman in labour is like a woman on a log floating downstream on a wide, wide river. Helpers can stand on the river bank, shouting encouragement, but she is alone on her log, in the river. Fathergod has drained the river, chopped up the log, and he pokes the woman from time to time, impatiently waiting for her to finish. She is alone, and there are no well wishers; their hands are tied and their mouths are gagged – they've been arrested. She lies prone, pushing against gravity, shaved, her legs splayed like a centrefold so Fathergod can see her mystery. Unaware that the mystery is one of participation, not voyeurism, he misses the point and sharpens his scalpel.

Words spoken by a mother to her newborn son as she cuts the umbilical cord:

I cut from your middle the navel string: know you, understand that your birthplace is not your home . . . This house where you are born is but a nest. It is a way station to which you have come. It is your point of entrance into this world. Here you sprout, here you flower. Here you are severed from your mother, as the chip is struck from the stone.[29]

The story of motherhood has rarely been written by mothers;

the psychology of the child-mother relationship is written focusing on the child's, not the mother's, trauma. Mothers are to blame for everything and yet do not deserve praise when things go well. In patriarchy mothers are guilty. They are blamed for rising crime figures, for vandalism, for infantilising or castrating their sons, or for not teaching them the rules.

Susan Brownmiller, writing about rape, cites the case of the Boston Strangler. Psychiatrists made a profile of him, saying he would have had a 'seductive, punitive, overwhelming mother', that he was probably homosexual and consumed by mother-hatred. When Albert DeSalvo was caught it was revealed he was genuinely attached to his mother who was in fact not overwhelming or suffocating. His father, however, was a brutal drunk whom DeSalvo hated. His father had regularly beaten his mother and her children and had once broken all the fingers of her hand, whilst knocking her teeth out. He had intercourse with prostitutes in front of his children and had abandoned the family when Albert was eight years old.[30] (It is not clear why Albert didn't kill men; perhaps he was too afraid of them.)

The relationship of mother to son is not always according to the patriarch's fantasy. Adrienne Rich, for example, writes evocatively about a summer spent with her three young sons without an adult male, without the rule of the father:

we fell into what I felt to be a delicious and sinful rhythm . . . we ate nearly all our meals outdoors, hand-to-mouth; we lived half naked, stayed up to watch bats and stars and fireflies, read and told stories, slept late . . . we lived like castaways on some island of mothers and children . . . I remember thinking: This is what living with children could be – without school hours, fixed routines, naps, the conflict of being both mother and wife with no room for being, simply, myself.[31]

I write of mothers, today, on a bitterly cold winter's day, in London, deep in recession. The shock of seeing young men sitting on the pavements wrapped in thin blankets has faded for me. An old, black woman is talking to one of these boy-children; she's giving him food and a can of coke, telling him

he must keep warm. He looks embarrassed. I feel a rush of
pity, grief and longing for her mothering, her unselfconscious
tenderness. And anguish for the motherless sons and daughters of the Fathergod overwhelms me.

The mother who is at the beginning and at the end of all
life is degraded and enslaved by patriarchy, but her numinous
love cannot be eclipsed. Whatever the fathers tell us, in our
hearts it is our mother's truths we long for. We might glory at
the transient pleasures of Fathergod, but as we lie sick and
bleeding we call for the mother, remembering those hands
that first tended us and held on to us so tightly.

> Your children are not your children.
> They are the sons and daughters of Life's longing for
>   itself.
> They come through you but not from you,
> And though they are with you yet they belong not to
>   you.
> You may give them your love but not your thoughts,
> For they have their own thoughts.
> You may house their bodies but not their souls,
> For their souls dwell in the house of to-morrow,
> which you cannot visit, not even in your dreams.
> You may strive to be like them, but seek not to make
>   them like you.
> For life goes not backward nor tarries with yesterday.
> You are the bows from which your children as living
>   arrows are sent forth.[32]

THE MAIDEN

'The original witch was undoubtedly black, bisexual, a warrior, a wise and strong woman, also a midwife, also a leader
of her tribe.'[33] When we think of maidens, we think of light-
haired girl-children with soft voices, delicate, sensitive and
pretty insubstantial. When witches talk about maidens we
mean the mirror opposite. Girl-cubs (*arktoi*) of Artemis were
chosen at nine years of age and wore the saffron bear-robes,
learned to hunt and to dance the pack of she-bears. They
were fierce, they were wild, they were strong and athletic.

Artemis, queen of the Amazons, liked her women tough and they started their training early. Pre-pubescent girls learned archery, to ride wild horses, to wrestle, to scry, to measure and to perform all the sacred rites, in short, to be warrior-priestesses.

Diana-Artemis, Goddess of the Witches and Amazon Warriors of ancient Thrace, Libya, Macedonia. Lesbian goddess, riding the clouds; huntress, tamer of lions; also thousand-breasted Artemis of Ephesus and dark crone of the cross-roads Hecate. Hers, the face of the waxing, waning, dark moon. She flourished in the Bronze Age around the Mediterranean, in Marseilles and Syracuse. In Ephesus a temple was built by Amazon warriors around 900 BCE in the shape of a beehive. Her rites were conducted by *Essenes* (castrated male priests) and *Melissal* (bee) priestesses. The Black Diana was kept at Ephesus and on her head was the diopet, the sacred Neolithic stone. It was smashed by a Christian in 400 CE in the mistaken belief that he had destroyed the 'Demon Diana.' Statues of the Black Madonna found in Mediaeval Europe are believed to be of the Black Diana, who can be traced back to the Black Egyptian Goddess Isis.

In Rome, Diana was protectress of the downtrodden and disenfranchised, the slaves, outlaws, thieves, of women. Amazons of north-west Africa (now Morocco) were called Gorgons and Medusa was one of their queens. The myths of Gorgon slaying may refer to actual battles fought with Greek patriarchs, just as they fought Macedonian Amazons. They wore goat-skin tunics and carried magic serpents in their pouches. Suetonius said that Amazons ruled over a large part of Asia (as late as 500 CE the Black Sea was known as the Amazon Sea).[34] Herodotus, a Greek historian of the fifth century BCE, spoke of Libyan Amazons. These warriors were said to have been the first to tame horses and were famed for their skills on horseback. Barbara Walker[35] claims that Amazons founded the cities of Smyrna, Ephesus, Cymes, Myrine and Paphos, which were all centres for matriarchal worship. They came to the aid of matriarchal Troy. Their queen Penthesileia was killed in battle by brutal Achilles who violated her corpse, thus showing his contempt for the rule of women. He wanted to 'immobilise her wrathful spirit'.[36]

Called the Beautiful Ones, the souls of dead Amazons had shrines built to them by the Trojans and for centuries sacrifices were made to them. Theseus, king of Attica, kidnapped the Amazon Queen, Hippolyta, and forced her to be his bride, contrary to all Amazon customs. Thus began the patriarchal takeover. Enraged, the Amazons ravaged the Greek coast and besieged Athens. The Greeks and the Amazons became hereditary enemies and the latter joined under queen Artemisia with Xerxes to fight the Greeks at the battle of Salamis in 480 BCE.

The islands of Lesbos, Taurus and Lemnos were said to be islands of women. The warriors of Taurus sacrificed any man who landed on their shores and legend had it that the women of Lemnos had risen up and murdered all their husbands at once. These women lived entirely without men, only consorting with the opposite sex at ritual times in order to conceive.

The Valkyries were the Amazons of Northern Europe, together with the warrior queens of the Celts and the Irish. Traditions of women warriors abound. Lewis Spence[37] is clear about the lineage of witches:

I believe it [witchcraft] to have had its beginnings in a caste of women associated with horse breeding or cattle-raising, or both, as the entire folklore of the cult has reminiscences of association with the horse and with domestic cattle. In some such caste, I think, as that of the Amazons of classical lore may possibly have been the prototype of the witch cult. The tendency of the witch to bespell cattle, her obvious power over flocks and herds, and her traditional aspect as a horse-using sorceress has led me to believe that somewhere in North-West Africa a female religion arose out of the usages of such a body of women as I describe, which later lost its significance with respect to pastoral affairs, and became purely and simply magical and occult. That it was thus of 'Iberian' origin is also highly probable.

Amazons are maidens, are virgins in the sense they belong to no one; they are the wild hunting bloody maiden form. But Persephone or the Kore – another name for Persephone – is another story.

lady of the wild things

THE MATRIARCHAL MYTH OF PERSEPHONE

Persephone, according to pre-patriarchal myths[38] is maiden to the mother Demeter. (The grain-mother was originally Cretan.) Persephone, the grain-maiden, is the new crop. Demeter brought to Attica two gifts: the grain and the rite of initiation. The Homeric Hymn to Demeter, written around 700 BCE, is a story written about the celebration of the Eleusian mysteries.[39] It was called the Rape of Persephone. But in the pre-Olympian myth there is no mention of rape. The Mystery is believed to have come from the Egyptian Isis cult and transmitted to Athens via Crete. 'Concerning the feast of Demeter ... It was the daughters of Danaus who introduced this rite from Egypt and taught it to the Pelasgian women.'[40]

Egypt was a matriarchy which worshipped the goddess Isis. As Queen of Heaven Isis passed freely in and out of the underworld. The role of Egyptian women is summed up by Sophocles speaking of the daughters of Oedipus:

Ah! They behave as if they were Egyptians,
Bred the Egyptian way! Down there, the men

Sit indoors all day long, weaving;
The women go out and attend to business.[41]

In Athens the dead were called Demetreioi (Demeter's people).
She received people back into her body when they died. The
womb which births the child takes it back in death. For this
reason only the mother mourned her dead. Weeping over the
death of her child, Demeter initiated the cult of mourning
which was carried out in deep, subterranean caves. (Virgil,
describing the underworld, uses the term *matres atque viri* –
mothers and men –; after death only the mothers remain.)[42]

According to Athenian law, burial sites were sowed with
wheat to purify them and to give them back to the living. The
seed of the pomegranate in turn gives birth to the fruit.
The first pomegranate tree sprung from the blood of Agdistis,
the bisexual, primordial Great Goddess. When she was emas-
culated the blood from her wound fell on the earth and the
first tree sprung up.[43] Souls nibbled the pomegranate seeds
which were left on Attic graves.

Persephone was also called Phesephatta, goddess of the
underworld in Attica. It is likely that her 'rape' was a re-
working of the myth which told of the invasion of the northern
barbarians.

The myth, according to Charlene Spretnak, runs as follows.[44] In the beginning, the world knew no winter. Flowers
and fruits blossomed and ripened in a continual cycle (the
Garden of Eden). People moved from hunter-gatherers to settled tribes and the goddess Demeter, who watched over her
people, gave the gift of grain (wheat) to the women that they
might further prosper. Persephone, her daughter, watched
over the crops with her mother. She was especially fond of
the young plants, the green shoots of wheat. As the crops ripened in the summer sunshine, Persephone wandered the
hillls gathering narcissi, hyacinth and myrtle for Demeter,
and red poppies, which grew between the wheat, for herself.
On her wanderings Persephone met the spirits of the dead
hovering around their earthly homes, restless. Persephone
asked her mother why there was no one in the underworld to
receive the newly dead, to welcome them and make them at
home. Demeter told her that the underworld was her domain

but she felt the living were more important. Persephone became haunted by the suffering of these spirits. She could no longer enjoy the beauty of the earth, thinking of their suffering. She resolved to go into the underworld herself and receive these spirits. Collecting three poppies and three sheaves of wheat she was led by Demeter to a cleft in the earth. Her mother gave her a torch and slowly, alone, Persephone descended into the underworld. Snaking down the dark, dank passageway, Persephone made her way in silence until she heard the moans of the dead. Rounding a corner she found an enormous cavern filled with tormented spirits, the dead wandering and moaning in despair. Standing on a low, flat rock, Persephone prepared her altar which comprised Demeter's torch and a bowl filled with pomegranate seeds (food of the dead). As each of the spirits approached her she anointed them with pomegranate seeds and said:

You have waxed into the fullness of life
And waned into darkness;
May you be renewed in tranquillity and wisdom.[45]

For months Persephone received and blessed the dead. Meanwhile, Demeter grieved the loss of her companion, her daughter. She roamed the earth hoping to find her emerging from one of the secret clefts in the earth. She sat and waited, while the earth grew barren; seeds were planted but no growth occurred.

One morning a ring of purple crocuses grew (purple is a colour of mourning) and surrounded Demeter as she sat on the hillside. Astonished that any living thing should ignore her interdict, she leant forward to hear them whisper, 'Persephone is coming, she returns!' Demeter leapt up and rushed through the earth to meet her. As she passed by, leaves budded and flowers burst out, and the earth erupted into life again. Birds sang, animals shed their winter coats and Demeter wove a cloak of white crocuses for Persephone. And from that time forth, every year mortals would wait with Demeter as Persephone, now Queen of the Underworld, gave succour to the souls of the newly dead.

THE CRONE

There is something in the darkness that waits for us women, which gives us life. Without the winter stillness no seeds could grow. Before the birth there is the long, pregnant pause, the gestating of ideas, building of forms. The aching, when-will-it-ever-be-over cries of the darkest hours are but a hairs-breadth from dawn. The darkness is the nightmare land, but also the place where life begins, with untold riches, the mysteries. For without Hecate's torch or Persephone's need to give succour to the spirits of the dead, there is an imbalance; too much light. Too sweet, bloodless.

> Half lived lives
> walking into darkness
> Engaging the Muse
> who becomes
> The Gorgon's head
> Engaging her

We need conversations with the dead. Hecate of the wild things leads us down into nightmare, down into life. 'Three-headed, nocturnal excrement-eating virgin, holder of the keys [maiden?] of the underworld, Gorgon-eyed, terrible dark one.'[46]

Ravens, crows, snakes, spiders, bats and all manner of creepy-crawlies slither and swirl around the crone. Night-mares, the horses, the Crone, death-goddess rides as she swoops down and picks up souls to take to the land of the dead. Barbara Walker describes the Indian Dakini who 'was supposed to take the final breath of the deceased into herself with the "kiss of peace".' And other psychopomps (Shamanic ritual figures) of the pre-Christian tradition, the Slavic vilas, Teutonic Valkyries and the Celtic Morrigan, had the power to rebirth dead souls by sucking them into themselves with the final kiss, and that death in their arms could be ecstatic.[47] The Crone was the sweet kiss of death, the glamorous spirits of the air, the flying serpent, the castrating witch devouring men's genitalia, drinking blood, weaving shrouds, wandering the labyrinths of the dead. Shaman, she passed freely from the world of the living to the world of the dead, slithering down on the world pole, the tree of life, flying as crow or dragon, she learned the secrets of death and rebirth, of healing, and worked in the world above with the sick and dying.

But she was also the tribe repository of wisdom, of lore and legend, weaver of dreams, woman of the wild seas, keeper of the sacred fires and stirrer of the cauldron, the vessel of life. Running with wolves, haunting crossroads, goddess of the sour and bitter, she was the nest-destroying mother who had the evil eye of piercing judgement, the ancient aesthete who left behind things of the world, of childhood and family, and took to the roads, the hills and the forests, living in shadows, baying at the moon. Hecate of the wild things, queen of the night, sweet mistress of all that flourishes in velvet nights. Drinker of blood, keeper of the dead, erupting and chaotic force who periodically destroys old forms that new life might grow. Spiritual pruner and watcher over time. Some call her the dweller on the threshold, reader of the runes, spinner of fate. The crones who knitted and who sat by the guillotines as the corrupt aristocrats lost their heads during the French Revolution were ladies of Hecate, crone, flesh-eater, with her bubbling cauldron of blood and milk, life, death and life. Hers was the great round, ending so it might begin again, beginning that it might end. Aware at the summer solstice when night draws nearer and death is never far away, and at the darkest winter moment when the warm winds of summer beckon. Terror of that which is the most beautiful, most sublime, turning into its mirror image, slime-ringed, serpent-haired raving fury, spitting venom with a cloak of bats, frogs and toads hopping beside her, snakes and lizards on her arms, nightmare, mother of the night, when brave knights' armour tarnishes and bold words and deeds come to nothing. Whose face do warriors see at the moment of death? The Crone, always the Crone, providing comfort, succour or sweet release from fear and pain.

Lilith, who was found in Sumer, Babylon, Assyria, Canaan, Persia, and in Arabic, Teutonic and Hebrew mythology, was known as Vampire lady, End of all Flesh, screeching owl, serpent, dog. 'Lilith is an instinctual, earthy aspect of the feminine ... It is a pulsating, throbbing, primal, wordless

36

state of being.'[48] She chooses the desolate wilderness and the company of demons rather than be subject to, or lie underneath, Adam.[49]

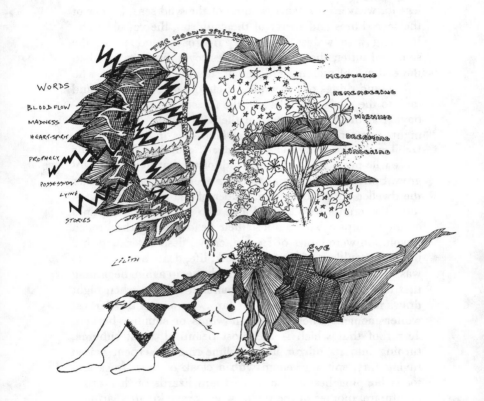

Wild cats will meet hyenas there,
The satyrs will call to each other,
There Lilith shall repose
And find her a place of rest (Isaiah 34:14)

Wandering in the wilderness, crawling, howling, making animal sounds . . . connected to the Goddess in her orgiastic rites, riding to the very edge, throbbing, pulsating, flesh-tearing, sexual abandon. She is the alien woman; honey is said to flow from her lips[50] through the mystery of her adornments (she has no hands and feet; they were cut off by God for seducing Eve); she fornicates with men who sleep alone. She also hangs out by a crossroads 'like a despicable harlot, and takes up her position to seduce the sons of man.'[51]

> Eve is the life nourishing side of the instinctual feminine, while Lilith is its death dealing opposite . . . Lilith rules the Equinoxes and the Solstices. Like Hecate, her powers are greatest at the instinctual crossroads of a woman's life: at puberty, at each menstruation, at the beginning and end of pregnancy, motherhood and menopause.[52]

The Patriarchs imagined a war between Eve and Lilith. Eve can have her needs met in relationship; Lilith cannot. Lilith is forever childless and without love, free-ranging and wandering wild and windy places, while Eve is safe at home. They regard each other jealously, but they are not enemies. Grown women see the need for both faces of the moon, the split root.

> There was a time when you were not a slave, remember that. You walked alone, full of laughter, you bathed bare bellied. You say you have lost all recollection of it, remember . . . you say there are no words to describe it, you say it does not exist. But remember. Make an effort to remember. Or, failing that, invent.[53]

4

WITCHCRAFT FROM PRE-HISTORY TO THE BURNING TIMES

Many volumes could be written about the history (herstory) of witchcraft and Goddess worship, and many points of view encompassed. History is never objective; it is necessarily coloured by the prejudices of the writer, her cultural, racial and political position. Add gender to this heady mix and the subject becomes emotive, hysterical (from *hyster* – womb), and passionate. For when we discuss witchcraft we are talking about our mothers and the mythic Great Mother, about whom no one is ever neutral. The story of witchcraft tells of the battle of Father-right against Mother-right, and the Fathers' (Patriarchs') war against the feminine principle as she is expressed by nature, cyclical life and the body of Woman.

We have to understand the happenings which have shaped current practices in both myth and actuality, although as we move further back into Foretime[1] our reading of the signs becomes increasingly subjective. Myth and legend, however, do tell us about the culture which they reflect, and as such cannot be discounted in the absence of 'hard evidence'.

In her epic studies on the Goddess in 'pre-history', Marija Gimbutas[2] has painstakingly unearthed evidence of matrifocal, if not matriarchal, societies. Goddess-centred religion is said to date back to Paleolithic times when the goddess of fertility was worshipped.[3] Cave paintings and Goddess figurines depict the Goddess in her Great Mother aspect with ample breasts and belly, sometimes pregnant. The Great Mother was worshipped in all cultures, albeit with different names.

Witchcraft takes its teachings from nature, and reads inspiration in the movements of the sun, moon, and stars, the flight of birds, the slow growth of trees, and the cycles of the seasons.[4]

Witchcraft developed more than 35,000 years ago, with the thawing of the Ice Age. As the ice moved southwards the tundra filled with life. Herds of beasts roamed the plains. Hunter-gatherers walked the land. Shamans attuned themselves to the spirit of the herd, 'and in so doing they became aware of the pulsating rhythm that infuses all life.'[5]

Priestesses embodying the Mother Goddess and priests embodying the Horned God performed rites, worshipped the changing seasons and observed the movement of the stars, eclipses and other natural phenomena. They were the teachers of the tribe, the law-makers and judges, the healers and midwives. In short they represented divine authority, mother and father figures to their people. As the ice melted and the grasslands spread further southwards, the tribes turned to fishing and herbcraft. They developed new tools and slowly isolated families collected together in small villages where the shamans and priestesses cared for the spiritual and material well-being of their people.

THE EARLY DAYS OF GODDESS WORSHIP

No one knows for sure how witchcraft came about. I suspect it evolved from two main sources. The first was the religion of the Goddess, which was the religion of pre-history. From her worship, many mystery traditions evolved. Witchcraft is predominantly a religion of women and as such it can be said to represent a matriarchal tradition. Witchcraft encompasses many of the skills a matriarch embodies. Observance of seasonal customs, divination, healing, plant lore, myth telling and starcraft. Probably these talents developed over many centuries through empirical experience. Women were custodians of these arts because their lives were more home-based and concerned with the spiritual life of the community, the rearing of children, agriculture, pottery, weaving, and care of the sick and dying. The absence of leaders in witchcraft mirrors the ways women tend to organise, that is co-operatively rather than through hierarchy and domination. I see witchcraft developing through groups of women in communities exchanging skills, swapping recipes and comparing experiences.

After the destruction of the temples of the Goddess, her priestesses melted into the rural communities where they carried on their worship hidden from the jealous eyes of the patriarchs. They passed on their traditions to lay women and the ancient lore was passed down from mother to daughter, until the witchcraze broke the connection.

In her book *Woman as Healer*, Jeanne Achterberg describes a Danish Shaman, Thorbioga, who was especially honoured and became a legend:

> She was dressed in a gown of green cloth, buttoned from top to bottom, had a string of glass beads about her neck, and her head covered with the skin of a black lamb, lined with the skin of a white cat; her shoes were made of calf's skin, with the hair on it tied with thongs, and fastened with brass buttons; on her hands she had a pair of gloves, of a white cat's skin, with the fur inward; about her waist, she wore a Hunlandic girdle, at which hung a bag containing her magical instruments; and she supported her feeble limbs by leaning on a staff, adorned with many knobs of brass.[6]

As life became more settled the priestesses and shamans worked earth magic, working with power lines or ley lines and celebrating the four great quarter days and the four festivals. Huge stone monuments were used to mark out burial mounds and compass points and to form a focus for rituals.

> With each ritual, with each ray of the sun and beam of the moon that struck the stones at the times of power, the force increased. They became great reservoirs of subtle energy, gateways between the worlds of the seen and the unseen.[7]

These tribes of pre-history travelled far and wide, and there was a cross-fertilisation of ideas and religious practice. Robert

Graves[8] recounts the history of the matrilineal tribe of Tuatha de Danaan. The tribe invaded Ireland in the middle of the Bronze Age, having previously been driven northward through Greece as a result of an invasion from Syria, and reached Ireland by way of Denmark. The date of its arrival is recorded as 1472 BCE. The Tuatha de Danaan worshipped the Goddess Danu. Their shrine at Argos was the religious capital of the Peloponnese until its capture by the Phoenicians.

Recorded in the Irish Book of Invasions, and confirmed by Bede's *Ecclesiastical History* is another invasion 200 years after the Danaans. These people came westwards from Thrace, through the Mediterranean and out into the Atlantic. They landed at Wexford Bay and were met by the Danaans who persuaded them to move on to northern Britain. They were known as the Picts (Pixies). The women of the tribe participated in battle like the Amazons.

Graves[9] suggests a close connection between the ancient British, Greek and Hebrew peoples. He claims that around 2000 BCE a sea-faring tribe was displaced from the Aegean by invaders from the north-east and south-east, and that some wandered north along established trade routes and reached Britain and Ireland, whilst others went to Syria and Canaan. Thus,

> modern Catholicism, is, despite the patriarchal Trinity and the all-male priesthood, based rather on the Aegean Mother-and-Son religious tradition, to which it has slowly reverted, than on its Aramaean or Indo-European 'warrior-god' elements.[10]

Warrior tribes swept through the plains of Europe throughout the Bronze Age (the first invasion into Thessaly was about 1900 BCE) forcing the peaceful goddess worshippers to flee to the mountains. They continued with the Old Religion, celebrating the festivals and using poetry, myth and magic to teach. The Poetic Colleges of Ireland and the Colleges of the Druids were related to the fairy folk and preserved the traditions through song and poetry,[11] as these fragments of a poem, 'Cad Goddeu' (The Battle of the Trees) beautifully demonstrate.

> I have been in many shapes,
> Before I attained a congenial form.
> . . . I have been a drop in the air
> I have been a shining star.
> I have been a word in a book.
> . . . Enchanted for a year
> In the foam of water.
> I have been a poker in the fire.
> I have been a tree in a covert.
> There is nothing in which I have not been . . .
> When I was made
> Of the blossoms of the nettle,
> Of the water of the ninth wave,
> I was spell-bound by Gwydion,
> Great enchanter of Britons . . .[12]

The tales and romances were told by Welsh minstrels who had not been co-opted by the church but, as Graves notes, were 'popularly credited with divinatory and prophetic gifts'.[13] They were descended from the original Welsh master poets who were excluded, or who chose to exclude themselves, from the courts of their conquerors, the Cymry. The Cymry came from the north of England in the fifth century CE and held in bondage the many smaller Welsh tribes of Goidels, Brythons, Bronze Age and New Stone Age peoples and aboriginals. These minstrels wandered the land entertaining under trees or in houses and kept alive an ancient literary tradition which Graves claims goes back to the Stone Age.[14] Their poetic principles are summed up in the Red Book of Hergest: 'Three things that enrich the poet:/Myths, poetic power, a store of ancient verse'.[15] These poets, who were judges and priests, were called *fili* in Irish (seer) and *derwydd* (oak seer) in Welsh. They were feared as well as respected:

> But let a man offer the least indignity to an Irish poet, even centuries after he had forfeited his priestly functions to the Christian cleric, and he would compose a satire on his assailant which would bring out black blotches on his face and turn his bowels to water, or throw a 'madman's wisp' in his face and drive him insane.[16]

The monotheistic patriarchal religions, culminating in Christianity, began their bloody domination of European culture. At the outset their inroads into the matriarchal religions were slow but gradually the ruling classes converted and then by force or persuasion they converted their serfs. In Britain and Ireland, however, it was a process of assimilation and compromise. In Ireland, in particular, the new Christian beliefs were co-opted by the priests of the Old Religion with hardly a blink of their collective eyelids.[17] Those who had been the Druids, ancient forebears of the shaman priests and priestesses, became the poets who studied 12 long years, learning by memory history, myth, secret languages and law. Their poems came from the Otherworld and a poet's initiation was like that of a shaman,[18] a solitary journey where the mysteries were taught by experience and understood at all levels of being.

As the Greeks, a Northern tribe some time previously known as the Achaeans, moved southwards they encountered pastoral tribes who worshipped the Triple Goddess.[19] At first the invaders were won over to the worship of the goddess. 'The Greeks learned that this magic worked, and discarded their patriarchal ways.'[20] The Greek male god Dios was adopted by their goddess, Hera, as her son and re-named Zeus. As more tribes moved southwards, the two traditions met head-on and '. . . cultural warfare became at this point a very conscious campaign'.[21] The leader of the Achaeans declared that Zeus had no mother and a religious war ensued. The battles between Zeus and his wife Hera (a name of the Great Goddess) reflect the war between the patriarchs and the Mother Goddess. With the sack of Troy (around 1200 BCE) Greek power was further limited. About 200 years later an Indo-European tribe swept down into Asia Minor and Europe, killing, sacking and burning their way through the peaceful matriarchal cultures. Those who were able to escape the barbarian hordes fled in all directions. The nineteenth king of all Ireland, Heremon (circa 1267 BCE), was one of the tribe of Milesians from Spain which was said to have come from Greece in the second millennium BCE and to have visited Crete.[22]

High priestesses of Rhea and Athena were hung from an

oak tree by their hair with anvils tied to their feet until they swore to accept Dios as supreme and foreswear Rhea. Fifty Pallantid priestesses of Athens leapt into the sea rather than submit to the new patriarchal religion. Urgent discussion amongst the invaders resulted in the Pantheon being 'fixed', as Zsuzsanna Budapest puts it. Zeus became the almighty ruler while Poseidon was moved from forests to the Ocean. The Triple Goddess as nymph was married off to Hephaestus the smith and re-named Aphrodite. The Goddess as maid was called Artemis, huntress of the wild. But she was made twin to Apollo (who was originally a mouse God) to increase his status. The Athenians and Boeotians were outraged as Artemis was their goddess and they demanded a bigger role for her. She was then given her name of Athena back, but only by being re-born through Zeus's head. This denial of her mother showed the patriarchal intention to kill off matriarchal opposition by a false re-working of biology.

In the underworld 'the patriarchs went wild'.[23] Hecate, triple goddess of that Queendom, was abolished. But the resulting public outcry caused the patriarchs to accord Persephone as wife of the new ruler Hades, brother of Zeus. Budapest claims that 'Her marriage was . . . nothing less than Rape. And so the stage was set for a sexist society. The entire Western world lifted the values and male domination structure from the Greek model.'[24]

A similar story was re-enacted throughout other parts of the world. In Egypt, for example, Ra deposed Hathor and Isis, while in Babylon Marduk brought forth the whole universe. In Christianity, the cult of the Virgin Mary replaced worship of the Goddess and the story of the Divine child was fitted into Goddess myths. Eve, whose name means *havla* (life), was the goddess in her mother form eating the apple which represented wisdom, and with her companion, the serpent, a death and rebirth symbol.

In England, priests often led the dance at the great festivals of Sabbats[25] and the shamans and priestesses became Wiccans or shape-shifters (from the Anglo-Saxon to shape or bend). They continued working with divination, prophecy, healing, poetry and teaching. Earth magic was still practised within the cult of Mary, while the sacred wells of the Goddess were bathed in by Christians, Celts and Druids alike. Women worshipped the Goddess in a thousand small ways in their daily lives:

> decorating tables, wearing laurels, taking omens from footsteps, putting fruit and wine on the log in the hearth, and bread in the well . . . Women call on Minerva when they spin, and . . . observe the day of Venus at weddings and . . . call upon her whenever they go out upon the public highway.[26]

Within the courtly traditions of the Middle Ages Mary was praised as a goddess and many of the exquisite cathedrals were built in her name. But at the same time she became firmly established as subject as:

> For the first time in history the mother kneels before her son; she freely accepts her inferiority. This is the supreme masculine victory, consummated in the cult of the Virgin – it is the rehabilitation of woman through the accomplishment of her defeat.[27]

Until well into the Middle Ages, witches were used both privately and publicly for divination, healing and weatherwork. Walker recounts how, in 1382, the Count of Kyburg hired a witch to stand on the battlements of his castle and raise a thunderstorm to disperse an army of enemies. Churchmen said witches could control the weather 'with God's permission' and were not punished for this until the Renaissance.[28] But the terrible political, social and religious upheavals of the Middle Ages resulted in peasant uprisings, and severe penalties for those who challenged the status quo. Plagues decimated the population in Europe, while the Crusades uprooted millions of people and disrupted the ordinary cycle of life. Wars between fledgling nations created lawlessness, with robber barons pillaging the countryside and there was famine and anarchy in the streets.

The end of the Middle Ages heralded three centuries of the most unspeakable cruelty, directed at those who were perceived to threaten the stability of society. Conspiracy theories are notoriously hard to prove but though we can never be sure, it is probable that the witchcraze was a conscious campaign by the ruling classes to consolidate their power. It has also been suggested that it was an unconscious projection of inner conflicts. Whatever the reason, women, Jews and all other outsiders were considered fair game as victims. They were hunted down ruthlessly, tortured and died in their millions. The worst excesses of Christian repression took place on mainland Europe, within and around the battle between the Protestant and Catholic arms of the church.

Thou shalt not suffer a witch to live (Exodus 22:18)

Like a dark shadow, the burning times are forever branded on our minds. We cannot forget that our foremothers were tortured; we cannot forget their pain and the paralysing fear all European women felt as the Inquisitors went about their bloody trade. We cannot forget this, nor should we. Such wounds leave deep scars. Our collective psyche, our knowledge of ourselves as women has been beaten and terrorised out of us. The deadly message we imbibe with our mothers' milk is that to be female is not to be sacred. We are the source of all life, but profane, dirty, disgusting and useless. We remember. How could we do otherwise?

I feel afraid. I remember, how I remember, the smell of burning flesh, the hair catching alight, the awful awful agony of your feet slowly burning up. I remember the jeers of the men who watched, and the frozen dread of the women and children who were forced to watch my ending. Breathing in the smoke, I remembered the advice a crone gave me: breathe in the smoke, you will die quicker, breathe it in. Breath of life, breathe in the acrid, sickly sweet, fumes of your own flesh roasting. I remember. How could I forget? Yet at that moment, the peak of agony, the searing, shooting, wrenching pain, worse than any rack or thumbscrew, I remembered the words of the prophet of these blind and wicked men. Incredulous, I said them to myself, over and over and over again:

'Forgive them, Mother, as they know not what they do.'

5

THE RISE OF THE FATHERGOD

Pope Innocent VIII's Papal Bull,[1] *Summis Desiderantis Affectibus*, published on 5 December 1484, heralded the beginning of the Catholic Church's campaign directed against witchcraft. The Bull discussed the growing 'problem' of witchcraft, outbreaks of which had been reported all over Europe, but particularly in the Rhinelands and the mountainous regions of Italy. At that time Europe was a highly dangerous and unstable place. There were great epidemics of the Black Death and other plagues; it has been estimated that up to one quarter of the population of Europe was wiped out by the Black Death of 1348. This was also the time of the crusades when millions of people, kings and commoners alike, left their homes to make the perilous journey to Palestine. Not many crusaders survived and those who remained at home experienced terrible hardship. Famine raged over the countryside, while crops were left to rot as peasants fled from both marauding armies and the spread of pestilence. High taxes were levied to pay for the expensive wars and many of the common people were left to starve or be conscripted into their landowners' armies. Although there were local dukes and barons, anarchy was the norm as petty feuds were waged between landowner and landowner, with lands being annexed and then given up again. Many of the 'regular' soldiers who had previously policed the countryside were killed in the crusades, either in battles or as a result of the plagues which swept through the armies. Matilda Gage estimates[2] that seven million men were killed during the crusades. This meant that the various relatively small kingdoms were decimated and that the people who were left were unable to defend themselves from invasion and brigandry at the hands of wandering mercenaries.

There was continual bickering between rival factions of the church and at one time there were even two popes. One arm of the church was keen to maintain the Christian creed of poverty and chastity but it was vehemently opposed by a more materialistic faction, which was renowned for its corruption and greed; it wielded power by financial tyranny and by generating fear in the minds of the ordinary people. Large taxes were levied by the church on an already over-burdened populace and these monies were used to support the extravagant lifestyle of many clerics. Heretical movements had sprung up all over Europe and continually aggravated the body of the Church. One group would be put down, only for another to immediately spring up in its place. For example, the Fraticelli were a splinter group of Franciscans who declared the Church itself was the anti-Christ. They were hunted down and ruthlessly massacred. Every inhabitant of the village of Magnalata was murdered and the village razed to the ground under the orders of Pope Martin V.[3]

People rebelled against the strictures of the church and its distortion of the teachings of Christ. It promised no comfort to its followers and offered no solace for their suffering. Instead, it preached that suffering was the will of God and the penalty for man's – and especially woman's – sins. People naturally resented these prophets of doom and gloom, particularly as many of the preachers did not seem to share their miserable lot. St Bernard, for instance, dryly remarked: 'Whom can you show me among the prelates who does not seek rather to empty the pockets of his flock than to subdue their vices?'[4]

Barbara Walker claims that in the twelfth century monasteries turned themselves into wine shops and gambling houses, nunneries became private whorehouses for the clergy and female parishioners were seduced by priests in the confessional.

Witches were attacked by the church for several reasons. First, they were women and the Christian doctrine was trying to replace the worship of the feminine principle with the masculine. Women, as representatives of the Great Mother were mistrusted and suspected (rightly) of not supporting the deification of godthefather. All women were in fact suspect, queens and commoners, young and old alike, and none could be trusted.

Having established a toehold in society, the Church set about taking over. To consolidate its position Christians set out to remove as much power and money as they could from the hands of the laity, and from women in particular. No other religion could be tolerated alongside Christianity, because it was too weak to face any challenge. Least of all from the pagans and witches, who represented the Old Religion which Christianity was trying to destroy. Europe was Pagan in its heart long after the so called 'conversion' of its peoples who paid lip service to the Church but were not easily dissuaded from their age-old customs. For a beleaguered church it was a life and death struggle, which later became an addiction to blood and terror. The Church was in danger of running away with itself as it conquered new lands and found more and more 'enemies of God'.

> ... in times of rapid change ... the rulers of society felt their status threatened and proceeded ruthlessly against those they feared. Heretics, witches, and Jews were the most visible non-conformists; and these groups were subject to the most bitter persecution.[5]

The Papal Bull was followed by the publication of the *Malleus Maleficarum*,[6] written by two monks, Kremner and Spregner. They were instructed by the Pope to mount a campaign aimed at uncovering and punishing those who were found to be practising witchcraft. The *Malleus* was written in three parts: the first dealt with the proof, by argument, that witchcraft existed; the second gave instances of where witches had been sighted and explained how it was possible to identify a witch; and the last section contained the legal machinery for examining and sentencing guilty witches. To aid the legal process, canon law was combined with civil law which:

> increased [the] ferocity of criminal procedure and punishment, condoned the extraordinary power of the civil author-

ity to institute summary procedures and extraordinary punishments, permitted secrecy, instituted new and less restricted categories of evidence, and created the idea of the *crimen exceptum*, the crime so dangerous to the civil community that the very accusation acted to suspend traditional procedural protection to the defendant and opened the way for the most ruthless and thorough kind of persecution undertaken to protect the state from its most dangerous enemies. Not only treason, but magic and witchcraft and other offences became exceptional crimes by the sixteenth century.[7]

Thus a police state was born. The Church, law and state combined in uneasy alliance to keep the population at bay by instituting a reign of terror as a way of controlling dissidents. This offensive was on a scale previously unknown; the ruling classes had always oppressed the poor but these new laws allowed for institutionalised mass-murder. More women died at the hands of the Catholic Church than men died in the Holy Wars. Matilda Gage estimates that, during the following three centuries, nine million people, the great majority of them women, were put to death. In Langedorf in 1492 to 1496, for instance, all but two of the adult female population were charged with witchcraft. And in addition to the 'official' deaths there were the suicides, the death from starvation in prisons as the accused awaited trials, the starvation of families as a result of the death of their breadwinners (as no one dared to help for fear of being accused of guilt by association), not to mention the unofficial lynchings. In 1590 Henry Bouget reported Germany was 'almost entirely occupied with building fires for witches . . . Travellers to Lorraine may see thousands and thousands of the stakes to which the witches are bound'.[8]

Because of the social and economic instability at that time, it is easy to see how the fear of witchcraft could spread throughout a vulnerable and ignorant population. Feeding on people's fear of the supernatural and their belief in secret enemies, the Inquisitors and their agents terrorised whole communities, whipping up fear and hatred so that it was not long before enemies would denounce one another, and rivalries, feuds and squabbles over land or property would end up with one or both of the contestants in the Inquisitor's cell. The prime motive for many denunciations was profit. When arrested, all property and goods of the accused were seized by the Church and nothing was ever returned. The accused also had to pay for their own torture. For example, in Scotland, they were charged six shillings and eight pence for branding on the cheek. Even the dead were not safe; they could posthumously be charged with heresy, their bones dug up and burned, and all their property confiscated. No business was safe, or family wealth. The dependants of witches were left destitute and no one dared help them. Suicides also had their property confiscated. Those who felt pressure from above would in turn oppress those beneath them. Women and children were the obvious target. The misogynist teachings of the Church sanctioned woman-hating and actively promoted the murder of millions of women and children.

To the church, women were the embodiment of matter: earthy and of the world, whilst men were believed to be closer to God and the holders and dispensers of spiritual truths. But within the understanding of most ordinary people the reverse was true. They saw women as having access to these supernatural realms. It was women, not men, who could hex and heal, using unseen 'forces'. The church tried hard to quantify and regulate the natural world and 'put in order' the world of spirit. Women were seen to be inherently more anarchistic, more fluid, more open, challenging and confronting. To men with a rigid, fascist view of the world, such freedom of thought was both dangerous and terrifying. Women allowed for the possibility of chaos, up-ending the orderly world-view of mediaeval man. And as such, women were seen as a corrupting influence. They had the power to turn men's thoughts away from God and lead them to the Devil.

Charles Godfrey Leland, who made contact with Italian witch traditions, wrote the following in the appendix to his book *Aradia*:

The perception of this [tyranny] drove vast numbers of the discontented into rebellion, and as they could not prevail by open warfare, they took their hatred out in a form of

secret anarchy, which was, however, intimately blended
with superstition and fragments of old tradition ... The
result of it all was a vast development of rebels, outcasts,
and all the discontented, who adopted witchcraft or sorcery
for a religion, and wizards as their priests.[9]

Within the Craft it is not believed that many of the nine
million murdered 'witches' were actively involved in pagan
religion, any more than that all but a very few German Jews
were really conspiring against Hitler. Persecutions of minori-
ties, or rather anyone who is 'other' – women, blacks, Jews,
Muslims, gypsies – have a depressingly familiar ring and seem
to be common to all times and all cultures.

Anyone who supposes that the absurd and disgusting details
of demonology are unique may profitably look at the alle-
gations made by St Clement of Alexandria against the followers of Carpocrates in the second century AD ... or by
St Epiphanius against the Gnostic heretics of the fourth
century AD ... or by St Augustine against certain Mani-
chean heretics ... In these recurrent fantasies the obscene
details are often identical, and their identity sheds some
light on the psychological connection between persecuting
orthodoxy and sexual prurience. The springs of sanctimony
and sadism are not far apart.[10]

The truth of the witchcraze is probably that these murdered
women were 'indigestible' in some way, to quote the feminist
philosopher Mary Daly:

The witch-hunters sought to purify their society (The Mystical Body) of these 'indigestible' elements – women whose
physical, intellectual, economic, moral and spiritual inde-
pendence and activity profoundly threatened the male
monopoly in every sphere.[11]

Some women, clearly, were witches as we understand the term,
while others were healers, psychics, midwives. Others were
beautiful women, ugly women, old women, single and lesbian
women, rich women, poor women, but most of all uppity

women. Christine Larner, for instance, has found in her re-
searches of the Scottish witch trials that one half of the accused women were unmarried and that the accused had the
quality of 'smeddum' which referred to her spirit and refusal
to be put down.[12]

Superstitious belief in evil witches persisted until well into
the eighteenth century; the last English witch trial happened
in 1712 and the last official witch burning in Scotland was in
1727. And today, unofficially, witches are still harassed. In
1928 a family of Hungarian peasants beat an old woman to
death, claiming she was a witch. They were acquitted of
murder as the court said they acted from an 'irresistible com-
pulsion'.[13] Torture, the weapon par excellence of the Inquisition, was officially sanctioned in 1257 and remained a
recourse of the Catholic church until 1816, when Pius VII
abolished it. The Inquisition remained active until 1834, however, especially in Latin America where members of the
indigenous population were tortured to death unless they converted to Catholicism. An Inquisitor was always sent alongside
missionaries. The Church has no regrets. Cardinal Lepicier
supported by Pius X declared:

> The naked fact that the Church, of her own authority, has
> tried heretics and condemned them to be delivered to death,
> shows that she truly has the right of killing . . . [w]ho dares
> to say that the Church has erred in a matter so grave as
> this?[14]

For those who blink and imagine the Inquisition was the
product of less enlightened times, they need only cast their
minds over dictators of the recent past –Hitler, Peron, Musso-
lini, Franco, Trujillo, Duvalier, Marcos – to realise they were
or are Roman Catholics, while Stalin was trained for his priest-
hood in an equally dictatorial church. The inescapable conclusion is that the Inquisition lives on.

The Inquisitorial rules for trial were:

1. The procedure was secret.
2. Hearsay was accepted as proof of guilt.

3. The accused were not told the nature of the charges or allowed legal representation.

4. Witnesses were kept concealed.

5. Perjurers, excommunicates and children could give evidence.

6. No favourable evidence was allowed; those who spoke for the accused were arrested as accomplices.

7. Torture was always used; if there was a confession, torture was used to validate it.

8. Names of accomplices had to be admitted under torture.

9. No accused person was found innocent.[15]

THE MODERN REVIVAL OF WITCHCRAFT

It is the writers and poets who are the heralds of new cultural movements. Three writers in particular were responsible for the current upsurge in interest in witchcraft and neo-paganism. Margaret Murray published *The Witch-Cult in Western Europe* in 1921. She was an Egyptologist and anthropologist. Studying statements made by witches tried by the Inquisition, Murray claimed witchcraft was the ancient religion of Western Europe. She said that Diana was the Goddess of the witches, and for this reason called it the Dianic cult. Witchcraft was practised by commoners and nobles alike and the two main festivals were those of May Eve and November Eve. The religion was said to be pre-agricultural and concerned fertility of both animals and crops.

Murray saw witchcraft as a religion celebrating the thirteen full moons (*esbats*) and eight main festivals. She developed her theories in her later books, *The God of the Witches* (1933) and the *Divine King in England* (1954), particularly that relating to the sacrifice of the King in a yearly fertility rite. Like many a woman scholar she was fiercely attacked and dismissed as a crazy old woman; she published at the age of ninety. Even so her theories found resonance and held sway for a considerable period of time. Only recently have her findings been looked at once more. Credence is now given to the fact that trial reports were confessions given under torture and as such may say more about the torturer and his sexual fantasies than about witchcraft.[16]

Margaret Murray's work has fallen from favour because she made her deductions from the transcripts of witch trials, which were confessions extracted under torture. As such, they cannot be claimed to be reliable evidence. Nevertheless, Margaret Murray was a pioneer and she spurred others on to make their own investigations.

If Margaret Murray has been discredited then another pivotal folklorist, Charles Leland, has been dismissed out of hand. He wrote the *Aradia or The Gospel of the Witches* in 1899. An American, he lived with native Indian tribes, studied with gypsies, learned the Celtic tinkers' language and was president of the first European Congress of Folklore in 1899. In Italy he met Maddalena who claimed to belong to an ancient family of witches. She brought Leland a book (of Shadows) which Leland said was a translation from the Latin. It talks of the union of Diana, Queen of the Witches, with the sun, Lucifer and their daughter, Aradia, who was sent to earth to teach witchcraft to the oppressed peoples of the earth. Leland claimed that at that time whole villages in Romagna practised the craft. In *Aradia* the Charge of the Goddess appears:

> Now when Aradia had been taught, taught to work all witchcraft, how to destroy the evil race [of oppressors], she ... said unto them:

> > When I shall have departed from this world,
> > Whenever you have need of anything,
> > Once in the month, and when the moon is full,
> > Ye shall assemble in some desert place
> > Or in a forest all together join
> > To adore the potent spirit of your Queen
> > My mother, great *Diana*. She who fain
> > Would learn all sorcery yet has not won
> > Its deepest secrets, tell them my mother will
> > Teach her, in truth all things as yet unknown.
> > And ye shall be free from slavery,
> > And so ye shall be free in everything
> > And as a sign that ye are truly free,

Ye shall be naked in your rites, both men
And women also: this shall last until
The last of your oppressors shall be dead[17]

Ironically enough, it was the political aspect of his work that caused many of the more conservative members of the Craft to discredit him. Thus T C Lethbridge and Raymond Buckland say it is political propaganda and Doreen Valiente claims it was for this reason, together with its sexual frankness, that Leland was marginalised. Feminist witches, however, find Leland a sympathetic writer and fully agree with his assertions that when patriarchy is running amok the feminine principle rises up to subvert the status quo.

Robert Graves' *The White Goddess* is another book found on most witches' book shelves and like other cult figures he has suffered the vicissitudes of fame. Once hailed as a benign father figure to Wicca, his scholarship has also come under attack. Graves was a poet, who said that: 'The function of poetry is religious invocation of the Muse'.[18] Graves claimed no divine revelations for his book but by his own admission 'a sudden overwhelming obsession interrupted me ... my mind ran at such a furious rate all night, as well as all the next day, that it was difficult for my pen to keep pace with it'.[19] He wrote the first draft of the book, 70,000 words, in just three weeks, and is clear about the price exacted by his muse, The White Goddess: 'Who am I, you will ask, to warn you that she demands either whole-time service or none at all?'[20]

Graves claimed that covens had always existed in Britain, 'European poetic lore is, indeed, ultimately based on magical principles, the rudiments of which formed a close religious secret for centuries'[21] but attributed their growth in recent times to the scholarship of Margaret Murray. He wrote about the mainly Irish Celtic tradition and worked with an ancient poem concerning the Battle of the Trees. Using powerful poetic imagery, Graves described the legends of Celtic Ireland. He did not claim to be a witch neither did he have much respect for witches, but as a poet the poetic imagery of magic had always fascinated him.[22] In *The White Goddess* Graves talks eloquently about the need for the Goddess to be re-awakened to counter Apollo:

> the Organizer, God of Science, usurps the power of his Mother the Goddess of inspired truth, wisdom and poetry, and tries to bind her devotees by laws – inspired magic goes, and what remains is theology, ecclesiastical ritual, and negatively ethical behaviour.[23]

It is clear why Graves is beloved by feminist witches, although it is doubtful he would have recognised his Muse amongst them. His contempt for modern life without the muse is stark and his poetic sensibility is disgusted by the degradation of modern living:

> 'Nowadays' is a civilisation in which the prime emblems of poetry are dishonoured. In which serpent, lion and eagle belong to the circus-tent; ox, salmon and boar to the cannery; racehorse and greyhound to the betting ring; and the sacred grove to the saw-mill. In which the Moon is despised as a burned-out satellite of the Earth and woman reckoned as 'auxiliary State personnel'. In which money will buy almost anything but truth, and almost anyone but the truth-possessed poet.[24]

MODERN WITCHES

Witchcraft was kept alive within families mainly in rural areas. In England the repeal of the Witchcraft Act in 1951 allowed witches to 'come out of the closet' and witchcraft entered the public domain after 600 years of repression.

Gerald Gardner (1884–1964) was a practitioner of witchcraft rather than a writer about the subject. He was an amateur anthropologist who spent many years as a civil servant in the Far East as well as running rubber and tea plantations. On his retirement to Hampshire (a county well-known for witches), he contacted local witches and in 1939 he joined the Fellowship of Crotona and thence was initiated into Wicca. Because witchcraft was still illegal, his book, known as *High*

Magic's Aid, but published under the title of *Witchcraft Today*, was written under the pen name of Scire in 1949. With the repeal of the Act in 1951 Gardner came out into the open and was much criticised by fellow witches for so doing. They argued that his account of the Craft was not definitive. He described witches meeting in covens run by high priestesses worshipping the Triple Goddess and Pan, or god of the forests. He claimed they worshipped naked in a circle of nine foot diameter and raised power through dance, chanting and meditation. They celebrated the same eight festivals Murray had previously described. Gardner claimed that he was taught fragments of the old religion, which, being incomplete, he supplemented using his extensive knowledge of the occult. Attacked for not being 'pure' Wicca, Gardner was sincere in his heartfelt desire to preserve the Old Religion which he felt was in danger of dying out. He was said to have hired Aleister Crowley to re-write some of the rituals, although this is refuted by other sources.

The controversy surrounding Gardner centred on whether or not he was initiated into an ancient lineage of witches or whether he, together with Aleister Crowley and Doreen Valiente, had made up the rituals. Probably both were true. Any ancient knowledge, unless it has been kept in academic aspic, is bound to degenerate and become corrupted and after 500 years would surely be in need of updating or at least rendering intelligible to contemporary worshippers. Any creed has to be relevant for its adherents, and by all accounts Gardner's co-worshippers were elderly middle-class English whose rituals reflected their cultural background.

What Gardner did was start a debate amongst witches as to their real heritage, and claims and counterclaims of ancient lineages of witches emerged. This debate has been thoroughly researched by Margot Adler in her book *Drawing Down the Moon* and I do not propose to repeat her findings. She documents the twentieth-century witchcraft revival and its flowering in Europe and the United States during the last 20 years. Quoting innumerable first-hand sources of those initiated by their families she comes to the conclusion that there can be no proof as to whether present-day witchcraft is related to an ancient Craft or the witch trials of Europe or whether it is a modern invention following anthropological and ethnological research.

In their book *The Western Way*, Caitlin and John Matthews discuss the modern pagan revival and its relationship to the Old Religion:

> If there seems to be an unexplainable hiatus between the Foretime's Old Religion and the modern Craft, it is because the links are either invisible or plainly were never there. Yet if there is any successor to the shaman then the most likely candidate is the revivalist witch.[25]

They quote the example of a male witch, George Pickingill, from East Anglia (1816–1909) who traced his lineage from a witch, Julia of Brandon, who died in 1071. George founded some nine covens over a period of 60 years, some of which may well still be in operation.[26]

The argument as to whether our witchcraft traditions are 'authentic' seems to be the usual male intellectual posturing, debating the number of angels on a pin head, Apollo run riot . . .

Bonewits, writing in 1971,[27] divided witches into the familial, the gothic and the neo-pagan. The familial witches were those whose traditions were handed down from mother to daughter, who mainly came from rural communities and practised what I would term earth magic, controlling the weather, making crops grow, healing, charming and so on. He called the gothic witches those who were tortured and killed during the Witchcraze who, he claims, are the modern counterparts of the Satanists who act out the shadow or repressed side of Christianity. His last category, the neo-pagans, are part of the witchcraft revival of Gardner *et al.* who are pagans, feminists, etc. I would tend to agree about the familial and the neo-pagan, but I feel the gothic witches, who have always been around, were probably not representative of the majority of those who were killed and that the trial reports reflect the sadomasochistic fantasies of the torturers and the judges rather than practices the women on trial were accused of.

Witchcraft today remains an eclectic mix of Pagans, feminist

witches, Goddess-worshippers and others. There is no movement as such, and no leaders except those who appointed
themselves. Through the networks of the Women's Liberation
Movement runs the thread of feminist or matriarchal spirituality. Feminist witches are the indirect descendants of both
the Amazons and the priestesses of the ancient world.

6

STARCRAFT AND THE MOON

> The Queen of Heaven . . . she, too, loved the solitude of the woods and the lonely hills, and sailing overhead on clear nights in the likeness of the silver moon looked down with pleasure on her own fair image reflected on the calm, burnished surface of the lake, Diana's Mirror.[1]

The moon, stuff of poets, mystics and goddess-worshippers for millennia. Her progress from sliver of silver to fat, golden, harvest moon to deep, rich darkness, the monthly journey through our skies is a cyclical mystery played out in our most linear of worlds.

Peoples everywhere have watched the moon. She symbolises the sacred, the mysterious female, woman's connection to her rhythms, and all that is mutable, fluid and strange; she is shape-shifter, deluder, queen of the glamours, haven of souls. The Sioux called her the Old Woman Who Never Dies, the Persians, Metra, the mother whose love penetrates everywhere. Ancient Britain was called Albion, land of the Milk-White Moon Goddess. The *Vedas* (Hindu sacred texts) say souls return to the moon at death, thus agreeing with the Pythagorean and Orphic sects of the ancient world. She was a female gateway, of Yoni, through which souls passed on their way to the paradise fields of the stars. She sheltered the dead and also unborn babies. The moon controls the tides. Myth had it that you can only be born on an incoming tide, and that the dead die on an outgoing one. In Scotland young women would only marry at the full moon and would curtsey to her saying, 'It is a fine moon, God bless her.' African women pray to the moon saying: 'May our lives be renewed as yours is.'

The periodic need to shine brightly and to withdraw is inherently female and reflects the phases of the moon. The

Tao Te Ching wisely says: 'He who knows the masculine but keeps to the feminine will be in the whole world's channel.' The change from fire to Moon worship was presaged by the destruction of Atlantis. Sybil Leek writes that the Mayans recorded that 64 million people died when Atlantis was destroyed: 'Twice Mu jumped from its foundations. It was then sacrificed with fire. It burst while it was being shaken up and down by the earthquake.'[2] She also quotes Plato as saying that Poseidonis (Atlantis) sank 9000 years before his time when the precession of the equinoxes moved from Leo to Cancer.[3] Thus the Dianic moon/mother cults were born and Wicca flourished. With the moon came water cults such as sprinkling and baptising. Shape-shifting lunar consciousness balanced the fire-worshipping solar civilisations. Myth has it that Atlantis perished because of the abuse of sex-magic and corruption of its priests. The Chaldeans had a lunation cycle based on the houses of the moon and the 12 signs of the zodiac. Ishtar, their main Goddess, the All Accepting One, was said to carry the 12 zodiac signs on her girdle. Isis, the Egyptian Great Goddess, was Mother of the Moon, the keeper of the Mysteries that connected Egypt to the traditions of Atlantis. The moon boat carried souls from the underworld to be redeemed by light. The Christian church realised the importance of the moon and built the Vatican on mount Vaticanus, which was a shrine sacred to the Great Mother. Mary is known as the Moon of our Church, Our Moon, the Spiritual Moon. The most important festival in the Christian calendar, Easter, is celebrated on the first Sunday after the full moon of spring.

CALENDARS AND THE MOON

Each 28 days the moon describes a cycle. From swollen, fecund full moon to the faintest slice of new moon to darkness, no moon. From the cycle the moon also describes a yearly cycle of 13 moons. The moon provided the first calendar; women watched the moon as they waited for their bleeding or for new life to emerge. Menstruation and mensuration derive from the same root. Thirteen lunar months give a year (13 x 28 = 364), plus one day. Hence the Wicca measuring of a year and a day for blessings, curses, mourning, etc.

Mensuration was a knowledge of the menses as women, anxious or fearful of pregnancy, counted the days before they bled. The seventh day of each lunar phase was considered especially important, as were new, full moons and the quarter days, and a holiday was given on those days (the forerunner of the Sabbath). Menology was knowledge of the moon. Moon calendars went from noon to noon, which is why Pagan festivals are always the day before Christian ones. The 13 lunar months relate to the Christian contention that 13 is an unlucky number; in many cultures, however, 13 is seen to be most auspicious. 'However safe the way may be, nothing can be done without the benefit of Luna . . . making in any month the four seasons of the year.'[4]

THE ASTROLOGICAL MOON

In traditional astrology[5] the Moon is of vital importance. Decumbiture, the ancient art of diagnosing sickness using astrology, relied on the movement of the moon to predict the course of the illness and to determine the right method of treatment.[6]

In natal astrology, the Moon is one (together with the sun) of the two 'lights' and is a symbolic representation of the feminine principle, the Great Mother as well as the biological mother. It tells us how the person relates to the feminine principle, how she nourishes herself, where she feels at home, how she feels, what moves her, how she escapes. The Moon is instinct, some say the unconscious (although it might be argued that Pluto has taken over this role). She represents our childhood. As we grow older we tend to become like our sun-sign, but as children we are more lunar.

Albertus Magnus says she is: 'conveyor of the virtue of all the other planets, coming next from her to us.'[7] The Moon rules the fluids in the body: tears, lymph, menstruation and its cycle, the breasts, breast milk, the reproductive cycle, childbirth and fertility. The Moon shows our emotional responses and how these affect our health. It rules the stomach, an organ well known to be affected by the passions as well as the menstrual cycle which directly reflects emotional imbalance with pre-menstrual tension or excess bleeding, cramps, block-ages, etc.[8]

MENSTRUATION AND THE MOON

Persian women said the menses first came into being through Jahi the Whore, she who defied the heavenly Father.[9] She began to menstruate after sex with Ahriman the great serpent. Afterwards she seduced the first righteous man who had lived alone in paradise with only a bull for company. He knew nothing of love making, so she taught him. In Greece, men-strual blood was the 'supernatural red wine'[10] given to the gods by Hera. The aboriginals painted stones with red paint saying it was menstrual blood. Thor reached the land of enlightenment and eternal life by bathing in the blood of the Goddess. Celtic kings became gods by drinking the red mead of queen Mab, and to be stained red meant to be chosen by the Goddess as a king. The British goddess of flowers, Bloed-wedd, whose whole body was made of flowers, was called blood wedding. Egyptian Pharoahs became divine by ingest-ing the blood of Isis. Taboos were the demons produced by menstruation, especially the Gorgon who had serpent hair and wise blood. Victorians claimed that children conceived during the menses would have occult powers. Old women likewise were believed to be filled with magical powers because they retain their magic blood, they became clan leaders and sham-ans. It was said that if a man approached a menstruating woman he would lose his wisdom, strength, energy, and vitality. The cauldron of Cerridwen and the Holy Grail were seen to be full of blood, the mixed drink of Eleusis may have been blood and milk, the two precious fluids women produce.

The time of the first onset of bleeding, menarche, is a magical time for young women when their physical child-hood ends and psychically the door to other worlds opens. The time before and during her menstruation are the most magical for women, best spent in the company of other women lest our unbounded magic scorch and destroy; it is only men that the Gorgon stalks. Menstrual huts and seclu-sion gave time for women to gather, free from the burdens of running the home. Women living together generally menstruate at the same time; they tell stories, do dark magic and cleanse themselves of contaminating influences. A young woman menstruating for the first time enters the world of women's magic, steps over the threshold of another world. When we menstruate, we dream, we are more creative, and if we are denied psychic space we go crazy. Doctors call this pre-menstrual tension,[11] but witches know it is lunacy. Crawling about on all fours and howling like a wolf is a good menstrual antidote to masculine linear consciousness. Eating raw meat and stalking the streets with your Gorgon mask is better still. No mugger I know would take you on.[12] It freezes the blood in their veins and turns them to dust.

Ficino, writing in the sixteenth century at the height of the witchcraze, recorded the contemporary wisdom of the moon.[13] He called the moon the 'most moist of Planets, far removed from dryness and abstraction, in touch with experience, saturated with feelings.'[14] He says the moon has more to do with nature and the body as gardeners plant by her cycles. She shows both growth and decay. He enjoins us to watch closely this fast-moving planet which will ensure good timing and a full awareness of the body and soul. He claims that those with an integrated natal moon have regard for the natural rhythms of the soul and not the ego. The new moon to the first quarter represents youth and new beginnings, the first quarter, full youth and maturity, the full to the second quarter is maturity and old age and the last quarter to the new moon is dying and dissolution.[15] So her changes affect our changes and the dynamic of life: fullness, newness, waxing, waning, death. Ficino describes the lunar spirit as: 'a young woman with horned head, on a dragon or bull, with serpents over her head and under her feet.'[16]

The moon and the snake represent the shedding, chameleon nature and the moon and the bull as fertilising nature. The moon reflects and receives energy. She takes direction from the depths and channels the spirits of the other planets. The way back to the light (the sun) is through the shadows. The moon pours itself out, emptying as it begins to wane. The process of entropy, ending, decay, death, is seen as part of a larger pattern, the emptying is important, so personal life is emptied as well as filled, that is, there is as much darkness as light:

Lunar would empty us of those purposes and plans, as well as the interpretations and explanations, that keep life busy on the surface with no guarantee that there is movement within. Emptying, naturally, does not feel as good as filling up; it seems uncreative and unproductive ... Farmers who watch the moon know when to let things ripen, fall off the tree, cure and ferment. The psychologically attuned person observes the soil of his soul with equal sensitivity, knowing that nature wanes with the moon and falls into total darkness.[17]

Death is always close to creativity, the moon is darkness, sterility and emptiness as much as she is light, fecundity and growth. A paradox. Solar evolution is a resistance and denial of death and decay, moon wisdom knows things must die for life to begin. The moon is only full for the briefest of moments.

LUNACY

Prophets and poets, priests and lovers, hetairas[18] and Amazons, mothers and sibyls all know of the madness of the moon. Plato called them the four frenzies,[19] those inner figures or archetypes, which speak to us of the irrational, the chaotic, the moon's deep shadow. The poet works with music, dance and imagery to arouse the sleeping serpent, to bring peaks of ecstatic union and troughs of darkest night. Without the muse life is bland and mechanical; we suffer depressions and become inert. The priestess teaches us the mystery of the sacred, life's numinosity, the madness of myth and parable. Through ritual the soul contacts its deepest mysteries. Life without ritual and meaning empties into the mechanical, the soulless inanity of material existence. The lover takes us through fiery passion to the burning ground of love. Through desire for the divine, love leads us to our mirror image, to the highest and holiest. Lack of love kills our spirit and impels us to search for ballast to fill our hungry hearts. The prophet takes us above our mind to unity and tells us of the future, she shows us the fates spinning our destiny, the Moirae. She teaches us to 'know the ennui and confusion of surface experience, and feel the psychic bruises caused by conflicts between deeper movements and surface expectations.'[20] She teaches that reality is a dream.

Lunar consciousness is the voice of the oracle:

> This is . . . an oracle shared by Night and the Moon; it has no outlet anywhere on earth nor any single seat, but roves everywhere . . . The voice was the Sibyl's . . . who sang of the future as she was carried about on the face of the moon. (Plutarch)[21]

As our society has polarised into solar god-consciousness so witches hold that lunar awareness is vital to redress that imbalance. Witches watch the moons, especially the full and new moons which are powerful times for magic and for endings and beginnings.

FULL MOON

The full moon is a time of culmination, of fruition, of celebration. A time of revelation, illumination. The past will be central. There may be a sense of division. (Remember the sun is opposite the moon, symbolising a splitting of energies.) Relationships may be all-important or rejected because they do not match ideal expectations. It is also the time of greatest light, literally, if the sky is clear, and more so if there is no artificial light. However bright the lights of technology burn, nothing on earth can replace the awesome, still, cool light of a full moon over a calm sea. Moonlight is the most magical of lights. Sunlight can burn, but it is universally seen as hostile, unrelenting, scorching. Whereas moonlight heals and soothes; it causes things to grow; it bathes the land in an ethereal, shimmering luminosity which bends and distorts. Priestesses of the moon watch her and notice her actions on themselves and those around them. The effect of the full moon is said to last for two-and-a-half days before the exact full moon and two-and-a-half days afterwards, the energies building to a peak and then tapering off. Full moons are more powerful still for you if they come within two degrees of any planet you have in your natal chart,[22] and their effects may last for several weeks. If at all possible, sleep in moonlight;

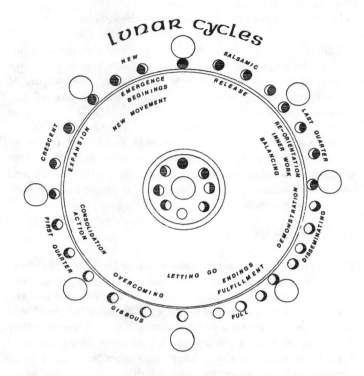

leave the curtains undrawn. Use moonlight to cleanse and make magical objects potent (Tarot cards, wands, chalices, etc.). Traditionally, a crystal ball has to be exposed to the light of 13 full moons before it is ready to use.

The full moon is a time for reflection and meditation, a time to go inwards as perception is heightened.

THE DARK MOON

The darkness is feared, loathed and abhorred by patriarchal, solar consciousness. Dark skies, dark skins, the sinister left handed, the occult, sexuality, the unconscious, old age and death, all bring into relief the otherness, the difference, the anarchic behaviour of those who don't fit the patriarchal mould. The dark moon is a time of inwardness, traditionally women bled at the time of the dark moon going into seclusion. They wove words and spun spells and sat in deep conversation with their inner selves. If the full moon is the mother, the new moon the maiden, then the dark moon is Hecate, Kali, Medusa, Cerridwen, the Morrigan picking over corpses. She is the death card in the Tarot, the Hermit, the Hanged Man (see Chapter 12). Snakes and spiders are her familiars as well as black cats, wolves and crows. No wonder she is feared. The dark moon is a potent time for hexing and binding spells. Z Budapest states that 'A witch who cannot hex cannot heal'[23]. Hexing witches do their most in the dark of the moon, they meet in the shadows, not in the light of the full or new moon. More than any other part of ourselves, we need to integrate, own and acknowledge our shades. The dark moon is the time for banishing deadly ties that bind you to old, outworn selves, for cutting free from obsessions, compulsions, for bury-ing the hatchet by understanding the fear of your oppressor, or for making a final break. In the dark moon we dis-member in order to re-member. And soon the new moon comes.

NEW MOON

This is when the sun and moon are in exactly the same spot. The moon is not visible as the sun blocks it from view. The astrological new moon is about two-and-a-half days before the new moon is visible in the sky. For the purposes of witch-craft the sighting of the new moon is the time rituals are done and the actual time of the conjunction of sun and moon is the dark of the moon, those three days in the month when there is no moon, the most terrifying or restful of times.

According to Arab custom, whatever you are doing when you see the new moon, you are doing the right thing. It is a good omen, a sighting of hope after the darkness. In the West people turned over coins in their pockets when they saw the new moon; this was deemed to be lucky. New moon magic is for beginnings, new projects, the seeds sown at the dark moon will begin to sprout. Ask for help to get your projects off the ground. Now, until the time of the full moon, is the time for action, movement, dynamism, from full to dark is culmination, receptivity, growing. So go out and put your dreams into action.

Each moon will be flavoured by the astrological sign it finds itself in, which is why witches have to know the basics of astrology to work with the energy of the moon.

THE EXPERIENCE OF THE FULL MOONS

Below I set out my personal observations of the full moons as they move through the 12 signs of the zodiac. Each person's experience will vary according to his or her receptivity to the energy of the full moon and her environment. The full moon in deep countryside will generally be experienced as beneficent but in urban areas the energy often jars with the manic pace of living. Women who are spiritually tuned, wherever they live, will respond positively to the heightened energy of this time.

For the purpose of ritual or spell-making it is necessary to understand the different energies of the moons. Make your own observations, how you and those around you feel, and notice how the public at large react, to build up your own picture of each moon.

The moons can be divided into the four elemental types:

Earth Moons (Taurus, Virgo, Capricorn)

Earth moons deal with issues connected with stability, security, social traditions and pragmatism, around the need to organise a structure. They are less happy with feeling and sensations.

Fire Moons (Aries, Leo, Sagittarius)

Fire moons are enthusiastic, optimistic and initiate changes. They are impulsive, full of naivety, self-centredness. They have lots of energy, can be bad tempered and irritable.

Air Moons (Gemini, Libra, Aquarius)

Air moons analyse feelings. They are connected to fore-thought, objectivity, expression, communication, writing, phoning, talking, reading, travel and movement.

Water Moons (Pisces, Scorpio, Cancer)

Water full moons are the most witchy and feel the most disorientating. Vulnerability and fear are heightened; there is great emotional intensity, and the past is important. This is a time to do love rituals and fertility spells.

The full moon is always the opposite sign to the sun, so when the sun is in Aries, the Moon is in Libra; when the sun is in Scorpio, the moon is in Taurus. New moons, conversely, are both in the same sign; new moon in Aquarius means both sun and moon are in that sign. Newspapers usually print the phases of the moon and the star sign column will tell you the 12 signs of the zodiac and when they begin.[24]

FULL MOONS

Aries. Energy, courage, initiation. Letting go of anger and aggression, selfish habit patterns, self-destructive anger. Do courage work, warrior rituals, to initiate new projects. Break through depression and inertia. Good for initiations. Be bold, cheeky, daring, lustful, angry and impatient. Aries is an autumn equinox moon.

Taurus. Love, money, homes, property, fertility. A moon to build, to put down foundations, to do creative work. Follow on from the fresh beginnings of the Aries moon. Ground and make concrete practical plans, lists, frameworks, sow seeds. It is sensual. Do money spells, fertility magic, build houses, plan out gardens.

Gemini. Writing, communication, ideas. A learning moon, time to deal with letters, get messages across, make contact with people, write, ring, phone, fax people who are important to you. Meet, travel short distances, buzz around and chatter. Magic to make good misunderstandings, to clear the air, to get your ideas across.

Cancer. Family issues, the home, fertility. Feelings run high with this moon. Watch out for depressive thoughts, picking up other people's bad vibes, ruffling other people's feelings, being oversensitive, touchy, tearful. Do love spells, banishing bad magic, work for the family. Good for divination and cleansing rituals, consecrations and baptisms. Cancer is a winter solstice moon.

Leo. Fame, creativity, luck. A theatrical moon, lots of glitter and glamour, lots of noise and energy, lots of razzmatazz. There is also selfishness, if not egomania. Thing big: big rituals, big projects, big shows. Use the energy to expand your life to be at the centre of things. Do creativity rituals, let go of those things that block your creativity, remember the things that make you special.

Virgo. Health, purifying the body, clearing up bad vibes, magic. A quiet moon, so fast, do cleansing rituals, banish sickness and toxins. Let go of negative thinking and worry over work problems. Virgo has an affinity with pets; if yours has a problem do work to clear it. Banish fear, worry and negative thinking. Do work in the garden, on the land, with your pot plants.

Libra. Love, creativity, celebrations. It is a refined moon. Listen to music, dance, paint, write poetry, meet and mix with influential people, ask for favours, contact the great and the good. Flatter and charm. Stay light, be beautiful, mingle. Do spells if the muse has deserted you, meet other witches, other covens, let go of all that is ugly and unbalanced in your life. Sparkle.

Scorpio. Power, revenge, courage, hexing, warriors and battles. A heady mix, this moon. Sibyl Leek[25] suggests there are more murders around this time of the year than at any other. This is when you see car drivers attacking each other, punch-ups in the streets, drops of blood on the pavement in the morning. I head for the hills if I can, or walk the streets head down, armour on. This moon is supposed to have been Buddha's birthday and is a festival in the East.

Sagittarius. Travel, study. It is a moon of big ideas and a good time to start off on a long journey, begin a course of

study, philosophise, think. This is a time to get your Goddess
teachings across, to broadcast your beliefs, to start a debate
amongst friends or colleagues about spiritual and philosophi-
cal issues. It is a time to let go of meanness, pettiness, quarrels
and misunderstandings. This day has been named Great Invocation Day.[26]

Capricorn. Career, status. A serious moon, by and large. It
is a time for remembering that the apex of the year heralds its
nadir. Make plans now, throw out deadwood, prepare for
autumn work, bring in your harvest.

Aquarius. Study ideas for starting projects. So network
with friends and meet as many members of your clan as you
can. Move around. Try to resolve disputes, clear up misunderstandings, as people will be at their most logical now. If
you are in a coven or group deal with issues about how you
organise, have debates and discussions, resolve power issues.
Do ritual work for building networks, for international support and unity for large humanitarian issues, and let go of
petty personal concerns.

Pisces. Love, clairvoyance, dreams. Sibyl Leek has suggested
that more suicides occur at this time than at any other time
of the year. With a Pisces moon you run the risk of dissolving
into the primordial ooze, which may be good or bad depending
upon your circumstances. You will be more sensitive to mind-
expanding substances and you should remember you are no
worse than you ever were. Scry, read the runes, do Tarot
readings, dream and whisper to spirits. Don't attempt to do
practical things as your co-ordination and rational powers are
at their lowest ebb. Hang loose, save humanity. Do rituals for
the planet. But beware when summoning up spirits; your
psychic powers are intensified now, so be careful what you
ask for.

7
RITUAL

Ritual is a pivotal force in most people's lives. From the everyday rituals of waking and sleeping to the complex social rituals of religious festivals, political celebrations and the celebration of milestones in our life's trajectory. Ritual provides a sense of order, a continuity and connection with the community we live in and enables us to identify our place within it. As our society breaks up and changes, we increasingly feel marginalised and excluded from those rituals. Many of us groan with the onset of Christmas and New Year, which are perhaps the empty rituals of family gatherings or a time when we realise we are lonely and separated from loved ones.

Christmas, one of the two main rituals celebrated within the loosely defined Christian culture, has for the most part, become an empty, expensive, alienating experience bearing little relationship to the traditional celebration at the nadir of the year with its anticipation of the coming summer. Christmas and birthdays tend to remind us of our loneliness and dislocation from our culture, our tribe. Those we feel closest to are often not our blood kin but friends or those who share our interests.

Many people have decided that rituals are empty, meaningless pastimes, with no place in everyday life. Ritual is, however, vital. On a personal level a certain amount of order and routine is necessary to keep sane. No one can live with complete anarchy; patterns always emerge, however chaotic they might be, which the psyche regards as routine and into which it can relax. The early morning cup of tea and the late night bath, for instance, both mark divisions in the day, touchstones through which we can assure and reassure ourselves that all is as it should be, however far from the truth that really may be.

All women of menstruating age are aware of their monthly cycles. Events in their hormonal ebb and flow mark the passage of time and energetic high points and low inward-looking days may also coincide with the moon's phases. Women who live together after a time begin to menstruate in unison so that the life of the community is caught up in their rhythms and their differing moods of withdrawal and action. If this reflects the moon's phases then nature in her cycle reflects and enhances the cycle of the community. Thus ritual is born. For meaning is ascribed to the waxing and waning of the moon as it coincides with the mystery of menstrual bleeding. The bleeding becomes a dark time, a time when the mystery is at its height, a time when magic is in the air and women withdraw deep into themselves and are inaccessible to their men and their children. If this coincides with the time when there is no moon in the sky[1] then the mystery deepens still further. Menstruating women have withdrawn from the tribe into their menstrual huts, and the light has gone. The dark moon becomes a time of abandonment, a time when menstruating women congregate and do ... What? Their strongest magic perhaps? Their secret work, their seditious talk? This time passes quickly enough and then the crescent moon appears in the sky, bringing its new, silvery light, its wavering beams, the promise of more light, new growth, the offer of hope and possibility, tentative beginnings. There is a collective sigh of relief, the women come out of seclusion, the shadows have been forgotten and the community comes to life. Hope is restored.

The moon waxes, it fattens, like the belly of a pregnant woman it becomes the outward expression of fertility, a symbol of fecundity, of growth, of fruition. As the moon size increases its light spreads further afield and brings into relief the magical nighttime shadows. The bright, silver-blue moonlight changes the outlines of familiar daytime objects, distorting their contours, making them larger than life, unfamiliar, 'glamoured.'[2] As the moon waxes to full, the harvest of the new moon's surge of energy is gathered in, and there is a feeling of culmination, of harnessing the forces of nature as she glows her most magnificent, symbol of all that is glorious and immanent in woman. The moon culminates, the brightest

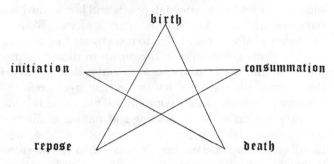

Five Stations of the Goddess

night arrives and brings with it a stillness, an out-of-time timelessness which takes the breath away. The sight of the full moon in a cloudless sky always causes gasps of wonder. Perhaps people shrink from its awesomeness, but it is a reminder, even in the most de-natured of cities, of the omnipotent forces of nature. You might land on the moon, but you cannot harness its forces. It waxes and wanes relentlessly . . . and you are of no account. The full moon is where the egg is shed and the baby born, where the fruit drops from the tree and the blossom opens. My friend Mary gave birth to her son, Luke, at the full moon; her labour was brought on by thunder and lightning.

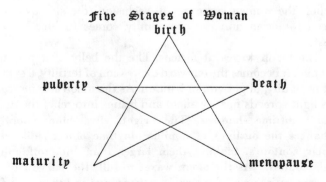

Five Stages of Woman

After culmination comes the slow descent, the moving downwards and inwards after so much lightness and expansion. There is still light, but it slowly decreases. After summer comes winter, from blossoming comes a withering. There is a buildup of the dark, shadows lengthen, life becomes heavy, ponderous, introverted. Women's bodies thicken, they become more silent, more thoughtful, more sensitive to the clamours of the outside world and increasingly impatient with it. Concerned with building the inner life, the concerns of the outer world become less engaging, the light less appealing, the shades more seductive. This is the time of letting go, of shedding the superfluous, the ephemeral, the unnecessary, paring life back to its basics, to the bone. And then once more we tumble into the darkness, to begin the circle again, the circle drawn in blood.

Witches celebrate this moon cycle, particularly the 13 full moons of the year. Full moon is a time of great spiritual awareness, literally of greatest light, where vision and insight are heightened and the conscious and unconscious parts of ourselves come closer together. It is also where the two lights are literally furthest apart, sun and moon, and the sense of separation is at its most extreme. Using the reflective nature of the full moon helps us to understand both our wholeness and separation.

CELEBRATING THE CYCLES OF THE MOON

Sabbats and Esbats

'Sabbat' comes from the same root as Sabbath, meaning sacred. Sabbats are the days and nights of the full moon and there are 13 in a witch's year. Esbats are full moon rituals. The year begins at Samhain, 31 October. Significantly, the year begins with darkness, the first moon after the visit to the ancestors, the day of the dead. From the Samhain moon the wheel of the year describes the circle from death to life and back to death again. Each month at the full moon we celebrate our achievements, we do big spells, special magic, giving thanks for the progress we have made and letting go of those things we no longer need.

Ritual for Full Moon

> . . . and once a month,
> when the moon is full,
> gather in My light.
> By dance and song
> and all sweet pleasures
> Celebrate my Mystery
> by the clear waters of the oceans
> and the still mountains
> by the rushing wind
> and the luscious copse
> thy will be done.
> And should you have need of anything
> call on me then
> For I am your Mother
> mistress of the seven seas
> guardian of the stars
> I sit on high mountain tops
> lie in the belly of the earth
> my winds lick your face
> and blend the trees
> There is no place where I am not
> Mistress.

Gather in a sacred place, either outdoors or indoors. Purify the air by burning incense, and welcome each woman, anointing her forehead,[3] her breast and her hands and feet, saying: 'Who is here? How do you come? What do you bring?' She will reply, giving her name, and say she comes in perfect love and brings perfect peace. Each woman takes her place in the circle. Wind up the circle by walking round three, five or nine times *widdershins*, that is, anticlockwise, moonwise. As you do, begin to hum softly, allowing the humming to move into chanting and let your voices weave in and out of each other, building a cone of power, creating a protected, sacred space . . . Standing inside the circle call on the spirits of the four elements:

Facing North call on earth and say:

Earth, earth, I call on you earth!
be with us tonight
envelop us with your power
enfold us with your strength
hold us
hold us

Facing South call on fire:

Spirits of fire, spirits of fire!
dance with us tonight
lend us your energy
give us your light
warm our hearts
warm us, spirits of fire
warm us!

Facing West call on water:

water, water
cool, crystal water
wild, rushing water
deep, dark water
bathe us
bathe us

Facing East call on air:

wind, wind, listen wind!
whistling wind, weeping wind
howling gale
balmy breeze
carry us.
carry us.

Then invoke the power or face of the Goddess with whom you
wish to work. Full moon is associated with the Mother Goddess. If you have no special work then invoke her:

By the sweeping of the clouds
and the rushing of the brook;
by the running of the hare
and the howling of the wolf,
Mother, I call you.

By all that is fair and fairy
and the hobgoblins' hidden lair,
by all that is wild and wanton
and all that is barren and bare
by the brilliance of the sun
and the darkness of the womb
I call you to me now.

By the softness of your voice
and the curving of your form,
by the perfume in your hair
and all that glints and shimmers
by the crashing of the cymbals
and the flight of doves,
I call you now.

When She is with you do your magical work. You may choose
to do a pathworking or meditation:

Journey to the Mother

*Close your eyes and go deep within yourself. Take a few deep
breaths... Relax your body and quieten your mind... Go
deep, deep, deep inside... You find yourself on the edge of a
lake... It's night, a warm breeze is blowing over the surface
of the lake; the moon is full, its silvery light is reflected in the
still water... Far away an owl is hooting... Fish plop as
they swim... You put a toe in the water... It is surprisingly*

*warm ... You wade into the water ... It covers your thighs ...
Then your genitals and belly ... And finally you can resist it
no longer and you dive into the inky blackness which envel-
opes you and you begin to swim, effortlessly, as if the water
is carrying you*[4] *... As you swim out you see a light in front
of you, high up ... You begin swimming towards the light ...
As you get nearer you realise the light is shining from a
tower set on an island ... You swim towards the island and,
arriving, you walk towards the tower ... Passing through a
small wood you find yourself at the foot of the tower ... There
does not seem to be any door ... You wonder how you will
get in ... You realise you can climb up the creeper growing
around the tower ... You try it out and it easily holds your
weight ... Swiftly you make your way up to the window,
climbing effortlessly and look inside ... It is a circular room,
and there are candles burning on a great altar. On the floor
a circle is painted with symbols around it. You climb into the
room and walk into the centre of the circle ... You sit down
and wait ... The High Priestess comes to you ... (Allow ten
minutes to follow the High Priestess. Let yourself go and be
directed by her.) ... Now she leads you out of her tower to
the water's edge ... A boat is waiting to take you across the
water ... Say your farewells as the boat slowly glides through
the water ... Arriving on the shore you step out of the boat
and slowly open your eyes ... Take your time and come back
into the room ...*

You may choose to discuss your work in pairs or in the group
(bearing in mind how long it takes to tell your story), or you
may move on to the next stage.

All stand and hold hands, centre (bring your energy back
into your body and feel your feet on the ground) and connect
as a group. Feel the circle of light passing through each one
of you. Be aware that on this night all over the world groups
are meeting to celebrate the full moon and connect with the

energies of love, light and power. Hold on to that connection for a while.

Then begin chanting again, raising power. Continue for as long as you can ... Beat drums ... Dance ...

Then send this energy to where it is needed in the world, send it off with love ...

Pause a while.

Pass round the bread, each woman putting a morsel in her neighbour's mouth saying, 'may you never be hungry' and passing on the rest of the bread. Then pass round the wine saying, 'may you never be thirsty,' letting each woman drink.

Finally, each woman kisses her neighbour saying, 'may you always be loved'.

Now feast and talk and deal with coven business or other matters, remaining within the circle. Eventually unwind the circle, walking three times clockwise, sunwise.

Blessed Be!

If spells have been done, collect all candles and spilled wax and other materials, plants, ribbons, leftover food, and throw them into a moving body of water (a river, stream or the sea). Walk away without looking back.

THE STRUCTURE OF THE RITUAL

Using other people's rituals has always been difficult for me; I work using my intuition rather than follow instructions and so prefer to follow the mood of the moment rather than learn long rituals by rote. But beginners do need a general outline within which to work before they can start to devise their own rituals.

Every ritual has most of the following elements which are generally performed in the following order:

1. Preparation

In many respects this is the most important part of a ritual. Good planning and meditation on the theme of the ritual will deepen the experience for everyone and make the magic strong and well-directed. If you are working in a group and plan to do a full moon ritual, work out its structure at the preceding new moon. This will give you enough time to do any research, collect any special materials, make incenses, anointing oil, etc. To start with, I suggest you work with the Goddess in her many names and guises, and assign members to research this. As you become more confident do rituals on specific themes, such as creativity, power, menstrual rites, motherhood and death. Decide in advance who is going to do what in the ritual, who will be the High Priestess, who will call the elements, be in charge of the altar, the food and the wine, and so on. It is important that each woman has a role, so no one person is responsible for too much. On the night of the ritual, bathe and wash your hair to let go of your ordinary concerns. Put on clean clothes or your special ritual robes. Set up the altar in a safe place where it cannot be knocked over, and where the candles will not get blown out by the wind. Put out a representation of the Goddess – it may be a model, a painting – which represents the phase of the moon you are working with (that is, Maiden, Mother or Crone). Put out the appropriate flowers for the season and candles to match. Decorate with ribbons, shells, wood, whatever comes to hand. Your altar is a focal point; it acts as an inspiration and an attractive force, therefore put all the love and energy you have into building it. Set the incense to burn. I like the altar builder to then walk the four corners of the room or a large circle if outside to purify the air and begin the magical operation by taking the incense around. Light the candles and set out the food and drink around the altar.

2. Welcome and making the circle

The High Priestess greets each member, asks who she is and how she comes (see p. 81) and the anointer anoints each woman with oils on her brow, her throat, her heart, her solar plexus (see p. 81), her womb and her hands and feet. Each woman takes her place in the circle. The circle is then cast. This is done by walking *widdershins* (anticlockwise) for three, five, seven or nine rounds. As this is done each woman meditates on the ritual. The circle is a protection for all the women inside it, nothing can get in, and if women want to leave before it is unwound, a door has to be made in it by the High Priestess which is opened and then closed afterwards.

3. Summoning the four elements and the Goddess

The four elements are summoned, usually beginning with earth (as described above, p. 81); if you know them you can use the names of the spirits which go with them, otherwise stick to the symbolism of the four elements (see Appendix C). The High Priestess invokes the Goddess using similar words to those on p. 82 (you will have to memorise this).

4. Raising a cone of power

The coveners then begin to chant and hum and bang drums if they can to raise power. Remembering spellcraft (see Chapter 10) you bring the Goddess into your circle and draw down the energy there. There is always a point at which the energy peaks and the chanting stops. Hold the energy within your circle and then send it off, if you choose to do that, as healing energy for peoples or places, or use it to heal the group if there have been rifts or sickness in any of the members. It is now that you will feel the breath of the Goddess.

5. Pathworking/spell making

Here the magical work is carried out. If you are doing a spell or have a particular theme for your ritual such as healing or creativity, now is the time to do it. Otherwise the High Priestess leads a pathworking, which should reflect the general theme of the ritual.

6. Grounding

Here, women may choose to discuss the pathworkings or the themes of the ritual. If you are learning Goddess lore someone teaches a little while. If there is coven business, this should be brought up now. Allow women time to speak, share, ask questions.

7. Cakes and wine

The food is passed around and the wine (or juice or herbal drink – alcohol is not obligatory), and any last business, thoughts or feelings are raised. The time-watcher indicates the time to close the ritual and all stand.

8. Farewell to the Goddess

The High Priestess bids farewell and thanks the Goddess for being with them. The four directions, that is, North, South, East and West, are also thanked and bade farewell.

9. Unwinding the circle

Finally the circle is unwound, moving in a circle the same number of times as at the beginning, only this time in a clockwise direction.

As a general rule, and especially if the coven is new or the coveners unused to magical work, don't make the rituals too long as the energy will dissipate and women will get distracted. Short and dynamic is better than hours of incantations. Also remember that this is a celebration! It is serious but joyful; leave the ponderous rituals to patriarchy.

NEW MOON

Astrologically the new moon is when there is no moon in the sky; but witches call this time the dark of the moon. For them, the new moon comes three days later when the first crescent is seen in the sky, and this is what I mean when I refer to the new moon.

The New Moon is a time for beginnings, for hopeful, optimistic, expansive magical work. It is a particularly good time for spell work that involves a new step, a change, planning and moving forward into the future.

Spell-making ritual

Wait until you see the crescent moon rises in the sky, then light a white candle on your altar, saying:

> Moon, moon, maiden moon.
> Welcome!
> Welcome to my home
> Welcome to my heart
> Welcome! Welcome! Welcome!

Then do your spell.

The New Moon is when we express ourselves through the things we do, and usually involves taking practical action, visioning the future, renewing, building again. Such path-working is useful for re-orientating or connecting back to your path if you have been blown off course or are feeling a little lost.

Back to Source

Take yourself to a place where you won't be disturbed for at least 20 minutes. Lie down and relax... Take some deep breaths and breathe out any tension you are holding in your body and allow yourself to slowly sink down into the floor... Let go... Allow the floor to hold you up, and sink deeper and deeper into yourself... You are walking along a seashore... It's nighttime... : The waves softly lap along the water's edge and a crescent moon is just visible in the sky... A warm nighttime breeze caresses your face; somewhere an owl hoots... You begin to slowly walk along the beach, with the moon always in sight... far off in the distance you see a light burning... Resolve to investigate... As you draw nearer you realise it is a bonfire burning on the sands . . . Sparks shoot up from the flames and drift off into the velvet blackness of the midnight sky. Drawing closer still, you see there is an old, old woman sitting by the fire . . . You draw nearer . . . She looks up and smiles encouragingly . . . Feeling the heat of the blaze you move towards her and greet her . . . From underneath her cloak she draws out a crystal ball and hands it to you . . . In it are images showing your next step. Watch them without judgement . . . When they have stopped spend a little while if you need to, talking to the crone. Take your leave and walk slowly away . . . Come back into the room and write down your findings.

DARK MOON

Hecate walks at the dark moon when energies are at their most hidden, most secret, most magical. Hexing is traditionally done at this time, when Persephone goes deep into the earth to receive the spirits of the dead, where she is impregnated by the sacred seed which bears the sacred child. It is the time of blood, death, inner landscapes, deep, dark unconscious forces, dreams and visions, hexings and hauntings. The Black Goddess, Kali, Hecate, Lilith and Morgana reign in the kingdom of the underworld, the Hel of the Scandinavians. Hel is the womb, the cave, the pit, the well. The ancient Chinese book of wisdom, the *I Ching*, says: 'The well cannot be changed. It neither decreases nor increases.'[5] Wellspring of life and darkest, deepest of waters, most frightening and profound, source of life and dealer in death, the dark moon challenges and confronts us, showing us the mystery of life and death.

88

Pathworking to the Dark Mother

Some women may find it better to do this pathworking with a friend or in a group as frightening material sometimes comes up. Or do it in a ritual.

Relax and lie in a darkened room, preferably at night when there is no moon. Close your eyes and take several deep breaths, relax and go deep, deep, into yourself... Imagine you are walking along a path, in a wood and that it is night time, very, very dark. There is no moon, no light, except for the canopy of stars overhead... All is quiet, all is still... You walk deeper and deeper into the forest... You become aware that you are not alone, that other women are walking in the same direction as you. Silently you make your way into the heart of the forest... Three paths meet and you can just make out the other women who are gathered there... Offerings of fish and eggs lie where the three roads meet... You join hands and begin to chant... Your voices burst through the silence of the trees and reach high, high, up into the heavens and deep, deep, into the earth... There is a great fluttering of wings, a rushing of wind... Hecate arrives... (Pause for 5–10 minutes to take in all around you.)... Connect with the other women... Holding hands close the circle... Walk away without looking back. Come back into the room and talk about what happened.

Rituals are opportunities for growth, for learning and for experiencing both our innermost selves and the breath of the Goddess. Be as creative as you can and build up the correspondences, especially with the plants of the season, candles, ribbons and any things which decorate your altar, or yourselves; the Goddess loves beauty. Likewise in your preparation work, take time to do research about the Goddess-form you will be working with, that is, maiden, mother or crone. Make notes and give them to the other coveners so that your group builds up its own book of shadows and its own tradition. This is how we will re-weave the past to make the future.

RITUALS FOR EVERYDAY

As we celebrate the wheel of the year and the monthly waxing and waning of the moon's cycles, so witches celebrate and hold sacred other pivotal times in the life of women. Childbirth, puberty, menopause fit with the moon's cycles and represent important times in a woman's life. We also celebrate love, loving partnerships, birthdays and passing of dear ones (death).

To welcome a new mother and child

On the first new moon 40 days after the birth, gather together the mother and child and all those who helped her during her pregnancy and labour (including the midwife, if possible). Decorate the altar with white and yellow flowers and white and yellow ribbons and candles. Burn some chamomile incense (or oil), and have some to drink as a tea or punch. The goddess mothers lead the ceremony: light the candles saying:

> Great Mother!
> Goddess of all life!
> We gather here today to welcome another mother and
>   child into your great clan.
> We, the goddess mothers undertake to guide . . . (name)
>   and teach her (him) your ways and mysteries.
> A child of the Goddess, we bless her, enfold her deep in

your arms and guide this new mother in your greatest
work.
Bless this child!
Bless her mother!
Bless our family!
And all humanity!

Clap and cheer. One goddess mother then anoints the mother
and child with sandalwood on their brows. The child is passed
around and each person gives a wish or blessing to it. Then
celebrate, feast and swap mother/baby stories.

Ritual for puberty

After a girl's first bleed at the new moon, gather together with
her friends who have also begun to bleed. Set the girls the
task of building the altar with objects they consider to be
appropriate to their first bleeding. Assemble women and
crones, friends and family. One woman welcomes them, preferably a crone:

Through the cycles of the moon
and its Great Mystery.
Through the turning of the year
in its simple majesty.
By the will of the Mother,
and the building of the Fates,
I welcome you . . . (names)
into this, the greatest of mysteries.
Bleed and never empty;
replenished always.
From you life ebbs,
in you the seed grows.
Enter my darkened realm
and the world of the mother.
Maidens! We salute you
and welcome you home!

The maidens are greeted one by one by the other women who
give them a small token and wish them well. Follow by feast-

ing, singing and dancing and telling menstrual stories, myths
and legends.

Ritual for the Crone

At the dark of the moon gather together new crones (who
have had no blood for several moons) and old crones. Make
an altar of dried leaves and flowers, stones, fossils, nuts, bones
and symbols of female wisdom. Light silver and brown candles. An old crone welcomes the new crones:

> Welcome sisters to the waning years.
> Into the deeper spiral
> of our profound teachings.
> As we unwind from long years of mothering.
> As we let go of the cares of the world.
> Let us gather
> deep in darkness.
> Let us celebrate hidden wisdom
> that our Crone Mother
> holds for us.
> We take our shadow
> into the light eternal
> and weave a cloth,
> a sacred tapestry.

One by one the new crones are greeted, share food and drink
and speak of the teachings and crone lore.

Birthday ritual

You may choose to do this alone or with friends. If at all
possible meet up with some friends at some point during the
day.

On your altar light a candle of your favourite colour, or one
of your aura colours, and burn some sweet-smelling incense
or oil (sandalwood, ylang ylang, jasmine etc.). Briefly think
through the last year from your last birthday to the present
one. See the year unfold and, without judgement, notice the
theme of the year. Pause a while to remember the things you

learned this past year, your successes and your failures. Then
let it go, saying:

> The year is past,
> the great round completed.
> Harvest gathered and new seed sown.
> Listen mother
> as I ask you
> for these gifts
> this next year . . .
> (list them)
> May you hear me
> and do my bidding.
> May I flourish
> this next year!
> Blessed be!

Then do a divination for the coming year, with Tarot, crystal
ball, *I Ching*, etc. Afterwards, party!

Trysting ritual

This is to celebrate the coming together of a couple, whether
lesbian, gay, or straight. On a new moon, all gather together
outside, if possible. Decorate the altar with fresh flowers,
white, pink and green candles and burn jasmine or ylang
ylang oils or other sensual incense. Have food and drink to
celebrate. One person welcomes the couple:

> Welcome lovers, welcome!
> In the sight of the Goddess
> and by this new moon
> we celebrate Venus
> and a honey moon.
> May these lovers who join
> before us tonight
> be happy and healthful
> and full of delight.
> As we celebrate, Mother,
> the Wheel of the year.

> Bless this new couple
> Whom we hold so dear.

All cheer the couple and toast them. Have music (live or recorded) and let the new couple lead the dancing. Follow with general merriment.

Ritual for death

This is really only possible if the person dies at home, otherwise amend this to do as an alternative funeral or remembrance service.

If you are keeping watch at a dying person's bedside, be sure to have lots of fresh flowers in the room, and keep on hand some chamomile oil to burn and white candles. As she or he dies, open the window, light the candle and bless the departing spirit:

> Fly spirit!
> Soar, high above the clouds,
> deep into the darkest space.
> Find your way back to the Mother,
> the sacred place whence you began.

Ring a small handbell three times, sprinkle the room with rosewater and set the chamomile to burn.

Then call friends and loved ones (leave the doctor until much later) and let them sit with the body for as long as they wish.

If you can, keep the body in the house and have the burial or cremation as soon as possible afterwards.

Wreaths of rosemary are traditionally worked along with myrtle and white and purple flowers. Mourning colours are white, purple and black. If you cannot have the funeral the way you wish, be sure to gather with like-minded friends to celebrate the passing of your beloved one. Tell stories of her/ him, reminisce, record things you did and did not like, faults as well as virtues. Read from sacred texts, if you wish, and be sure to include some singing and afterwards lots of eating and drinking. Next Samhain you will have an opportunity to

speak to the deceased should you have unfinished business
(see Chapter 8, p. 103). It is best to let the soul go after it
leaves its physical body. But if the death has been sudden or
violent the spirit may stay earth-bound to check that those
left behind are all right. This is natural; let it be.

COVENS, PRIESTESSES AND THE CRAFT

There are as many ways to organise a coven as there are forms
of witchcraft. I will speak of my experience both as a
member of a women-only coven and as a lone witch.

A coven is a group of witches, which may be 13, 5, 7 or 9
in number. A small group of three can also work well. Notice
the odd numbers. My experience with groups has taught me
it is better to have an odd number of women, so that the
dynamic quality of the group is maintained. This can mean
that at times the group is stressed, but it also means that it is
unlikely to be cozy and convention-bound. So aim for odd
numbers.

The first rule of groupwork is commitment. Which means
that however eloquently you speak, and whatever the depths
of your learning, if you do not come to the group regularly and
punctually, you will be a disruptive force. Some people cannot
manage commitment or punctuality and it is very hard to
reform these bad habits. Such a woman probably is better
being a lone witch, so as to not waste anyone else's time.
Covens can meet monthly on the full moons, or twice monthly
on the new and full moon. Set a time to begin and stick to this.
Many groups start at Candlemas (see Chapter 8, p. 109) and
run for a year and a day. It is wise, each year, to re-affirm your
commitment, or leave if the group no longer serves you.

The second rule is motive. What are both the collective
and individual motives of the women in the group? Are they
compatible? Some members of a coven might have religious
or political perspectives, others teaching and learning agendas.
These issues are best thrashed out at the outset, because they
will come up at some point in the life of the group and may
cause deep rifts.

The third rule is honesty. Be honest with yourself and with
the group members. This usually entails creating an environ-

ment of trust in which members can feel safe enough to be angry, vulnerable, contentious and so on. This, naturally enough, takes time to achieve, but it is facilitated by listening to each member, giving each member's words and opinions equal weight and being careful not to form sub-groups within the larger group. This is hard as members will automatically be attracted to some rather than to other members, but honesty implies integrity in the way we relate to others.

The fourth rule relates to gossip. Everyone likes tittle tattle and we all indulge in it, to a greater or lesser extent. But within a group context, especially one dealing with potent energies, gossip must be avoided. It is harmful and wounding and causes splits and suspicion. If a member is indulging in gossip, and particularly if it is divisive, the whole group has to confront the person and make it clear that this is not acceptable behaviour. Often a gossip feels she cannot have power overtly and so seeks it in a covert manner. If this is the case, try to give her status and responsibility which will satisfy her need.

Consensus is the next rule. Decisions should be made by consensus only, with *all* members agreeing with a decision before any action is taken. If there is not consensus then those who do not agree with the decision will feel resentful and excluded, which eventually will lead to splits and factions. Consensus takes a long time to achieve; be patient, it is worth it in the long run. Don't rush decisions through. Put aside time for a special meeting if the issue is important. If consensus cannot be reached, drop the issue. Alternatively, put one person in charge of an issue and allow her to decide for the best and report back to the group.

Fun is most important. There are no rules, no duties for fun. Worshipping the Goddess is a pleasure and should be joyful and uplifting. If it becomes duty bound or too serious, something is wrong. Make sure everyone gets to have fun in her own way, whether with trips out, readings, artwork, dancing, or cooking. The Goddess may be celebrated in a myriad of ways, not just through ritual and meditation.

At the outset you need to decide if you want a leader (High Priestess) for the life of the coven, or for particular rituals only, or whether you want it to be non-hierarchical. It depends how much experience the individual members have of both witchcraft and group work. Be practical, but also wary of someone who always takes charge, or who has an intimidating style. A mixture of led and leaderless groups I have found works the best. Rituals do need a focus, and unless the individual participants take on their roles fully, there will need to be someone to co-ordinate the happenings.

Each coven member is a unique and talented individual, whose creative input needs to be fostered and encouraged. All groups must be learning experiences, which broaden and enrich its members. Take stock of the talents of your group and make sure they are expressed, regularly and creatively, in praise of the Goddess. As the members learn and grow, so will the group as a whole deepen its experience. It might be an idea to make a list of the skills of the group members which can be referred to from time to time.

Inevitably at some stage conflict will arise. A group is as strong as its weakest link. Conflict often arises due to underlying feelings of exclusion, or the need to dominate or criticise others. This is usually well hidden under an issue which is merely a smokescreen for a deeper matter. If the whole group is not involved in the conflict, let the others try to scent out what the real issue is about, to get behind the words. If the conflict seems irreconcilable, separate the two parties and start another coven. In this way it is to be hoped that no deep rifts form because the conflict is not allowed to continue to the bitter end. It is always best to stop and consider practical solutions to a serious conflict than try to persuade or force the factions to agree. We cannot always agree, we cannot often change people's minds, but we can live in harmony with all the myriad differences that exist. To agree to differ stops wars.

The Goddess loves the generous and hates the meanspirited. Generosity is giving people the benefit of the doubt, ascribing to them good motives, sharing your resources, whether material, emotional, spiritual or intellectual. This means sharing your pain as well as your pleasure, your weaknesses as well as your strengths, and accepting and cherishing those of others.

Record the work of your coven in your own book of

magic. Write out the rituals, teachings and experiences of the members.

EQUIPMENT – TOOLS OF THE TRADE

A simple ritual made with great devotion is worth a million censers, robes and wands.

I come from the rustic, hands-on, nature-loving branch of witchcraft, so I value natural, seasonal objects and inexpensive, unembellished rituals. Because I see my practise of the Craft relating directly to the seasons of the year and the phases of the moon, most of the ritual paraphernalia I use comes from nature, or I make it myself. I buy the candles and essential oils to burn, but otherwise make my incenses and drinks; some witches make their own wine. My sense is this heightens or deepens the experiences and weaves the sacred more and more into daily life.

If you are dedicated and have time, make your own wands, cups and robes.

Your altar, which can be of any size – a shelf or windowsill or table and covered with a cloth, if you like, should be somewhere private and will probably have some of the following objects on it: a cup (handmade) of pottery, glass or silver. Fill it for libations, which represent the cauldron of knowledge and the element of water. A censer is needed to burn incense. It will be made of metal as incense gets very, very hot. Stand it on a tile so as not to burn the surface of the altar. This is the element of air. Use candlestick(s) which should be secure so that they cannot fall out and set fire to curtains or other objects nearby. This is the element of fire.

I use flowers, fruits in season, pretty leaves, barks, seashells, nuts; anything earthy will do to represent the element of earth. I try always to have fresh flowers on my altar. You may also have a wand, made from hazel or elderwood,[6] and an ordinary knife or *athame* (sacred knife), either of which are used to cast the circle and point out the four directions. A representation of the Goddess, a picture, statue, stone, something which brings her into your house, is also needed. If you read the cards keep them on your altar. I also put money I earn there before I spend it, as a gesture of thanksgiving. Any other sacred objects, or precious things, affirmations, prayers, poems or pictures, should be placed on the altar.

Use your altar as a focal point in your home. Light a candle when you feel sad, happy, lost or angry. Symbols accumulate power the more energy we invest in them. Your altar is a piece of the sacred which lives and breathes along with you, your companions and your home. Treat it as such; clean it regularly; add things, take things away; keep it a living, breathing, embodiment of the Goddess within you.

Blessed Be!

8

FESTIVALS OF THE YEAR

THE WHEEL OF THE YEAR

The wheel of the year, like the cycle of a lunar month, depends upon and reflects the changing seasons. The passage of the sun is charted through the 12 signs of the zodiac. The four quarter days of midsummer, midwinter and the spring and autumn equinoxes, and the cross-quarter days of the festivals of Beltane, Lammas, Samhain and Candlemas are the eight major festivals of the pagan calendar and are celebrated, along with the 13 full and new moons. The yearly cycle repeats the monthly cycle of death, regeneration, rebirth, fruition, ripening and death. This time it is the sun and her cycles which lead the dance, as she disappears in the dark winter months to reappear, tentatively, in the watery spring, in full-blown summer and then in the ripeness and warmth of autumn.

The rituals I discuss are taken from a variety of sources,[1] based on first-hand accounts of the lives of rural people in England. Much of their celebrating was related to their agricultural work and so was directly connected to the earth and its mysteries, particularly the cycle of fertility, impregnation, birth and death.

The year begins with Samhain, death and dissolution.

SAMHAIN–31 OCTOBER

Soul-day, Soul-day,
We've been praying for the soul departed;
So pray, good people, give us a cake,
For we are all poor people, well-known to you before;
So give us a cake for charity's sake,
And our blessing we'll leave at your door.[2]

Samhain was the beginning of the year in Anglo Saxon times,[3] and the whole of the month of November was associated with the cult of the dead. Samhain marks the final end of harvest and the beginning of winter, the dark descent of the year into the barrenness of the coldest months. Like the experience of death, flipping us from life into the dark shadow-land of mourning. Money was traditionally collected for the souls of the dead, so that masses would be said in their honour. Cakes were also baked to be given to callers, as the above rhyme testifies. Food was left out for the dead at crossroads and fires were lit. Beltane and Samhain were the two major fire festivals of Europe and in living memory fires were lit in the fields and burning brands carried around the perimeters while families prayed for their dead. The fires were said to light the soul's journey to the Otherworld. The fires of 5 November are really Samhain fires. Each person would pick a stone and toss it into the fire; if he or she failed to find the stone in the morning it would mean the person wouldn't live to see the next year's bonfire. Bonfire comes from 'bane fire' or 'bone fire', the fires that burnt up the rubbish to purify it.

Samhain was associated with apples, hazel nuts and trees; in the North of England it was also known as nutcrack night.[4] This was a time of apple-dipping and burning of hazel nuts. Hazel was a magical tree, a symbol of wisdom. Graves[5] describes a fountain, Connla's Well near Tipperary, over which hung the nine hazels of poetic art that produced flowers (beauty) and fruit (wisdom) simultaneously. The nuts contained all the knowledge of the arts and sciences. Hazel rods were used in divining water and buried treasure. It was one of the seven sacred trees[6] of the Irish grove, as was the apple tree which was considered the tree of immortality: 'Sweet apple-tree crimson in hue/Which grows concealed in Forest Celyddon.'[7] The apple tree led the soul into the land of the immortals who fed with the fruit of life and everlasting happiness. King Arthur was healed of his grievous wound in Apple Isle or Avalon, the secret island filled with apple trees. The apple cut crosswise reveals one of the mysteries, a pentagram (five-pointed star), symbol of the Goddess representing the five stations: birth, initiation, consummation, repose and death. Death to birth and back to death again. The pentagram

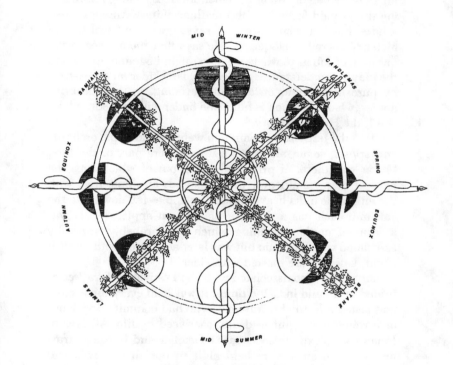

the festivals

also represents the planet Venus, the morning and the evening star. The nut in Celtic legend represents concentrated wisdom, something 'in a nutshell'. A hard shell protects a nourishing sweetness. That these two trees were sacred is revealed in the Triads of Ireland[8] where the death penalty was given for unlawful felling of two of the chieftain trees: 'Three unbreathing things paid for only with breathing things: An apple tree, a hazel bush, a sacred grove.' Graves gives the hazel tree to Mercury, sacred to eloquence. He says that the answer to the question of Job as to where wisdom might be found and where the place of understanding might be, is: 'Under an apple-tree, by pure meditation, on a Friday evening, in the season of apples, when the moon is full.' The finder will be Wednesday's child, the Hazel/Mercury.[9]

Often the festivities of Samhain were held in apple orchards and apples, sugar, ale and hazel nuts were part of the fare: 'A vat was there, of princely bronze, out of which runs the juice of merry malt; over the vat stands an apple-tree, with the multitude of its heavy fruits. The apples fall down into the vat, and each has a drink of ale and an apple.'[10] This was a form of apple wassailing which was probably originally associated with Samhain but was later associated with Twelfth Night. Guests were toasted with cider.

Samhain is also associated with the Festival of Tara[11] celebrated in Ireland in Celtic times. It was held every three years and lasted a fortnight. Any man who had committed violence or a robbery was put to death, sacrificed by fire. All fires in Ireland were extinguished on 31 October and burning straw or blazing brands were held aloft to banish old evils and welcome in the New Year. A great candle was lit from the last of the fires and the rites were held in candlelight. In the morning the people received the consecrated fire from the Druid priests and re-lit their hearth fires.

November was a month of mourning. The druids sacrificed a black sheep and offered libations to those who had died during the past year. The last sheaf was sometimes cut at Samhain (or at autumn equinox) and no one wanted to be the person to cut it; sickles were thrown at it for that reason. It was collected up and made into a corn dolly to placate the spirits of the Grain Mother and hung up in houses and places of worship. November was also known as the month of death and sacrifice (*Blot monath*) to the Teutons and Angles, and animal sacrifices took place.

For witches, Samhain is the time when the veils between the worlds are at their thinnest. The living and the dead co-mingle and we can talk to departed souls and learn the mysteries of Hecate's kingdom. For this is her festival, just as the dead are her realm. Sacred to Hecate are fish and eggs. Hecate suppers were left where three roads crossed, as gifts for the Goddess. Hecate who leads us into wild places, blood rites, decay and death, howling wolves and the dark moon. At the ending of the year old grievances should be resolved, debts torn up or paid, the slate wiped clean, ready for the new year. Hecate's tree is the willow and the root word for willow 'wike' is the same as that for witch and wicked. A witch's broomstick or besom is made from an ash stake which protects against drowning, with birch twigs, which entangle evil spirits, and willow, sacred to Hecate, to bind them. Druids offered human sacrifice in willow baskets (wicker) at the full moon. Willow is sacred to the moon, her affinity for water speaks of that. The willow is the tree of enchantment. Owls are sacred to Hecate and screech their loudest in November and then are silent until February. They are messengers of Hecate and she has given them the gift of prophecy, hence their reputation for wisdom, the crone wisdom of the Goddess.

Ritual for Samhain

If at all possible, do this ritual outdoors where you are unlikely to be disturbed, best of all where three roads meet. Do it as late as possible – around midnight is a good time – but the darkest hours before the dawn are best of all. Build an altar and decorate with apples, hazelnut twigs and the nuts themselves, willow branches, three painted red and black eggs in a wicker basket and some fish. Have black and red candles on the altar and a silver one for the Goddess. Burn sage incense, or other incenses that correspond to Hecate and the season. Be sky clad (naked) or dressed in red and black. Have red wine or a thick red herb drink (such as hibiscus or rose hip), well-spiced, with cinnamon, cloves, allspice, etc. Have a

cauldron made from iron or pewter or other fire-proof material
(not synthetic). Burn mugwort and mandrake. Cast the circle
in the usual way and then invoke the Goddess Hecate, pound-
ing the earth or floor. Whisper at first, then grow louder and
louder . . .

> Hecate, Hecate, Hecate, Hecate!
> Goddess of the marsh and heathland.
> Goddess of the sacred crossroad.
> Crone Goddess of wisdom,
> bringer of death, scavenger of souls,
> Queen of the Night, mistress of the shades,
> lady of the underworld,
> we call on you . . .

Now howling, beating the ground, banging drums and wailing,
bring up the Goddess from the land of the dead.

> Sweet mystery,
> dark knowledge,
> hidden wisdom,
> bringer of chaos and madness,
> we seek to enter your world
> to know you,
> we bring libations, we bring offerings.
> Show us your darkened face,
> your blood wise mystery,
> lead us into the shadows,
> into the darkest night.

She brings with her memories of past burnings, torturings
and betrayals. She brings pain, sorrow and mourning. She
brings rage, fury and frenzy . . . She brings peace, acceptance
and forgiveness.[12]

Stay with those things she brings; cry and howl, weep and
wail, scream and writhe, whatever she prompts you to do.
Hecate is the agony and the ecstasy, the Goddess of wild
places.

Each woman walks up to the cauldron and sits with it for
a time; it has burning coals inside it. Put a pinch of incense

on the coals and allow the smoke to waft around you, its sacred fumes filling you. Allow the visions and memories to come . . . Pass around the apple, cut crosswise, showing the mystery, and the red drink. Take some time to speak to others, those who have passed through the veil between the worlds, remembering and blessing them. Then offer up your personal sacrifice to the group, something you don't wish to carry with you into the coming year, a habit, a relationship, a thought-form (that is, an idea you have fixed in your mind which gets stronger the more you feed it with energy). Write this on a piece of paper, take this to the cauldron and burn it, saying:

> With fire I purify.
> With fire I burn.
> As the cycle of the year passes
> may I leave you behind.
> As the new year dawns
> will we separate.
> Blessed Be!

Thank the Goddess, and wind up the circle. Carry your offerings of eggs and fish to the crossroads and leave them. Walk away without turning back.

YULE – MIDWINTER

Yule is celebrated on the winter solstice, 21 December, the shortest day in the northern hemisphere.

> Oh the holly and the ivy,
> when they are both full grown.
> Of all the trees that are in the wood,
> the holly bears the crown.

Women of the village went around the houses (a' Thomassing) to collect wheat with which to make a Yule-time batch of cakes and bread, each woman being given a quart of wheat. The miller milled it free of charge in return for sprigs of holly and mistletoe. Yule was the time for the mummer play. There were many versions of the play but the same theme was in all of them. The male participants dressed in costumes of skirts made from rags, and large headdresses of rags and shirts of the same. It was a fight for death and resurrection, two men fought and one, the Fool – also known as the Holly-King or the Green Knight – was killed. A doctor came and raised him from the dead, he was called Beelzebub. It was the corn spirit who died, and the doctor or priest-healer made the corn grow again through his ritual acts. The old king dies and the new king is born. Hole[13] says there are records of mummer plays 850 years old and suspects they are pre-Christian.

Alms for widows were collected at Yule. Men dressed up as Hoddening horses in large white sheets and went through the village crying:

> Wissal, wassail, through the town,
> If you've got any apples throw them down;
> Up with the stocking and down with the shoe,
> If you've got no apples, money will do;
> The jug is white, and the ale is brown,
> This is the best house in the town.[14]

In Derbyshire and Cornwall, a Kissing Bunch was made. This consisted of two hoops, one passed into the other, decked with evergreens, and in the centre a crown of rosy apples and a sprig of mistletoe. It was hung from the central beam of the living room and kissing and romping went on underneath it. Here carols were sung.

The holly, ivy and mistletoe were all Yule plants. Mistletoe had a long association with the druids; their midwinter rites involved cutting the mistletoe from the sacred oak with a golden sickle knife. There was ritual emasculation of the king at the nadir of the year so that he might be born again. The sun king was killed to be returned to the Great Mother in the North (the land where the sun does not shine), and was born again. In Norse tradition, Baldur was slain by a mistletoe dart by Loki who dedicated the dart to his mother Frigg, the Norse goddess of sexuality, as long as it does not touch the ground. Hence it is always hung from the rafters and it is associated with kissing and sexual games. A boar's head was also sacrificed to Frigg at Yule, decked with bay, rosemary, laurel and mistletoe. Yule, like the Roman festival of Saturnalia, was where all rules were relaxed and a great deal of sexual license was permitted. Mistletoe was known as an aphrodisiac.

> The holly, dark green,
>   Made a resolute stand;
> He is armed with many spear-points
>   Wounding the hand[15]

Graves[16] gives the holly to the planet Mars and Tuesday. Holly was the tree of the Ass god of the Italians who was the Christmas fool and who is killed by his rival as he is in the mummer plays. The ass represents bodily lusts which a more purified initiate has dispensed with. In his story of the *Golden Ass*, Apuleius is changed into an ass because he forgoes the White Goddess and is lost in the witch cults of Thessaly, only to be rescued when he entreats Isis and is initiated into her cult.[17] Thus holly repeats the theme of sexual license and also of wounding.

The ivy girl and the holly boy fought battles on Yule morning; they sang songs and took forfeits. The last sheaf to be harvested[18] was wrapped around with ivy and called the Ivy Girl. The farmer who was last with his harvest was given the Ivy Girl; it was supposed to mean bad luck in the coming year. The ivy was seen to be the clinging wife, strangling the tree. In the Roman Saturnalia, the holly was Saturn's club and the ivy the nest of the Gold Crest Wren. On Yule morning, the first person to cross the threshold had to be the Ivy Boy (a dark man), and all sorts of games and ruses were played to make this so. Songs were sung by both the men and women in this struggle. The ivy bush was always the sign of the tavern which traces its association back to Dionysus, and ivy ale was a very intoxicating mediaeval drink. Ivy's spiral growth pattern is said to represent the resurrection, another explanation for the rivalry between the ivy and holly, which is the tree of death. Masculine death fights the feminine life, rebirth principle. Ivy is one of the five-leafed plants sacred to the Goddess, the others being vine, bramble, fig and plane.

I will pluck the tree-entwining ivy,
As Mary plucked with her one hand,
As the King of life has ordained,
To put milk in udder and gland,
With speckled fair female calves,
As was spoken in the prophecy,
On this foundation for a year and a day,
Through the bosom of the god of life,
and all of the powers.[19]

At Yule, witches celebrate the coming of the summer. At the darkest point of the year we look forward to the warmth and light of midsummer.

Yule ritual

Decorate the altar with holly and ivy wreathed with red and green ribbons, red and green candles, one gold candle to represent the sun and a black one to represent the darkness. Tie bunches of mistletoe with red ribbon, knotting them seven times, and hang them from the ceiling. Burn the incense of Saturn. Have a libation of mulled wine and spiced cake to pass around.

Cast the circle and invoke the Goddess.

Midwinter goddess,
Frosty Winter Queen,
Lady of the icicles,
Kind Mistress of hoar frost.
Listen as we call you,
On this darkest of nights.

In these barren months
where the sun is so hidden,
we gather here tonight
to celebrate the darkness
and the coming of the light.
The sun has disappeared
furthest underground.

It begins its ascent,
making the Great Round.

Bring us your mystery,
and let us celebrate
the glory of winter
and the rebirth of the sun.

Raise power by dancing and chanting or singing carols and
then act out the killing of the sun and its rebirth by the fool/
magician. Finish by feasting and passing round the wine and
spiced cake.

IMBOLC – CANDLEMAS

Celebrated on 1 February, Candlemas is the festival of lights.
It is a festival for when the first snowdrops peek through the
snow; it has an association with purity, innocence and new
shoots appearing through the winter chill. It is halfway between mid-winter and the spring equinox. Candles used to
be blessed on this day and distributed to women in the parish.
In a ceremony in Nottinghamshire a candle was set on a
rocking cradle near the altar, and the last baby baptised in
the parish was rocked in this cradle by the priest. Clearly this
was a pagan birthing ritual which was taken over by the
church. It resembles the tradition of Bride's bed, when the mistress of the house and her female servants would take a sheaf
of oats and dress them up to resemble a woman. She would
be put in a large wicker basket with a club beside it. The
women would then cry: 'Bride is come! Bride is welcome!'
This was done at night before everyone went to sleep. In the
morning the women would look for footprints in the ashes of
the hearth to show she had come. The custom was practised
in the Highlands of Scotland and in Cornwall, in the lands of
the Celts. Bride or Brigit had a strong following in Ireland;
hers was an all-female cult from which men were excluded
on pain of death. The centre of the cult was in Kildare where
a perpetual fire burned. Brigit's day was Imbolc.

I am the White Swan,
Queen of them all.[20]

The rowan tree was connected with the festival. It was known
as a tree of quickening, an oracular tree.

Rowan rod, forefinger,
By power of divination
Unriddle him a riddle;
The key's cast away.[21]

In the old days, Candlemas was the time when the Christmas greenings were taken down, not Twelfth Night.

Down with the Rosemary, and so
Down with the Baies, & misletoe:
Down with the Holly, Ivie, all,
Wherewith ye drest the Christmas Hall:
That so the superstitious find
No one least Branch there left behind:
For look how many leaves there be
Neglected there (maids trust to me)
So many Goblins you shall see.

Robert Herrick[22]

Candlemas ritual

Deck your altar with white and green flowers (the seasonal
flowers of the Goddess) – lots of them, especially snowdrops.
Entwine garlands of white and green ribbons among white
and green candles. Have pictures of the Goddess as creatrix
and beautiful objects, such as pottery, glassware and jewellery.
    Cast the circle and invoke the Goddess:

From the icy earth we call you,
from frozen lake and iron hill.
Pushing up through frosty forest
yellow, white and purple, crocus
colour in the leaden greyness,
splashing through the whitest snow.

> Goddess of this darkest season,
> Mistress of this sacred time,
> initiate us in your wisdom,
> carry us to your icy realm.

Raise power by chanting. Candlemas is the time for initiations. I feel initiation is more of a personal statement, rather than something conferred by others. Perhaps it is best done each year by members of a coven, all those who wish to stay for the following year.

One by one, each member goes up to the altar and meditates on this new stage and her contribution to the group. Then she turns, faces the coven and repeats her pledges. This is followed by feasting.

EOSTRE – SPRING EQUINOX

This was held at the quarter day, when the day was at equal length to the night, on 21 March. The Christian festival of Easter is held on the first Sunday after the full moon after the equinox, denoting its pagan roots. Eostre was the Goddess of the spring and the dawn. The spring festival was a celebration of the end of winter: spring flowers, new clothes. The old fires were put out and new fires were kindled by rubbing two sticks together. All the old fires had to be put out or, it was said, the sticks wouldn't catch. Then the grates were cleaned and polished and the fires lit from the sticks.

Easter eggs, hot cross buns and Easter bunnies are all pagan in origin, while dyeing eggs can be found in Norse, Egyptian, Greek, Roman and Persian customs. They were dyed with a variety of vegetable dyes such as onion skins, logwood, pieces of coloured rags, furze flowers. Eggs symbolise the world as encapsulated. The world egg is found in many ancient cultures. It is the symbol of initiation. The Goddess, having laid the world egg, needs the sun of spring to hatch it. For the spring festival represents the opening of winter into spring. In Egypt, Greece, Rome and Persia, eggs were dyed yellow, violet and pink and blessed by the priest. In England, however, the lord of the manor gave out eggs dyed red, green and yellow to his parishioners. In the account books of Edward I in 1290,

a purchase of 450 eggs was included in his Easter accounts
to be given to the poor.

> Please Mr . . . (name),
> Please give us an Easter egg.
> If you do not give us one,
> Your hen shall lay an addled one,
> Your cock shall lay a stone.[23]

Barbara Walker relates the story of the English King, Queen
and their courtiers creeping to the cross at Easter time with
eggs and apples (the pagan symbols of life and death) as late
as the sixteenth century.[24]

Hot cross buns came from the wheaten cakes eaten at the
spring festival of the Romans, Saxons and Greeks. The
Romans made these sacred cakes in honour of Diana, whose
festival was celebrated around this time. The centre of the
custom in England was Cambridge, where the Roman roads
of Ikneld Street and Amynge Street crossed and in that spot
was an altar to Diana. Here her sacred cakes were baked and
offered to the Goddess. Simnel cakes, made with lots of spices
and decorated with almond paste, were made by those who
could afford it and given to the poor. Easter bunnies represent
the moon hare of the Goddess. The hare was a taboo animal
in Britain which could not be killed. It was taken into battle
by Boadicea. (In Kerry in Ireland, even today the people won't
eat hare meat, which they call 'eating your grandmother'.)

Witches changed themselves into hares.

> O, I shall go into a hare
> With sorrow and sighing and mickle [little] care,
> And I shall go in the Devil's name
> Aye, till I be fetched hame.[25]

There used to be a Spring Mummer play between Thor and
Baldur: winter fights spring. Beau Slasher was the champion
of winter; he had an iron head, steel body, and hands and
feet made from knuckle bones. Spring fought winter and van-
quished him, heralding the end of winter's reign.

Springtime ritual

Decorate the altar with spring flowers, candles of pink and blue and yellow, and one Goddess candle. Have garlands of yellow, green and red ribbons and painted eggs of the same colour. Also have some small simnel cakes and light white wine for the libation.

Cast the circle and welcome Flora, goddess of spring:

> Spring Goddess, gentle maiden,
> stepping from the icy earth.
> Letting go of winter's fetters
> as the wide world breathes again.
>
> Chill winds rustle daffodils
> and blossom scatters,
> patterning the hill.
> Enter Flora!
> Enter spring.
> We welcome you once again!

Each woman takes an egg which is passed from hand to hand and contemplates the egg within, her potential self. Close your eyes and take a few minutes to be with that potential. Contemplate the new growth inside of you, the fruits of the dead wood which are cut back at Samhain. Take the image of the egg into your mind's eye and imagine it cracking open like a hen's egg. See what emerges. Share your insights with the group. Pass round the cakes and wine and give thanks to the Goddess.

BELTANE – MAY EVE

Celebrated on 30 April, Beltane was the great fertility festival of the witch's year. Philip Stubbes[26] wrote in 1583:

Against Maie every parish, town and village assemble themselves together, bothe men, women and children, olde and young, even all indifferently: and either goyng all together or dividying themselves into companies, they goe some to the woodes and groves, some to the hilles and mountaines, some to one place some to another; where they spende all the night in pastimes, and in the mornyng they returne, bringing with them birch bowes and branches of trees to deck their assemblies withal.

Every house was decorated with green branches, which were brought into the houses on May morning. The following day was a holiday. There was a fair during the afternoon and in the evening a May Ball for women servants. The women wore a lily-of-the-valley posy and the men morning dress with buttonholes, and they went around villages knocking at every door and would dance through houses, the women curtseying and the men bowing to bring in summer.

> And we were up as soon as any day O
> And for to fetch the summer home,
> The summer and the May O.
> For the summer is a come O.
> And the winter is a go O.[27]

The above words were the chorus of the Helston Furry which was traditionally a dance to Flora, the goddess of flowers and the spring. On May Eve, the May Birchers used different boughs and flowers to decorate the doors of each house in the village, which in code said what they felt about the occupants; for example, pear was fair, plum, glum, gorse morose, while those decorated with nettles and other weeds were the most unpopular.

Crosses made of rowan branches were tied to the tails of cattle to stop them being bewitched, for Beltane was when fairies were abroad.

> The spells were vain, the hag returned
> To the green in sorrowful mood
> Crying that witches have no power
> Where there is rowan-tree wood.[28]

May Eve was also known as mischief night, when shopkeepers' signs were changed, gates were taken off their hinges and practical jokes were played. Primroses were laid before the front doors of houses to scare away the fairies. Legend had it that the first fairy dance of the year was held on 2 May to celebrate the fairies coming out of hibernation; their last dance was on Samhain. If you drank water from a well after sunset on 1 May you would be captured by the fairy folk and imprisoned in the land of fairy for a year and a day.

May Day was celebrated by processions, the wearing of garlands, the lighting of bonfires and carol singing, on hill tops or from towers. (To this day, carols are still sung on 1 May on the Magdalen tower in Oxford.) Such festivities were brutally suppressed by the Puritans in the seventeenth century and were further affected by the change in the calendar with the loss of 11 days, which meant flowering May blossom was much less likely to be found on May Day. In Suffolk, too, an old custom of rewarding the first servant to bring in a bough of flowering May with a dish of cream had to be abandoned.

May Day celebrated the Green Man, Robin Hood and Maid Marion. Henry VIII, out riding with Katherine, one of his wives, one May Day morning in Greenwich, found a large band:

> of tall yeomen, clothed all in green, with green hoods and with bows and arrows, to the number of two hundred. One, being the chieftain, was called Robin Hood, who required the King and all his company to stay and see his men shoot.[29]

In Oxford there were processions like carnivals, with a Lord and Lady or King and Queen, a Fool with a pig's bladder on a string to hit the bystanders, a fiddler and all the town's chimney sweeps. A man with a shovel and a poker made a kind of music and two or three men carried collecting boxes. Everyone except the Lady had blackened faces and were decked out with ribbons and flowers. They collected alms for old chimney sweeps. In London and Manchester there were cart horse parades; the giant horses were decorated with flowers and garlands and shining horse brasses. (The original horse brasses were good luck charms, with crescent moons and stars.) The carts were decorated with laurel boughs and flowering lilac.

Red and white flowers were wound into garlands around the Maypole, reflecting the blood and milk mystery of the Great Goddess. The Maypole, an ancient fertility symbol, was brought from the woods on May morning. Stubbes describes this:

> They have twentie or fourtie yoke of oxen, every oxe havying a sweete nosegaie of flowers tyed on the tippe of his hornes, and these oxen drawe home this Maie poole . . . which is covered all over with flowers and hearbes, bounde rounde aboute with stringes, from the top to the bottome, and sometyme painted with variable colours, with twoo or three hundred men, women and children followying it with greate devotion. and thus being reared up, with handkerchiefes and flagges streamyng on the toppe, they strawe the grounde aboute, binde greene boughes about it, sett up sommer haules, bowers, and arbours, hard by it. And then fall they to banquet and feast, to leap and daunce about it.[30]

The Maypole in the Strand in London set up in 1661 was an amazing 134 feet high, having been raised by seamen from the docks using pulleys and anchors. The Puritans waged a severe campaign against all such pagan rites, which were banned one by one.

Beltane ritual

Decorate the altar with May blossoms, lilac, fresh flowers and green budding branches. Use lots of red and white ribbons, and red, green and white candles. Burn sandalwood or melissa incense. Have lots of sweet, honeyed food, cakes and pastries, and elderflower champagne. This is a big party. If at all possible, celebrate outside in orchards, woodland or even the local park. Keep a watch out for fairy folk. Begin once Venus, the evening star, has risen.

Invoke the Goddess as Maiden:

> Flower maiden,
> Blossom Goddess,

scent of summer,
rut of stag,
may we all share in your bounty
as we dance this magic night.

Sing, dance and celebrate the mysteries of love, beauty and fertility.

MIDSUMMER – 21 JUNE

Celebrated on the longest day of the year, Midsummer marks the turning point of the year. In Britain, bonfires used to be lit on hill tops in honour of the sun on Midsummer Eve and people danced around the fire. These fires were remnants of Druidic rites. In Greece, midsummer fires were lit in honour of Demeter, and her celebrants danced around them to banish evil and ensure a good harvest. In Ireland, the fairies were said to fly around the Baal fires on Midsummer's Eve to put them out so they could work their mischief. Afterwards the ashes were strewn on the fields to bring fertility to the crops. Men walked round the perimeters of fields with blazing torches. In London, fires were lit in the streets and the lamps burned all night over the decorated doors of the houses. Doors were hung with garlands of fennel, and St John's wort. Groups of maidens garlanded with roses and rue, vervain and trefoil, danced in the streets.

As Shakespeare wrote in *A Midsummer Night's Dream*, Midsummer Eve is a time of enchantments, of bewitchment and pranks. There were several plants with magical properties that had to be collected on that night. Fern seeds, so tiny they are almost invisible to the naked eye, are believed to make the gatherer invisible. There is a German story of a man who walked across a field with fern growing in it on Midsummer's Eve. Some seed fell into his shoes and he became invisible without realising it. Back home, he terrified his wife and children as they only heard his voice but could not see him. The seeds had to be gathered without touching the plant. Charles Hardwick[31] tells a story of three men who set out to collect fern seed on that night, when a darkened form in a cape appeared to them:

Darkness came down like a swoop. The fern was shaken; the upper dish flew into pieces; the pewter one melted . . . beautiful children were seen walking . . . and graceful female forms sung mournful and enchanting airs.[32]

Midsummer fires were always lit with oak, sacred to all the thunder gods, and the fires of Vesta, Roman goddess of the hearth. Midsummer was the time when the oak-king was sacrificed and burnt alive and winter's darkness anticipated. Lovers jumped over Midsummer bonfires together and threw flowers across the flames. Trysts were made and coupling took place.

Midsummer ritual

Decorate the altar with roses and vervain, and other summer flowers, lots of red, yellow and orange candles and early summer fruits. Burn solar incense. Have a deep, sweet wine or herbal drink and luscious summer fruits for the libation.

Invoke the Goddess of high summer.

> Summer sun which shines upon us,
> soft warm breezes as they blow.
> Meadows ripe with scented flowers,
> field, copse and hedgerow.
> The winds of summer lick our bodies,
> sunlight heals our frozen hearts.
> May the Goddess remind us
> of summer's lightness in the dark.

Raise power with song and dance and send it to farmers everywhere that they might have enough sun to ripen their crops and enough rain to moisten them. Finish with a libation and pass round the food.

LAMMAS – 1 AUGUST

Celebrated on 1 August, Lammas represented the gathering in of the first harvest. After Lammas come the dog-days of summer, when little gets done. This is the time for holidays

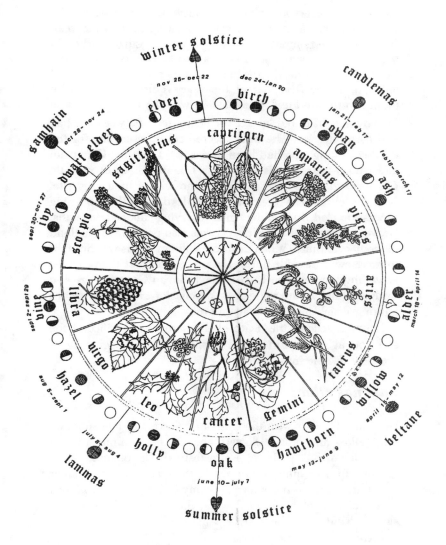

winter solstice

nov 25– dec 22   dec 24–jan 20

candlemas

samhain

elder   birch

oct 28– nov 24

jan 21– feb 17

dwarf elder   rowan

sagittarius   capricorn   aquarius

feb18–march 17

ivy   ash

sept 30–oct 27

scorpio   pisces

vine   aries

sept 2– sept 29

libra   alder

march 18– april 14

virgo   taurus

hazel   leo   cancer   gemini   willow

aug 5–sept 1

holly   oak   hawthorn   beltane

july 8– aug 4

april 25– may 12

lammas   may 13–june 9

june 10– july 7

summer solstice

the tree calendar

and rest, for everyone who is not harvesting, that is, but for those who harvest it is the hardest working time of the year. It is also a communal effort, long hours together worked in the hot summer sun. Lammas was also known as 'loaf mass.' Cutting the corn meant the grain would soon be milled and baked and the first loaf of the year would be given with thanks to the Goddess. Lammastide was the time when farm labourers went to old 'wakes' or hiring fairs between the hay and corn harvests. The wakes were held in mourning for the dead corn king who had been harvested, Lugh the Celtic sun god whose festival was known as Lughmass. Until recently *Lugh nasadh* was observed in Ireland with a mourning rite. It was celebrated as a festival of the dead, with the mourning procession led by young men carrying hooped wreaths. Graves[33] writes that this festival was also popular in England in mediaeval times. When the dead William Rufus was brought to the New Forest for burial the procession met the peasants bewailing the death of Lugh. The Tailltean Games of Ireland were originally funeral games of chariot races and sword fighting which took place at Lammas.

Lammas tells of the death of the hero, the sacrifice of the sun god at the zenith of his powers and the beginning of the slow decline into death.

Lammas ritual

Decorate the altar with the fruits and flowers of late summer, red, yellow and orange flowers and candles. Lammas is the going down, just as its opposite festival, Candlemas, is the coming up. Not quite autumn, but the season when summer is fading, Lammas has a hazy, dreamy feeling to it, the almost narcotic scent of honeyed flowers, the drone of harvest, the slow unwinding of the year.

Invoke the harvest goddess.

> Corn mother, grain reaper.
> Listen as we call to you!
> Our work is ending, the year is closing,
> the summer sun is going down.

Chant and raise power, sending it off to those projects and/
or people you know who need energy and support.

Take some time to review your own life and become aware
of unfinished business, tangles to be sorted, fruits to harvest.
Resolve to do this before the equinox. Pass around the wine
or herbal drink and feast.

AUTUMN EQUINOX

Celebrated on 21 September, the autumn equinox is the
second quarter day and finishes off the witches' year. It is
the celebration of harvest fruits and the dwindling summer
days. The last sheaf used to be dressed up as a symbol of the
Goddess, the maiden, the harvest queen, and was preserved
on the chimney piece. The youngest girl working in the fields
would cut the sheaf and carry her to the harvest supper. In
the far north east of Scotland she was called 'Cailleach', meaning old woman, and was dressed in a white cap and dress and
a shawl fastened with a sprig of white heather. Her apron was
stuffed with bread, cheese and a sickle. She sat at the head
of the table at the harvest feast and the young men danced
with her.

Autumn ritual

Decorate the altar with autumn leaves, berries of elderflower,
hawthorn, rowan and a corn maiden. Bake special bread with
raisins and honey and have a light dark wine or herbal drink.
Use brown, orange and yellow candles and a white one for
the Goddess. Burn an earthy incense, roots and barks.

Invoke the Goddess of autumn.

> Here are our fruits,
> here are our labours,
> here the work wrought in your name.
> Copper leaf and golden apple,
> sheaf of wheat sweet hazelnut.
>
> Here we bring our small libation
> made with love, our offering.

Mistress of the autumn harvest
come tonight and celebrate
the waning of the year.

This is harvest time but also seed sowing. Autumn equinox is where we dream deep the future of spring, the March awakening. After raising power take some time to plant those seeds within you. Dig deeply and send your hopes, dreams and wishes deep into the rich earth.

Blessed Be!

9

ETHICS

I have studied and worked in both feminist and orthodox traditions: Pagan/Goddess and Christian/Buddhist. My beliefs are an amalgam of the aspects in each system which I consider to be valuable and life-enhancing.

The views I hold are in most instances common to all Wicca traditions, but regarding some specific issues they differ. My ethics, as part of the general ethic of feminism and anti-racism, is more radical than traditional Paganism and Wicca but agrees with feminist witches and neo-pagan groups.

I do not consider witchcraft to be just a religion, replacing the Fathergod with the Mothergod. I see it more as a world-wide movement, comprising many different groups which respect and foster the growth and development of all peoples on the planet. This concern is expressed as much in the personal lives of the participants as in their direct action within their communities.

Much of our Western Mystery tradition was destroyed in the witch hunts and the repression which followed. Witches have had to do research, invent, copy and borrow the teachings of other peoples. It is for this reason that many of our esoteric systems come from other cultures, generally from the East. They come from China, India and Tibet, and recently from the Native American Indians, both from the United States and Central and South America and Mexico. There are real dangers: political, ethical and practical. First, these teachings have to be 'translated' for the Western mind, both literally as they often emanate from a different language, and figuratively as the cultures of which they form a part are very different to our own. The first pragmatic questions we need to ask are: Who has done these translations and do they follow the spirit of the texts? These are almost impossible to answer unless we know the original language. As most people do not, we have to take the primary precautionary measure of reading as many versions of the texts as we can. As regards women's spiritual traditions, male translators have often both trivialised and minimised the importance of their role within a given community. These misogynist translations of original texts have been left unchallenged until feminist scholars in recent years have begun to research the field.

The second, and even more important point, is that the West, as a dominant and racist culture, needs to practise extreme sensitivity with regard to any black culture. Otherwise there is a risk of the culture's spiritual practices being ripped off; their lands, language and culture having already been stolen by the West. This is particularly true of North American Indian spiritual traditions, which white North Americans are currently marketing like so many cans of Coca Cola while Indian women live on welfare. In her excellent article, 'For All Those Who Were Indian in a Former Life',[1] Andy Smith, a Cherokee woman, describes this co-opting of her spiritual traditions as: 'part of a very old story of white racism and genocide against the Indian people.' She points out that no genuine spiritual teacher profits from his or her teachings. The Indian tradition operates within the Indian community and cannot be extrapolated from that community. White feminists, she continues, want to be Indian to dissociate themselves from the genocide of the white race – but only partly Indian. They do not want the poverty, low life expectancy, alcoholism and the fight for treaty rights that are the daily realities for Indian people. By trivialising Indian spirituality, white feminists are enhancing the destruction of the Indian people. 'Experts' now contact these white women about Indian spiritual techniques, which further marginalises Indian women.

Indian women are perceived to be 'cool and spiritual' by white feminists who bully them into telling all about their spiritual practices, and who accuse them of being greedy if they don't. But these 'cool and spiritual women', whose life expectancy is 47 years and who face a 75 per cent unemployment rate, never benefit from the marketing of their own spiritual traditions. Rather, it is white women who run the sweat lodges, sell the jewellery, write the books, organise the conferences. Yet not one of the women who market women's spirituality is heard to campaign for Indian rights, or seen to be running conferences defending the Indian nation.

This situation is found throughout the developing world, in spiritual fields, in music, art, medicine, even cosmetics. Cultural exchange is great and good, but it must be an *exchange*. If Westerners want ethnicity then there must be some benefit provided by the West for the developing country which provides the ethnicity. The benefit does not, as Andy Smith points out, have to be a monetary payment, but payment in some form must be made – by whatever means available, perhaps by raising voices in protest against abuses or writing articles.

So we need to be careful who we listen to and to be aware of who is selling us their spiritual secrets and why. Not everything 'ethnic' is useful, helpful or even correct. Spiritual teachings so gained may be misleading or even harmful and the self-styled teachers deluded or even corrupt.

Living in a developing country, I saw how its spiritual leaders gave themselves hours of amusement by making up stories to tell researchers about their spiritual practices. Mostly ludicrous, these tall tales were nevertheless thoroughly digested and are no doubt to be found in doctorates throughout the developed world, proclaimed as academic truths. A woman friend of mine from that community told me the story of the egg, which perhaps will illustrate my point. This woman is one of the spiritual leaders of the community and a Japanese researcher asked to see her altar. On the altar was an egg. Eggs are used for many spells and healing rituals. When asked by the researcher what the egg was for, she replied, deadpan, that she always kept eggs on her altar out of the way of her children, otherwise they broke them. Exit researcher confused with her question answered. Enter laughing villagers.

In the West, we have our own traditions, albeit forming less of a direct link with the past than some cultures. In any study of ancient history there are examples of seafaring tribes (the Celts, Vikings, peoples from the Indian subcontinent, China, the American Indians) who met and exchanged ideas and spiritual practices which over the centuries have been interwoven to such a degree that the similarities exceed the differences. The Mummer plays of Hampshire, for example, are to be found in the Ga Ga of Haiti. We are all part of a time-space continuum which constantly doubles back on itself, makes loops and branches and weaves another tapestry.

These are the roots and branches of a worldwide spiritual reality, what Alice Bailey called 'The New World Religion'.[2] Her meaning, as I understand it, is that in cultural diversity we will discover a commonality of spiritual practice which will underpin the new world order which we all dearly hope will replace the culture of death and domination which has been imposed upon us.

For this to happen, we in the West have the most work to do in recovering our spiritual traditions. Our history is that of domination, bloodshed, cruelty and theft of the lives, lands and cultures of peoples less bellicose than our own. The guilt that many aware white people feel needs to be translated into positive action, reparation and bridge-building, in terms which can be accepted by those who belong to the peoples we have previously murdered, raped and looted. Our guilt gives us low self-esteem which is hard to own, let alone live with. Many choose not to face this but instead try to become honorary blacks to assuage their guilt, identifying with other cultures, whether Tibetan, Hindu or Native American, and at the same time trying to deny their own Westernness.

Rebuilding the spiritual core of our culture is the only way we have to find our way out of the materialist morass we have followed our deadly leaders into. It is also the only hope for a culture fast giving in to despair and nihilism.

As a peaceful, non-hierarchical, nature-loving, woman-centred spiritual practice, witchcraft has much to offer the lost and disillusioned. Our emphasis on personal value, community and self-determination engender a tolerance that the patriarchal religions of rule and domination can never share.

Patriarchal religions (Christianity, Judaism, Islam) have been at the vanguard of the culture of death which has been the bane of more pacific peoples for millennia. Their influence is finally waning. (The upsurge of fundamentalism, although worrying, I see as a last-ditch, desperate but futile attempt to capture a 'golden age' when a few men could rule whole continents by terror and bloodshed.)

The world is finally growing up. Although we are passing through a painful adolescence, the underlying mood is a rejection of the domination of Fathergod and a heartfelt need for the values embodied in the Goddess to be heard once more. We are now reaping the results of the ethic of god the father: obesity and eating disorders in the rich, while two-thirds of the world starves. Swimming pools and lawn sprinklers, dishwashers and washing machines are bought by the rich, while millions of babies and children die each year from drinking filthy water. The oldest wood in London, Oxleas Wood, was narrowly saved from being carved up so that a road could be built to pump even more poison into the air and the number of adults and children living in the metropolis suffering from asthma increases dramatically every year. The government subsidy of a nuclear power industry which is so poorly managed and corrupt that news of leaks of deadly radioactive material, which takes 15,000 years to become harmless, is delayed. Children breathing this air die from thyroid cancer. We live in a culture that would rather put small children behind bars than make the causal link between poverty, alienation and senseless violence and obscenely violent films and television.

At the root, Fathergod only cares for his chosen people, be they Jews, Christians, Moslems or Communists. The rest can burn. Like the Inquisitors who went around with huge bodyguards, the evil men behind all the injustice and cruelty in the world are faceless, removed from the wrath of the people. The puppets they manipulate, whether priest or politician, mask the worldwide network of drug dealers, pimps, arms salesmen and clergy. These men have brought us to the abyss and as we come to the end of the millennium, contemplating the end of our species, we perhaps have one last chance for sanity to prevail.

The enormity of the task which faces us often paralyses us with despair. But the perception of the enormity is the work of Fathergod and is a lie. It is not the men at the top who have the power (as they want us to believe) but us, the masses, who at present passively support the edifice. But each of us is pivotal.

There are many routes we can take as we plan our contribution to changing the world. Roberto Assagioli, a psychologist, talked of the seven ways to self-realisation, which mirror Alice Bailey's seven rays. They are the way of beauty, the way of will, the way of devotion, the way of concrete science, the way of active intelligence, the way of love-wisdom and the way of ritual. Witches are found on all seven rays and many work on more than one ray. The way of ritual, as its name suggests, is the making of sacred ritual, the finding of sense, meaning and wholeness through ritualised acts. The emphasis on connections, the seasons, the phases of the moon and the movements of the stars and planets, can help us to connect once more to the good, the true and the beautiful.

Research into the traditions which come from your part of the country. Unravel the past which Christian hands have buried and take pride in your culture and reclaim our Pagan heritage from the lie-mongers and tale-spinners. All Goddess religions share a commonality of beliefs and practices. Build on your indigenous practices and use them as a language to talk to others from different cultural traditions, thus helping us all to build an international network based on respect for life, and reverence for the Great Mother.

POWER

Fathergod and his necrophiliac followers have taught us that power is evil while demonstrating vividly the consequences of our powerlessness. Empowerment is the first stage on the path to self-discovery. Women, who for so long have been denied power and who may have wrested it out of the hands of men with great cost to themselves, find empowerment extremely problematic.

Magic is about manipulation of natural forces: 'The Science of the Control of the/Secret Forces of Nature'.[3] To work with magic is to have access to realms of power beyond the 'normal'. The restrictions of class, gender and race are irrelevant to the magical worker because the forces she is wielding are those of mind, which any trained person can work with. Aleister Crowley has said that magic is the science and art of causing change in conformity with the will. The first step in this magical operation is concentration, to be followed by visualisation. The mind is a potent tool and is neutral. It can be trained to work for good or for evil; it is all energy. Beginners in magic are often worried that if they develop magical skills they will abuse them and use their powers to harm others, or become lost in some occult siding of self-delusion. The worry is right and good. It is those who begin magical training without such worries who are the dangerous ones. In my experience it is never those who question their motives and doubt their integrity who become infatuated and enamoured of power.

We have grown up in a power culture, and however much we may have consciously eschewed its values, we have nevertheless imbibed the doctrine of power-over with our mother's milk. Constant and rigorous attention to our motives is vital.

Magical training often takes place in groups. Peer group assessment provides the opportunity (often painful) to learn how we wield power. Such supervision is the best kind of watching care. For many of us, our inner guides can talk to us and teach with a frankness we don't permit in others. If a climate of honesty and trust can be established then doubts can be raised in an atmosphere of mutual support.

THE DAILY REVIEW

This is an occult practice of great importance but which meets with tremendous resistance by our inner spiritual selves. Every night, review your day from the moment you got up. Don't judge or analyse, just let it pass before you like a reel of film. Take note of what was important, how you behaved in certain circumstances, how you made your choices and what they were. Try to be as impersonal as possible, as if looking at the day in the life of a friend. Try to see causal relationships between the choices you made, the things you did and how you did them (reluctantly, angrily, happily, etc.). What the review will teach you, if done over a period of many months and years, is the 'hows' and 'whys' of your life. How you make choices and why you do the things you do. The review will give you insight into your motives, and you will gradually realise who you really are, not who you would like to be.

As we develop our skills, so we take on the responsibilities that come with them. If our aim is to do no harm, then at some point we come to the realisation that our learning, our powers, need to be put to use for the general good of humanity.

Most witches are involved in some kind of activity which is life-enhancing and revolutionary in the sense that they are seeking changes in our imbalanced world. This may take the form of working on a one-to-one basis; counselling, healing, problem-solving and divination come under these categories. The witch seeks to comfort and facilitate the healing of damaged minds and bodies. Teachers seek to inspire and educate their pupils in the ways of the wise and so set them off on their own spiritual journey. Political and social workers aim to work with larger groups to right injustices and re-balance the imbalance of power. Our creative workers inspire us and cause us to reflect on life, to question its unravelling, and give us the gift of beauty, without which none of us can survive. And mothers give us new life and our future.

Patriarchal spiritual practice is about the development of the individual. Goddess spirituality, however, is community-based, even if you are the only witch (as far as you know) in Biggleswade. The basic tenet of patriarchal spirituality is separation: body from mind, spirit from matter, man from woman, the initiate and the lost ignorant ones, the priests and the laity. Goddess spirituality, however, emphasises the *connections* between things; the seasons, the phases of the moon and nature, the planets, goddess names, living, birthing, dying. Patriarchal religion denies death as a natural part of life and sees it as a reward or a punishment, burning in the fires of hell, wandering in purgatory or lounging in paradise. Goddess religion, on the other hand, sees our lives as a great round. We are born with the spirits of our ancestors (our Karma), we live our lives, paying respects to those spirits, we move on and then die to return to our ancestors (the other-world of spirits).

Spiritually we are evolving. Our cloistered lives have ended and we need to concentrate on the human family and its interdependence. This is the only way we can survive. Gluttony in the West causes starvation in the East. If we are honest we will admit to this. The world cannot afford the rich; mountains of corpses are the price of greed and avarice. We in the West have no more right to two-thirds of the world's resources than we have to machine gun our neighbours. And action starts here, in our hearts and minds, in the kitchen, in the workplace. And it starts in our personal lives. If we oppress and bully others, if we feel superior and discriminate against other people, all our work to end oppression elsewhere in the world will be in vain. The cry of the Women's Liberation Movement in the 1970s was 'the personal is political'. And women were not only talking about gender issues. Women treat other women as badly as men treat women. We, who grow up in a woman-hating culture, cannot help but hate our sisters who reflect our despised selves to ourselves.

Differences are easily found, but similarities are less easy to perceive, harder to digest and less comfortable to admit. It is easy to say that others are different, special, unworthy, but difficult to own these feelings about ourselves. The big lie of patriarchy is to insist on our difference and distinctness and to maintain that we can never get on with each other. But the great truth of the Goddess is that we are all one family, we are all related, a common blood flows through us and common experiences unite us.

We are currently unravelling millennia of lies built on the mass graves of dissenters. Of course we are afraid, and sometimes we slip back into old prejudices and beliefs. We know the dangers of countering the lie, but deep in our hearts we do know. We have all experienced the mystery of birth and we will all die, and all the layers and masks we use to protect ourselves cannot save us from these truths, however we colour them.

The Goddess is immanent, the Goddess is community . . . the phone rings, it is my friend Helen. I tell her I am writing a chapter on ethics and explain my deep disquiet about Westerners appropriating the spiritual traditions of other cultures. She practises Tibetan Buddhism, as I do; we have this in common, although our practices emanate from a different source. Her experience of working directly with Tibetans confirms my doubts, at the same time as it echoes my assertions. Tibetans feel that Westerners are ready for their teachings but will provide them only if Westerners respect the traditional methods used to teach them.

Many of the teachings are given orally to those who can receive them. This is not to say that some are the elect and others are not, but that unless you have done the preparatory work you cannot and will not be able to use the teachings. The teachings are sequential for good reason. This mirrors my experience of being unable to speak about certain aspects of my spiritual practice to someone who has not studied the basics. I do not want to withhold the truths I have found but there is not the language available if someone is not familiar with the teachings.

The spiritual is immanent in that it is woven into the very fabric of everyday life, which is an expression of the sacred. Tibetan novices painstakingly build an exquisite sand painting in a London museum only to pour it into the Thames when the exhibition closes. Sand goes back to the sea; in the great round it will wash up on some distant shore carrying the love that was painstakingly poured into it. For us in the West to respect community and begin to let go of our individualistic thinking is perhaps the greatest challenge we face. Indigenous spiritual traditions can show us how they have woven their spiritual beliefs into the fabric of their daily lives and provide us with clues as to how we might perhaps re-create this in our own fragmented culture.

RE-INCARNATION WORK

Past lives can shed light on present life issues. Often we meet people we recognise in some indefinable ways. People who become important in our lives may well have been known to us in previous lives. This is especially true of family members, who may have been known to us in former lives. These past relationships may explain the attraction or repulsion we feel for some people, or the sense of having a 'deep knowing' of a person we have just met.

If you are open to the idea of re-incarnation, you will be better able to see your present life in perspective. Life crises and seemingly random events can be understood more in the wider patterns of several lifetimes, which helps to place problems and preoccupations into perspective. Re-incarnation work is only useful if it enables and enhances this life. It is pointless unless it has a practical application. If you find yourself constantly repeating situations and attracting similar kinds of people who are not good for you, re-incarnation work may help you to trace patterns which might account for this behaviour. Maybe there is an important life-issue you need to work through which will keep recurring until you resolve it. Even if you do not believe in past lives, this work is valuable as a deep-level therapy looking at what images or archetypes are important for you, and what issues are currently asking for your attention.

Meditation: going back into the past

Take yourself to a spot where you won't be disturbed for at least 30 minutes. It is best to do this work with a friend or in a group, especially for the first time. If this is not possible, then pre-record the meditation with a tape recorder . . .

Lie down, loosen any tight clothing . . . and take a few deep breaths . . . on each breathing out, relax the body and let go of any tension . . . Sink deeper into yourself and feel your whole body weight supported by the floor . . . Be aware of your solar plexus and breathe into that area for a while . . . Notice a silver thread coming from the solar plexus, leading upwards . . . Take hold of the thread and move up out of your body, following the thread upwards, further and further away . . . Move out of the room, through the roof of the building . . . up above the street and then high, high in the sky moving over your town, your country and up, up into the heavens . . . Pause a while . . . See the stars around you . . . Listen to the sound of space, the exquisite darkness of the inky sky and the sparkling silver stars . . . Breathe in the rarefied air . . . Be aware that you are still holding the silver cord

which will lead you home whenever you wish ... Now you are going to go downwards into another time and another place, into another life ... Slowly you come down ... and see what is around you ... (allow ten minutes to explore where you are). Then slowly, taking hold of the silver thread, move up again into space and then come slowly back into the room. Take your time ... when you are ready ... write down what happened ...

This work is very intensive and is best done with a guide. To come to understand life issues which lead back into previous lives, it will be necessary to repeat this exercise several times. It is best to do this not more than once a week to give yourself time to assimilate your experiences. It is very deep work, so go carefully.

Back to birth

This imagery is useful in a similar way to the previous exercise, starting at the other end of experience.

Take yourself to a quiet place where you will be undisturbed for at least 20 minutes ... Lie down and loosen any tight clothing ... Take some deep breaths and relax your body ... Turn your attention inwards and downwards ... Sink deep into yourself ... deeper and deeper ... Visualise yourself as you were ten years ago ... Picture the clothes you were wearing and how your hair was cut, remember what you were doing ... Get a true picture of yourself ... Then go back another ten years ... Repeat the process ... Take time to

really feel this age ... Work your way back to the time you were a babe in arms ... Feel yourself as a tiny baby ... Now go back to the time before you were born ... Become aware of the choices your soul made before you were born ... what experiences you needed ... which lessons you needed to learn and obstacles you needed to overcome ... Take some time to answer any questions which might arise ... Then very slowly come back into the room ... Write down your experiences.

This exercise, like the one previous, gives another perspective on your life's problems and major issues. It is especially useful when a major life choice has to be made or when you feel you have lost direction.

ETHICS

'Do what you will and harm none.' (Traditional Wiccan)

A friend has been raped, she asks for your help. What do you do? Someone unemployed desperately needs a particular job and asks you to talk to the interviewer to make sure she gets the job. Do you agree? A married friend discovers her partner is having an affair and asks you to hex the other woman to get her to stop seeing her spouse. Once it becomes known you are working with magic a stream of people will arrive on your doorstep asking, and at times imploring, you to do this or that spell. They bring with them a whole nest of thorny ethical problems. Some witches say they will never do witchcraft for money; others earn their living this way. Many witches will never do hexing, others consider hexing rapists to be revolutionary acts. The Christian ethic invites us to turn the other cheek towards evil, not to retaliate, but it is those who hold all the cards who proffer this invitation, so not surprisingly we must be leery about accepting it. What, then, are our ethics?

The Feminist witch Zsuzsanna Budapest is clear about where she stands with regard to hexing. Writing in *Women of Power* magazine she talks about the issue of hexing rapists: 'It boggled my mind to have to explain to perfectly enlightened feminists that any man who attacks you and rapes you deserves to be hexed and it won't return to you tenfold.'[4] She describes a hexing ritual she and her coven performed against the man who raped one of the coveners. He was caught – and it turned out he had raped seven other women in the area. We are socialised (or, rather, brainwashed) into believing there is nothing that can be done about rape, violence towards women, nuclear power. Patriarchy encourages us to be passive so that we might remain imprisoned in our homes, with fear, and with despair in our minds.

As none of us are training for sainthood and all of us are humanly fallible, our ethical guidelines need to be as realistic as possible. My experience has taught me that revenge happens of its own accord and that however creative one might be, as far as revengeful thoughts are concerned, the fates usually come up with far better retribution. For this reason I never seek revenge, however justified I feel; I just wait. In my personal experience evil-intentioned people always construct their own downfall. Pride does come before a fall. This is on a personal level; in community, however, we have to take collective action to stop those who abuse us.

There is a Wicca tradition that spells should not be done for money, money in our Puritan culture being deemed a wicked substance. I would add a caveat to this, depending on the attitude the person has to money. Money, occultists assure us, is only concretised energy. Which means it is a neutral substance, neither good nor bad. It is the love of money which is the root of all evil, not money itself. If you are generous with your money and see it as a useful tool for the work of the Goddess, but not a means of self-aggrandisement or power over others, then getting more of it will only help the Great Work. Motives are important.

Love is another dubious area for spell work. Love magic works, only too well. Cast a spell to get a lover interested and you may have a besotted lover on your doorstep. What happens when you get bored with the one in love with you? Love spells are not to be recommended unless you are really, really sure . . . and how can you ever be that?

Magic is best used for the general good or for self-development. If your relationship with yourself is wobbly, do spells to like yourself better; no one can love you unless you love yourself. If someone has harmed you, send all the person's negative energy back and break your connection with him or her by doing the solar plexus meditation (see p. 160), or open the heart chakra (see p. 162). If you need work don't concentrate on a particular job, rather do a general spell to find work. In this way you will defend your interests without getting caught up in hexing or binding magic. You may feel a friend needs your magical help and have her best interests at heart, but doing magical work without her knowledge, whatever your intentions, is manipulative and must not be considered.

HONESTY

'Take what you want and pay for it.' (Spanish proverb)

If you lie and cheat, others will steal from you and mislead you. Obvious, we say, while we underpay our taxes, don't return the too-much change, shoplift books, take state handouts when we could work, use our friends for support and then not be there when they need us. These are all theft. Whatever the medium for barter, money, goods, energy, a Goddess ethic demands that we pay for whatever we take. We have to take responsibility for being honest, for speaking up when an abuse is taking place, for declaring our interest, or owning up to our faults and mistakes. This can be painful and is often seen to be disruptive, but for true relationships and a healthy community we need to feel the existence of trust, however uncomfortable and challenging. Constructive criticism often comes as a relief, while gossip and slander can be devastating. The former is done in a spirit of love, the latter as a divisive, power-over technique. As people gossip they collude in the ethic that creates outsiders and supports dishonesty. Constructive criticism operates within the ethic that relationship is all-important and communication paramount. Gossip demeans, constructive criticism empowers. Honesty enlarges, dishonesty diminishes, whoever we steal from. If we steal from shops, who in fact do we steal from? Others in the community. The store boss doesn't suffer, prices rise to cover theft, we pay because there is no such thing as a free lunch. We can hardly harangue greedy capitalists for despoiling the planet if we can't be bothered to recycle paper or glass, or if we buy plastic-wrapped goods because it's convenient. If we are aggressive or pull rank and intimidate we are in the same boat as the soldier with his gun. Which brings us to harmlessness.

HARMLESSNESS

Being harmless does not mean that we don't or can't defend ourselves, stand up for our rights and those of others, or that we are compliant and capable of being manipulated. Being harmless is integral to the belief in community and immanence. If we are all related and dependent upon one another, then harming a person hurts us. Aggression and violence perpetuate, as do love and compassion. What do we want more of? We embody harmlessness when we give people the space to be, when we really listen to them, when we see people, when we criticise but criticise constructively, when we encourage debate and only act with consensus. It is harmless to encourage new growth, change, freedom in personal relationships. But being harmless is not the easy option; it takes courage and long, hard practice. Practising harmlessness we leave things as they were before we came, we repair and mend, we let go and bury. Harmlessness is less about helping the blind lady across the road and more about helping our own blind selves see the light of day so that we don't hurt others. Sometimes harmlessness means getting angry; sometimes it means walking away until tempers cool. Being harmless is seeing the other's point of view while at the same time respecting your own position. Harmlessness comes from a real sense of our worth and divinity, which has no need for power-over as it has the far greater power-within.

SERVICE

Service, as defined by Webster's dictionary, means help, use, or benefit; contribution to the welfare of others; a good turn. We are being of service when we ring up sick friends, write letters of protest, clean up litter, run for public offices, are good plumbers or build networks in our communities. Many of us have a corrupted idea of service which comes from the distortions of the church which deemed service to be a distribution of largesse to an unenlightened mass who needed to be grateful. If you are doing service and it makes you feel morally superior (not just good) or it gives you power over less fortunate people than yourself but is not joyfully given without thought of reward, you are following the line of orthodox religions. True service is freely given, seeks no reward apart from that and, most importantly, encourages power and autonomy in those you serve. Dependency corrupts and bleeds away power. Servers listen to those they want to help and give them what they ask for, not what they feel they need. Again, service operates on the principle of immanence; if you help someone, when the time comes that you need help, it will be there. This is the logic of the Goddess, and I have seen it operate time and time again in my own life and in the lives of others I have known. Usually, the people I help are not those who help me, but I don't hold a list of checks and balances. If I am helped, by whoever it may be, then the help is the important thing, not the identity of the helper. Open-hearted, generous people reap the rewards of their conduct, while self-sacrifice and duty kill the spirit. Denial of selfish desires causes pain and conflict, transcending or substituting of those desires for service, liberation. The most self-nourishing thing a person can do is to nourish another. This is the paradox. Conscious self-nourishment perpetuates the separate, individualistic worldview and is ultimately alienating, however, satisfying it may be in the short term. Doing service, by nourishing another, however, feeds us on deep, deep levels.

May the power of the one life pour through the hands of all true servers.

May the love of the one soul characterise the lives of all who seek to aid the great ones.

May I fulfil my part in the one work, through self-forgetfulness, harmlessness and right speech.[5]

10

SPELLCRAFT

What is a spell? A spell is 'any kind of magical act intended to have an effect upon the physical world',[1] says Robin Skelton in his book *Spellcraft*. Webster's dictionary defines a spell as 'a state of enchantment, a strong compelling influence or attraction'.[2] Mary Daly in her *Intergalactic Wickedary* goes still deeper: 'a spoken, sung, or written word or set of words known by Crones to have Be-Speaking power.'[3]

Every child knows that if you close your eyes and whisper to the winds and stars you make a spell. Grownups often need their spells to be complex, detailed and much decorated for them to believe they will work. Take your pick. Witches veer from the childlike to the ritualistic, but underneath any successful spell is unbending intent.

UNBENDING INTENT

The quantity and quality of emotion and directed thought you put into your spell will determine its effectiveness. Love, hatred, rage, jealousy, envy and joy all focus the heart and mind to an incredible degree. When in love or in the grip of jealousy there is no space for other feelings, people or places; we live in the bubble of our hearts' creations almost invulnerable to others. To raise a storm or heal a sick woman, great concentration is needed, nothing less will do. This means getting clear, that is, checking out if you have conflicts about what you wish to do and putting all unnecessary thoughts and feelings to one side and focusing the mind on one thing and one thing alone. Is it a desire we are talking about, or a real need? Be careful here. Desire as the Buddha taught, desire and attachment, are the cause of all suffering. Do you really need this lover? That job? This revenge? Check out with people who know you well; your best friends will (if they are true friends) tell you if you're on the right track.

An experience I had early on in my training perhaps will illustrate the point I'm trying to make. I had been having a relationship with someone who I felt had done me wrong. The person was from quite a different culture to mine and deeply respectful of witchcraft (or perhaps afraid); in any case he was ripe for magical work. I decided I would take my revenge on him at the following full moon, which is a powerful one for me as it is the moon I was born with. On the night I was teaching a women's health class at an adult education institute and had to walk a long, straight road to get to the bus stop. A long walk, about half an hour. The moon was out, and low in the sky, it was a harvest moon, red gold, full and huge. It lay directly in front of me as I walked down this long, straight road. Directly in front of me. I couldn't avoid it. I began by thinking through the ritual I had devised, and the moon shone down on me. Her light made me uncomfortable, which is unusual as I was born on an exact full moon and feel familiar with that energy. As I paced out my route I began to have doubts about what I had planned; I wasn't as sure as I had been. Searching my mind, I found that I didn't really blame the man but was more angry at myself for being so unrealistic. The more I pondered the more it became clear that it was not clear. We were both to blame. My appetite for revenge had gone. By the time I reached the end of the road I knew that I could hex him. I had the power, but, and more important, that knowledge meant I no longer needed to do it. I had learned a great lesson. So when I reached home I collected up the things I had assembled for the ritual and burned them (purifying) and then threw them into a river near my home. As I let them go into the water I sent back to him the negative energy he had sent to me and made my peace with him. This was a spell that was not a spell. But it was a very important learning for me.

I see my spells as learning curves, which teach the spellmaker not only her art but also about herself. Anything is possible, with magic, anything, but only if your faith and concentration can move mountains. Watch the results carefully of your magic and you will understand more about what you need and how your desires conflict or help you to realise those needs. If you sow a seed you have to maintain the right conditions for that seed to grow, right environment, temperature, enough water, and so on, but ultimately you have to leave the seed to grow or not according to its will. Digging it up from time to time to see if it has started to root will not help the process; rather, it will probably kill the plant. Spells operate on the same principles. Prepare the ground, nourish them and then leave them alone! Forget them and carry on with everyday life. If they root it is the Goddess' will, if they die, likewise.

I discuss six types of spells: those for blessing, protection, health, love, work and money. I have found these to cover most areas of life and they are those most asked about.

BLESSING SPELLS

> May light sweeten in your lungs
> may your tongue shine
>
> May you be grateful to your body
> for the offences it forgives you
> may your body please you
> may your mind accept its forms
> and guide you among dangers and pleasures
>
> May you love yourself as you are loved.

> Blessing Spell (William Pitt-Root)[4]

This is one of my most favourite blessing spells; for me it encapsulates all the elements needed. The mind, the body and the feelings are all blessed in a non-judgemental way.

One of my own blessing spells invokes the Goddess:

> Bless this house
> and all who live within her walls.
> May you grow and prosper here,
> wise in the old ways.
> May your spirits soar
> and your bounty increase.

> May the larks of heaven
> and the angels of the deep
> enclose and protect you
> from all evil
>
> Bless this house.

Blessing ritual

On a Friday evening after the evening star has risen, bathe in a bath which has a few drops of sandalwood in it. Dry yourself and anoint your forehead, throat, heart and womb with musk oil and, lighting a white candle, say:

> I bless my body, fashioned in purity.
> I bless my mind wrought in beauty.
> I bless my heart full to overflowing.
> I bless my spirit which now fills me.

Repeat this three times.

PROTECTION SPELLS

White light protects. Whenever I am out and feel threatened I imagine myself wrapped in white light; it always works. Travelling on the tube or waiting for buses and trains if I feel some goon staring at me I imagine a huge mirror between us facing him so that he sees not me but a reflection of his pathetic self. It never fails! Such idiots always move off . . . they can't bear to look at themselves. City life necessitates wandering women should protect themselves, their cars and homes. Whatever form your protection takes, use rage as its bedrock. Rage, because we need to think about protecting ourselves from men who are out of control and hell-bent on harm. I walk a lot at night and if I feel I am being followed I tap into the Hag/Crone, the wild part of myself, and rage, imagining what I might do to an unsuspecting man should he decide to try his luck with me. No man ever has.

Two witch friends of mine had the following experiences, which will illustrate the power of protective magic. The first was travelling on the upper deck of a bus, late at night in a pretty wild and violent part of town. She was alone when about five or six youths came on to the bus. (A woman had recently been murdered in the area by a similar gang.) She was sitting at the front and they blocked her exit when she got up to leave. She faced them and they started hurling insults at her, getting more and more violent, calling her witch, hag, and so on. They threatened to kill her. She imagined herself to be a huge snake, I think a cobra, and faced them with her glassy stare. They continued to taunt her, but she remained unmoving. Gradually their boldness left them and, beginning to falter, they meekly let her pass as she left the bus.

The second friend left a train at a seemingly deserted station, only later noticing a man who had got off at the same time. He tried to talk to her, but she ignored him. He blocked off her exit and began threatening her. She covered herself in white light; the man lunged towards her; she kept imagining white light; he backed off; he lunged for her bag, but backed off once more; she stayed steadfast . . . He seemed to be trying to fight her energy, trying to grab her, but not being able to. Finally, uttering a few oaths, he rushed off.

These accounts reveal that protection techniques work, *but you need unbending intent for them to be successful*. Rage, as I said earlier, is a perfect vehicle for protection magic. When I leave my house for any length of time I seal the doors and windows with white light, and as I close my front door I seal it from the outside saying:

> May no harm pass this threshold.
> May my home be secure,
> inside and outside.
> Watch over it.

Purifying your home

When you move into your home, if someone moves out leaving bad energy behind them, or if you feel there is negative energy around, there is a simple purification ritual to deal with this. Also use the ritual after someone has been ill or when there has been a lot of tension in the place. In each room to be cleansed, place a blue candle in a saucer, firmly fixed. Place the candle on a large sheet of newspaper and draw a large circle around the candle with sea salt. Light the candle and, closing the door of the room, leave it to burn. (Check the candle from time to time to see it is safe.) When it has burned right down, carefully collect up the paper, taking care not to spill one grain of salt, and take it to a moving body of water. Throw everything in and walk away without looking back.

You can also burn sandalwood incense to increase the cleansing.

LOVE SPELLS

Love spells come with warnings, because quite often what we want is not what we need and nowhere is this more true than when we start talking about love, or lust. Be careful. I myself would not do a love spell to bind a particular person to me; I get bored easily and can imagine nothing worse than have a lovelorn soul following me about. And love spells can go horribly wrong if the object of your love really doesn't want you. If you are lonely and want a lover or a partner I suggest you concentrate on yourself. Love yourself and lovers will appear out of the woodwork or at bus stops or supermarkets.

Have a vague idea of what you are looking for in a lover; keep it vague and flexible, though. One friend made a precise list, down to the last detail of her ideal beau – who duly turned up having all those qualities she had envisaged as well as a wife, which was something she had not considered and which clearly lessened his appeal.

The blessing spell above is a good place to begin. After that you could consider the qualities you have to offer a lover – compassion, humour, warmth and so on – and really feel your way into them. Embody the principle of love and breathing and hold the feeling for as long as you can. Repeat the process once and then twice, and feel this love burst out of you and scatter far and wide. Repeat every Friday (the day of Venus), if you wish. But betweentimes don't think about it. Let it be.

HEALING AND HEALTH SPELLS

> Blessed is your body,
> proud and strong.
> Blessed is your heart
> as she soldiers on.
> Blessed is your belly
> as she holds your food.
> Blessed are your feet
> so lightly shod.

Sickness often brings us face to face with feelings of despair. If you have a serious and debilitating illness, a life-threatening one, the greater the fear and anger. However grown-up our theories about life and death might be, faced with our own mortality, fear rushes in. Death might be welcomed by the very sick and tired and by the elderly who feel they have had enough, but generally it is resisted and illness is greeted with feelings of fear and helplessness. For this reason it is not easy to do self-healing spells. I recommend you go to a group or call on a friend to help you. And perhaps this will be the first stage in your healing process, having the humility to call for help, admitting you are not in control and that all is not well.

Sometimes we are not so much sick as feeling generally unwell, low in energy. Then we might wish to do a spell to put ourselves back on par.

On a Sunday morning, light a golden candle, saying:

> Sun! Sun! Shine on me.
> Pour your golden warmth over me.
> Fill every cell and pore
> with your life-giving light.
> Bathe me in sunbeams.
> Regenerate me
> so that your fiery essence
> builds up my spirit
> that it might shine as you do.

If there is sunlight, stand in it for a while. Or else imagine the balmy summer's sun lifting your gloom and revitalising you. Repeat this spell on subsequent Sundays should you need to do so. For those of us who live in the darkened north, the lack of sunlight in the winter months challenges us to find our inner sunshine, to feel our inner fire highlighted by the outer cold. Yellow and orange flowers can help visually to make up for the lack of fire as does the wearing of brightly coloured clothes, burning red, yellow and orange candles and oils such as orange, cinnamon and ginger.

Healing ritual

Some witches work in healing groups, meeting on the new or full moons and do rituals for women who are sick. Usually the work has to be backed up using herbs, massage, healing or any of the other life-giving healing arts. The ritual may be a cathartic learning experience for the sick person, giving insight into the sickness or providing a gentle healing and nourishing, sustaining energy. Lone witches do one-to-one rituals or healing without the sick person being present.

The groups casts the circle (with the person or people to be healed inside) and call on a healing Goddess, the four elements, etc.[5] They raise a cone of power and then ask the Goddess that the woman (who should be named at this point) be healed. (She sits in the middle of the circle.) The coveners may or may not want to touch her as they channel healing energy, which can be very powerful. The group waits until it feels the healing is finished and the person being healed moves to one side to allow the next woman to sit in the centre. If it is the coveners themselves who feel they need healing, they should go to the centre of the circle one by one to receive the healing energy. Those who are being healed may wish to talk about their experiences, to the whole group or perhaps one-to-one with a covener; in either case time and space should be allowed for this. Then thank the Goddess and the four elements and wind up the circle.

WORK SPELLS

In times of high unemployment, women need to be sure of paid work and witchcraft can help to make this possible.

Remember the unbending intent, and then however impossible, or whatever the odds, magic makes things possible. You
just need razor-sharp focus and a heartfelt desire. Unemployment causes feelings of failure, self-pity and self-loathing as
our society judges us by the paid work we do; without a job
we are seen as useless, non-people. Some greet times of no
work as opportunities to study, take a rest, re-prioritise their
lives and change direction. Others, who cannot survive on
state benefits, especially women with children, need money,
as others depend on their income. Building up self-confidence
is the first step to someone valuing you enough to employ
you; it might well be the only step required. So witches work
with self-confidence. Women generally lack confidence, under-
value their skills, accept less than they should and compromise, because they do not have good self-esteem. No one can
give this to you, but neither can it be taken away. (It can be
undermined but, if healthy, it will bounce back up again.) It
burns away inside each one of us. Self-esteem comes from
self-love.

Take 30 minutes where you will not be disturbed and have
two sheets of paper. On one sheet with red ink write the things
you like about yourself; your skills, your talents, your good
qualities. Let yourself go from the sublime to the ridiculous,
list every little thing you can think of which is good. On a
second sheet with black ink, write all the bad and horrible
things about yourself (this will be very easy – you may need
a second sheet). Let rip, all your bad habits, failings, vanities,
all the things you do conspicuously badly. When you have
finished, put both sheets out in front of you. Light a white
candle and a blue candle, saying:

> Mother, here are my good points
> (read them out),
> and here are my failings
> (read them out).
> Only You know the truth.
> I need work for my talents
> which will encompass my failings.
> I need work in order to eat.

I need work in order to live.
I need work to do your will.

Then take your good points and your bad points and burn them in the blue candle (without burning your fingers, the carpet, etc.) and collect the ashes in a bowl. Carry them, wrapped up if you like, to the nearest body of flowing water (river, canal, sea), and throw them in, saying:

Thy will be done.
Let me find work.

MONEY SPELLS

Many witches say you should not do spells for money. I would say that it depends on why you need the money and what you intend to do with it. Buying materialist goodies is not a good reason for a money spell, but paying for an important course of study or a trip you need to make is fine by me. As I have said before, money itself is neutral, it is the *love* of money which is the root of all evil. Doing spells to get money for the work of the Goddess helps to redirect money from the forces of evil (patriarchy) toward the forces of good. But your motive is all-important, as is the energy with which money is surrounded. You must be very clear about this and ask yourself honestly about your motives. Money will come if it is appropriate; let it be.

On a Sunday morning light a yellow candle, saying:

Goddess of plenty,
bringer of bounty.
I ask you now.
Listen as I ask.
I need money for . . . (specify)
Hear me,
Goddess of plenty.

Then visualise money as golden matter being used for your project or cause. Be specific, see exactly how the money will be spent and focus on the work that will be accomplished. Repeat each Sunday until there is no longer a need.

11

DEVELOPING PSYCHIC SKILLS

This chapter looks at some psychic skills which most people can develop and are an essential part of a witch's repertoire.

VISUALISATION (PATHWORKING)

There is an occult as well as a psychological truism that something which cannot be visualised cannot be actualised. Roberto Assagioli[1] did a lot of detailed work around visualisation, albeit for psychology, but then magic and psychology have a lot in common – although some psychologists might deny this. He developed a series of laws relating to the subject, some of which are as summarised below:

1. Images and ideas tend to produce conditions and external acts which correspond to them.
2. Attitudes, movements and actions tend to evoke images and ideas.
3. Ideas and images awaken emotions and feelings which correspond to them.
4. These emotions and feelings in turn intensify images and ideas which correspond to them.

Thus Assagioli believes that ideas and images feed, and are fed by, our feelings and a closed circle is set up. The more we think a thing, the more we feel attached to the idea; the more the idea is likely to manifest, the more we will feel attached to the idea and therefore the more we will think about the thing. Urges and drives tend to demand to be expressed, directly through activity or indirectly through symbolic action. This is where magic comes in. By performing a symbolic action which we have previously imagined, we are giving expression to a deeply felt need. Witches use imagery (pathworking) both to change their internal environment (what goes on in their inner world) and to alter their relationship to the outer world. Pathworkings are used for many situations but their usual aim is for deeper self-knowledge which will enrich and aid everyday life.

PATHWORKING TO FIND YOUR INNER GUIDE

The following takes about 20 minutes. Go to a place where you will not be disturbed. Pre-record the meditation, or do it in a group with one member guiding the rest, or in pairs taking it in turns.

Lie on the floor, loosen any tight clothing and relax . . . let the floor carry your weight and take a few deep breaths to release any tension in your body . . . Imagine you are in a meadow, on a warm summer's day. Look at the plants growing around you, feel the soft, warm breeze on your skin . . . In the corner of the meadow is a gate. Walk over towards the gate and pass to the other side . . . On the other side is a path. Look at the path and decide whether you want to take it. If you do, start to follow the path upwards . . . It is slowly winding up a mountain . . . As you walk along the path, notice what is around you, any plants or trees or animals and how the air is. . . . As you slowly climb upwards, the sun is still shining, walk up at your own pace . . . As you near the summit you become aware that the air is becoming clearer, more refined and there is a faint echo of music . . . As you move further and further upwards the music becomes louder, it is like the tinkling of water in a fountain . . . Finally you reach the summit. You pass through an archway and you come to a temple courtyard with a fountain at the centre . . . You stop to rest by the

fountain ... As you do so, you are aware of a figure coming towards you ... This is your guide. Greet her or him and listen to what she or he has to say to you ... You may ask her or him any questions you wish ... Take some time to get to know her or him ... (pause for ten minutes – allow the image to develop in its own way without any mental effort.) Then be aware that it is time to leave ... Your guide will give you a parting gift and confirm that you can return to her whenever you wish ... Slowly make your way down the mountain, carrying your gift, back into the meadow ... Then open your eyes and come back into the room. Write down your experience.

The guide is your inner teacher who is there to advise you whenever you need some help or clarity about an issue. The more often you visit her, the deeper your relationship will become. She can help you with extremely practical issues or deeply esoteric matters.

Visualisation can also be invaluable for analysing dreams and for homing in on a physical problem which you don't understand. For dreamwork, take one aspect of the dream, a person or situation, and become that person or situation. Speak out, explain why you are there, what you need, what you have to say. In a similar manner, with a pain, for example, a headache, visualise the pain, give it a colour, a face even, and allow it to speak to you. The pain has something to say to you; give it a voice. You could even start a dialogue between the pain and yourself ... Experiment, be creative.

Once a relationship has been established with your guide you can move on to work with more subtle bodies.

THE ETHERIC BODY AND THE CHAKRAS

The word *chakra* is Sanskrit and means wheel. Like the English word it can mean a literal turning mechanism, or the metaphorical wheel of destiny, or perhaps the Wheel of Fortune of the Tarot deck. The chakras are seven wheel-shaped

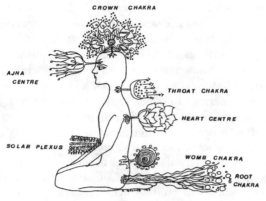

THE CHAKRAS & THE ETHERIC BODY

energy centres which are found in the etheric double of the body. The only body the majority of people are aware of is the physical body, but we also have an etheric body, an emotional or astral body and a mental body, as well as the overshadowing soul, which co-ordinates everything. The etheric body is an energy field through, and with, which we interact with both the physical world (as the etheric connects to the physical body) and the world of more subtle energies. It acts as both filter and template. It steps down the high current of spiritual energies and makes them readily able to be assimilated by the physical body, and forms the template on which the physical body is moulded. As our etheric body becomes more refined, so our physical body changes. The life force comes through the etheric body and vitalises the physical body, it literally colours it. When our life force is low, our aura becomes cloudy and dull and physically we appear washed out: grey. Our etheric body can be 'seen'[2] as a 'mist' or 'glow' around the physical body. The etheric body will be bright or cloudy, patchy or uniform, depending upon the psychic or spiritual health of the person. Spiritual energies can flow like a torrent through the body or trickle like a stream, depending upon how obstructed the etheric body and the chakras themselves are.

The chakras are like small wheels which rotate and vibrate. They are often likened to flowers. C W Leadbeater[3] describes them as similar to bell-shaped convolvulus flowers the stems of which spring from the spine. Sanskrit texts, notably that of Patanjali,[4] talk about the chakras having a certain number of petals, the best known being the crown chakra which is referred to as the 'thousand-petalled lotus.' The flower analogy is used when referring to the condition of the chakras. Some are opened fully, like a flower in full bloom, while others are bud-like or slightly open. Whether dazzling centres of light or small greyish depressions, these seven chakras transmit and receive vital energy which itself emanates in seven different types.[5]

The chakra system is only one of several which explain the etheric double or the subtle world of energies in which we live – not the world of illusions where we think we live. Carlos Castañeda's Don Juan describes us as luminous beings, connected to things and people through luminous fibres. There are the worlds of the tonal and the nagual, the real and the illusionary.[6] Don Juan spends years trying to get Castañeda to 'see' the real world and leave his perceptions of 'reality' behind.

Each magical system has its own explanation of these two worlds, some more complex and elegant than others, but the basics remain the same. There are always two planes, one of which we are conditioned – pressured – to believe is the one and only reality, and the actual reality, the world of children and mystics, poets and prophets . . . and witches.

Magic happens here, in the upside-down world of real reality, although here it is not deemed to be magic, only common sense and logic. But conditioned as we are to see only with our eyes and think with only the most mechanistic parts of our brains, it is hard, hard, work to be in this other, real world.

As much of our Western esoteric teachings were destroyed in the witch hunts, the teachings about the true nature of reality necessarily come from other cultures, generally from the East, from China, India and Tibet. Recently they have also come from Native American Indians of the United States, Central and South America and Mexico. As stated in the chapter on ethics, there are dangers of taking on the spiritual traditions of another culture, politically and ethically as well as practically.

As I have been trained in the Eastern traditions I will use

Eastern paradigms, weaving in my personal experiences and observations of years of running workshops and doing healing and esoteric work.

There are seven major chakras, which are, starting from the bottom: the root chakra, the spleen or womb, the solar plexus, the heart, the throat, the third eye and the crown. There are no definitive explanations of the chakras, just teachings and interpretations of the translation of ancient texts, and although I agree with all basic teachings about the chakras, I might disagree with specific details. Check out other sources and work on your own or in groups, and do meditations to find your own truths.

THE ROOT CHAKRA

The root chakra is to be found at the base of the spine and corresponds to the nerve plexus of the pelvis and coccyx.[7] As its name suggests, it is through the root chakra that we, literally, root ourselves, connect to those things that are material, earthy, familiar and instinctual. For this reason the root chakra is ruled by the moon, which represents our instincts, our basic drives. This chakra is awake in most people and connects us with those things we consider to be 'home'. For most people this is a familiar environment and company, but it can be any thing which provides us with security and a sense of well-being. Here, meaningless rituals, compulsive behaviour and addictions all operate, for these ritualised behaviour patterns reassure people who feel fundamentally ungrounded. Without a good relationship with our roots it is very difficult to operate effectively in the world. Often those attracted to the occult or the esoteric have a very ambivalent attitude to the material world. In its most fearsome expression, mediaeval clerics declared that all that was matter, female and natural was base and less than human. Our Western culture is a result of that thinking, as we poison the earth that houses us and the bodies which enclose us. Yet at the same time, the material, in the form of money, is deified. Money, as Freud observed, is really shit, and both money and shit are root chakra matters.

The root chakra relates to the colour red and to the moon.

Meditation on the root chakra

Sit comfortably, don't lie down, and support your back, if necessary. Close your eyes and take a few, deep breaths. Check out your physical body, turn your attention inwards, relax tense parts and breathe regularly... Be aware of the base of your spine. Look at the colours you see there. Notice the condition of the chakra, how much energy there is around it, how open it is... Then be aware that there is a root which grows out of this chakra, which grows out and down, down, down into the earth... Find this root and notice how it looks. Is it well cared for and healthy, or is it thin and sickly-looking, or is it solid and impenetrable? Using your imagination adjust the root: thin it down, thicken it up, feed it, do whatever needs to be done. Then take a few minutes to feel how it is to be firmly rooted, secure and attached... Now imagine going about your everyday life feeling this way... See what a difference it makes – to your work, your relationships, your attitudes... Come back into the room and make notes of what you discovered.

THE SPLENIC OR WOMB CHAKRA

In Western systems this chakra is associated with the spleen, but in Eastern traditions with the sexual organs and reproductive functions. Given the Western patriarchal attitude towards sexuality, it is little wonder that spiritual teachers do not focus on the sexual aspect of this chakra. Most men don't need this area stimulated – quite the reverse. For women, however, the womb and sexual organs are the centre of life energy, in many respects the centre of women's being. Children we have had, who have lived or died, are connected to us here. It is here, too, that we may also be connected to sexual partners, for good or ill. Any sexual trauma, rape, surgery, difficult childbirth, will also be remembered at the womb chakra. Troublesome wombs, with cramps, growths and pains, can be approached through this chakra, as well as sexual problems and fertility. My friend Mary Swale, a mother, tells me she feels the connection to our mother's and our daughter's wombs, like Chinese boxes, womb within womb. Carrying your own children reminds us deeply of being carried in our mother's womb, when she remembered hers, and so on, back to the very first ancestral womb. In a direct line. There is a deep gateway here into ancestral time.

The womb chakra relates to the colour orange and to the planet Mercury.

Meditation on the womb chakra

Lie down and take a few deep breaths to relax... Focus attention on your womb... See what condition it is in, take some time... See if any feelings come up as you go deeper into your womb... Let them come... Allow images and memories to come, let them appear and disappear without judging them... Then imagine a stream of golden light washing through your womb, healing and cleansing it... Hold the light there... Then let it go... Repeat the process, holding it for longer... Then let it go. Be aware that this is the centre of your energy, where you absorb light... Come back into the room and write down your experiences.

SOLAR PLEXUS CHAKRA

Situated above the navel, the solar plexus chakra is connected to the coeliac plexus and the digestive system. It is here we experience 'gut reactions' and many of the subliminal and unconscious messages that people exchange are given out and received by the solar plexus. It is a huge receiving centre and may easily get clogged or be overwhelmed by energy. It is here we connect on an everyday level with people and also where we relate through basic feelings. Anger is expressed here and envy, resentments, self-pity and depression all come from the solar plexus. We can be drained of energy through the solar plexus, with our vitality slowly leaking away or having our energy sapped by other people who 'drain' us. The condition of our solar plexus tells us about our relationships with other people and theirs to us. Physically the solar plexus relates to the organs of digestion: the liver, gall bladder, stomach, pancreas and intestines.

The solar plexus chakra is associated with the colour yellow and the planet Venus.

Meditation on the solar plexus

Lie down and take a few deep breaths . . . Let go of the tension in your body . . . Direct your attention inwards to your solar plexus . . . Look at the general condition of this chakra, its colour and any images or feelings which come up for you . . .

any people you find there . . . You will notice cords coming out from your solar plexus. They connect to people in your life . . . See who these people are, and whether these cords are helpful to you or whether they drain you or hold you back . . . You can remove the harmful cords. Don't cut them . . . just gently pull them out; they will come out like pond weed from water . . . Let them float away . . . Send them away with light. Slowly come back into the room and write down your experiences.

The three chakras discussed above are open in everyone and are known as the automatic centres. They have opened during the course of evolution, and their energies are available to everyone. The following four chakras, all located above the diaphragm, are opened in varying degrees, depending on the emotional, intellectual and spiritual development of the person concerned. In this sense they are less automatic and more subject to conscious control. Some suggest 'working' on opening up these chakras, which I personally feel is unwise. It is far safer and more effective to check out how they are and then, in your everyday life, endeavour to express those qualities you wish to develop in yourself, such as love, compassion, charity, and so forth.

THE HEART CHAKRA

The heart chakra, or centre, is to be found in the centre of the chest at the back, and is connected to the cardiac and pulmonary nerve plexuses. As its name would suggest, the heart centre is concerned with love, but it expresses an unconditional love, compassion, love of humanity, nature, beauty, spontaneity, joy. This chakra is open in most people who are aware of others outside their immediate circle, of the needs of humanity, of service, of the interconnection and interdependency of all life. The feelings we usually regard as being about love mostly originate from the solar plexus, not the heart. Because the heart frees the loved one, empowers her, it does not bind and tie her down in a world of responsibilities and obligations. Love has no connection with fear, or jealousy or pride; she does not hurt, she heals. This love, then, is an ideal we can strive toward, which we may have glimpsed fleetingly with our children or loved ones, which we feel about nature or have experienced briefly in mystical union. The heart chakra is connected with the physical heart and the lungs. The heart centre is where the life thread is attached to the body; too great a shock can weaken the connection, depriving the person of life energy or spirit. When a person dies the thread is pulled out; this is the flash which is sometimes visible at death.

The heart chakra is connected with the colour green and the sun.

Meditation on the heart

Lie down and relax ... Focus attention on your heart. See what colour it is, what shape, and what images or feelings come up for you ... Let them pass by, noting them but not judging . . . Be aware of the colour green, apple green, and bathe your heart in this colour . . . Feel it healing and opening your heart . . . Stay with this for as long as you can and then come back and note your experiences.

THE THROAT CHAKRA

Situated at the base of the skull and physiologically related to the pharyngeal plexus, the throat chakra is concerned with expression, voicing thoughts, feelings, poems and prophecies. This is where we express ourselves – or where expression gets blocked. This chakra works together with the spleen/womb chakra, encouraging creativity and helping its expression. The throat chakra is related to how we communicate verbally with others, through speech and song. Chinese healers pay particular attention to the voice and relate it to their five-element system. They talk about the groaning voice which is associated with water, and fear, the weeping voice of metal and grief, the singing voice which is earth and sympathy, the shouting voice which is wood and anger and the laughing voice which is fire and joy. Besides our physical appearance, our voices are what are most remembered by other people. They evoke an image which is often more true than the way we look. The human voice has tremendous power, to heal and hurt. We can all be seduced by a rich, deep voice and repelled by a whining one. Our voices also express power: mythology claims the stone megaliths of Stonehenge were raised by magicians chanting and witches raise cones of power with their voices.

The throat chakra is related to the colour pale blue and all ills relating to the throat and voice.

Meditation on the throat chakra

Relax and sit comfortably, bending your head slightly. Take a few deep breaths and breathe out tension from your body . . . Turn your attention inwards to the area just below your skull at the back of your neck . . . Relax the tense muscles there and breathe into them . . . Be aware of a centre of energy, a

*depression, a pool or whirling vortex . . . Slip in and see what
you find there . . . Look for a flower-like structure . . . When
you have found it, see what kind of condition it is in . . . Ask
it if it needs anything . . . Be aware of an iridescent blue colour
bathing the whole area . . . Stay with this for a while . . . Then
slowly come back into the room. Record any thoughts or
feelings.*

THE BROW CHAKRA

Situated between and slightly above the eyebrows, the brow
chakra, or ajna centre as in the diagram on p. 155, relates
physically to the carotid plexus and to the pituitary gland.
Sometimes called the third eye, this centre is concerned with
clairvoyance, literally meaning 'clear seeing'. True clairvoyance comes from this centre, but much so-called channelling is
a mixture of self-deluded wishful thinking, imagination and
picking up thoughtforms from the astral (emotional) levels
via the solar plexus. True clairvoyant messages are non-per-
sonal, non-judgemental, carrying neither praise nor blame,
and have a quality about them which is distinctive. Working
with spirit guides is only as useful as the guide itself; not
all Tibetans, Egyptians or American Indians were evolved
spiritually or were even particularly interesting. Be sceptical.
The best channelling has been done by people who had no
interest at all in such work, and certainly did not sit in circles,
neither did they profit from the teachings that came through
them.[8] Many clairvoyants become obese, showing that their
relationship to the physical is problematic. Overeating may
be a way of protecting oneself from the physical environment.
Those who are more sensitive and open than others may well
feel more fear and constantly sense the violence and danger
in our world; they eat as a way to cushion their experience.

Magical work begins with the brow chakra. From here we

project our energy outwards, in particular our thoughtforms. We travel on the astral plane and project ourselves into other worlds and other realities. None of this should be attempted until we have a firm relation to the physical and sound heart chakra. Meditation happens with the brow chakra, as does thoughtform building, but the heart has to be open first as will without love is dangerous.

The colour connected to the brow chakra is indigo, as are all diseases of metabolism, the hormones and some brain disease.

THE CROWN CHAKRA

The crown chakra is found at the top of the head and is related physiologically to the pineal gland. In the enlightened, the crown chakra grows to a large size and radiates light; there are the haloes of the saints, the growth on the Buddha's head, the light in the head of mystics. As soon as someone becomes able to assimilate spiritual energy, this chakra awakens and opens. Taking hallucinogens opens this chakra prematurely and sometimes the inflow of energy takes people on trips from which they never return. In this connection, it could be argued that the mass ingestion of hallucinogens in the 1960s and 1970s opened a lot of crown chakras. Although the results were in many cases fleeting, I feel that it did alter the consciousness of a section of the population which the burgeoning spiritual movements testify to. Although some are less useful than others, the renewed interest in things of the spirit to some extent counteracts the deadening effect the church has had on the spiritual life of people living in the West. The crown chakra will develop as a natural progression from working on all the preceding chakras. It is the result of many long years of sustained effort, of integrating and understanding the personality and coming to terms with our personality shortcomings.

The planet ruling the crown chakra is Saturn, who is sometimes called the Lord of karma, meaning work yields its own rewards, that good things are worth waiting for. No instant enlightenment lasts, although the experience may be profound. The reality is that spiritual work is tiresome, repetitive, boring and mostly unrewarded in the short term. In the long term, however, and particularly as we approach old age and death, spiritual work becomes the only reality worth pursuing, however erratic the progress might be. The colour associated with the crown chakra is purple.

THE ASTRAL BODY AND THE ASTRAL PLANE

The astral (emotional) plane, the land of dreams and nightmares, connects us to the feelings of our group, country or planet. As such it is a dangerous world, because there are arguably many more negative than positive feelings. This is the land of desire, of miasmas, of fogs; it is also the place where energetic workers usually begin their training. Dreamwork, astral travelling, psychic skills, aura-spotting, pathworking, all initially occur on the astral plane.

The aura is the electromagnetic field which surrounds all things. It can be photographed by Kirlian photography, and some will see and/or feel it. It is superimposed on the etheric body and has seven layers, five of which are usually visible. The first four layers tell of the energetic condition of the physical, emotional and mental bodies and the imagination and intuition or higher mind. The fifth tells of the spirit. The sixth and seventh layers relate to cosmic energies.

You can learn to see and/or feel auras fairly easily. You need to scan the person, not look directly at them but leave your gaze slightly out of focus. If you normally wear glasses take them off. It is easiest to see the aura around the head and shoulders, especially if the person sits before a white or pale-coloured wall. Don't concentrate; gaze blankly somewhere in the middle distance between you and the other person. More often people sense the colours, rather than see a clearly defined patch of blue or yellow. We read auras when we meet someone. We can see at once if they 'radiate' or seem in a grey mood or a brown study. Trust this sense.

Bright vibrant colours mean clarity and energy, dull, muted tones mean confusion, depression and sadness (see the Correspondences in Appendix B). Dark patches mean there have been 'wounds' to your aura, and that you are leaking energy in these areas. You can change your aura at will and become a glowing body or disappear into grey mists. We do this unconsciously when we feel depressed or chronically lack self-confidence. No one takes any notice of us and we become invisible. Our auras become muddy and blend in with the background. Sometimes this is very useful, especially if you are in a situation which feels dangerous or you just want to avoid the drunk in the street. Likewise when we feel good about ourselves, we're in love, feel ebullient, people notice us, they feel drawn to us. Sunlight naturally hinders the former and aids the latter, but we can change how we project our energies. It takes energy and, if we are very down, brightening up our auras for a while is hard work. But sometimes the brightness sticks, and for a few hours we forget how low we feel.

HEALING

Healing is a natural ability that everyone is born with, but most people suppress and discard this gift by the time they become adults. Children are natural healers; they know that placing healing hands on a forehead can help pain to go away, and they tend not to get enmeshed in the complicated power relationships the healer often finds herself in.

The techniques of healing are simple enough; most of the training is about getting the healer out of the way. Healing is done with spiritual energies which come through the healer but do not emanate from her; she is the messenger but not the message. Sadly, many people working with healing energies, and not only healers, forget this. Working with energy does not make you special in any way, any more than plumbers and mechanics are special. It's a skill which a healer develops, practises and applies, just like any other; moreover, it is a skill which *everyone* has.

So the first principle of healing is learning detachment. Detachment from your own hopes, feelings and aspirations both for yourself and the one you are healing, or it might be a cat or a plant, or even a car. There is no reason to limit yourself . . .

Centring, getting clear

Sit down in a comfortable place where you won't be disturbed. Take a few deep breaths ... Be aware of your body ... Focus on any tension you are holding ... in your jaws, your shoulders, your arms, your legs ... Focus in on your crown chakra. Feel it open slightly and a golden light gently fill your head, and then move down through your whole body and out through your hands and feet ... Stay a while with this image. You become a channel; the energy flows through you and comes from a source greater than you ... Be aware of your other chakras opening as well, especially your heart chakra ... Now change the colours flowing through you, from gold to green ... Feel the energy of green flow through you ... Then soft blue ... then rose pink ... sunset yellow ... crimson ... indigo ... purple ... and then back to soft gold. If you are not going on afterwards to do healing, close all your chakras off, one by one, starting with the crown. Imagine them closing like flowers ... Take a few minutes to centre.

The technique of healing

Some healers like to work hands on, actually touching the patient; others work with the aura several inches from the surface of the body. Thorough training is needed if you feel drawn to work with the very sick, but for simple first-aid problems with children, pets, plants, etc. you can safely follow the guidelines set out below:

Before you begin working, make sure you are clear in your thoughts. Empty yourself as far as you can of your feelings. Centre yourself and open up. Feel the healing energy come through your hands and place them on or near the one in need of healing. If the problem is a headache, for example, place your hands on the head or around it. Do nothing, just open up and let the healing energy pour through you. Green is a good colour to start with, apple green. Feel it coming from a source outside you and flowing through you into your patient. Don't talk, stay alert but try not to think, just empty yourself of thoughts. You may sense you need to heal other areas as well, listen to your inner voice ... don't over-tire yourself, however. When you feel enough is enough, stop. A little healing is better than too much. You can always do more later. Finish by clearing the aura of the one who is being healed. With both hands scan the whole body and clean the aura as if brushing away a fine layer of dust or sand. Afterwards, always wash your hands to cleanse them of any energy you may have picked up. Then close down your chakras.

12

DIVINATION – THE TAROT

The fortune teller on Brighton pier is arguably a descendant of wild witch-amazons. The reader of the runes, tea-leaf scryer, palmist and diviner, astrologer and aura-gazer all answer a deeply-held human need to know what the future holds. Diviners are a caste apart and, like witches, have access to other worlds. Alternately feared and revered, they, too, live in shadow lands and converse with spirits.

In recent years, divination, especially by Tarot cards, has blossomed. There is a thirst for such knowledge, fuelled perhaps by the many choices we are faced with in our lives and life's increasing uncertainty. Divination answers that need; if a good diviner is consulted the enquirer will also discover more about herself. I have decided to concentrate on the Tarot method of divination, of which I am very fond and for which I have a great deal of respect. It is very difficult to write a small chapter on so vast a subject. I have decided by way of a compromise to talk about the history and background of the cards and their meanings as I understand them. These meanings may, or may not, agree with other interpretations; there is no definitive interpretation of the Tarot, which as I see it is the beauty of the system. It can be looked at from a Jungian perspective, or through Gnostic eyes; it can be seen as an occult system; Kabbalistic teachings sit well with the cards as does astrology; and very many other teachings. There are almost as many Tarot packs as there are ways to wisdom.

To cover all these areas would do a disservice to the profundity of their teachings and would in fact serve no one. I have instead chosen a narrow path which I hope will serve as a beginner's guide and stimulate further study while at the same time provide new insights to those already familiar with the cards.

BACKGROUND TO THE CARDS

One of the gifts of the Goddess was numbering, measuring and mathematics. In *Innana*,[1] Demuzi says of his sister 'And took the lapis measuring rod and line in her hand.' Women, priestesses of ancient Sumer, were in charge of the measuring of time. Of moons, of cycles, one month, nine months, reading the signs at eclipses, observing the cycles of the year and their festivals. Numbers were the domain of the sacred; measuring, calculating, sizing were women's work. Sacred geometry is found throughout the world, from Mayan temples to the Pyramids. The philosophy of numbers was brought to the West by Pythagoras who was an initiate of the Egyptian temples. The sacred books of Thoth, written in pre-history, contained myths, rituals, religions, esoteric medicine, sacred geometry, astrology and all the knowledge that was needed for initiation.

The Jews received sacred texts from Moses who was initiated in Egypt. The sacred texts comprise the Kabbala and the Tora (Tora = Taro). The gypsies claimed that the ancient Egyptians and the Hindus were the remnants of the lost tribes of Atlantis, and that Pythagoras made the same claims.[2]

Legend has it that after the burning of the great library at Alexandria by the patriarchs and prior to the onset of the dark ages the wise gathered together in Fez (Morocco). They pondered over the best way to preserve their ancient learning without it becoming available to the uninitiated whom they thought might abuse its teachings. They finally settled on 22 pictures which held the key to the Mysteries. These became the Major Arcana (Greater Mysteries) of the Tarot. Court de Gebelin writing in 1781 in *Le Monde Primitif*[3] said 'it contained the purest knowledge of profound matters.'

Legend has it that in the temple of Ptah in Memphis in Egypt images were found on gold plates which resembled the Tarot trumps. All the Mystery traditions taught divination as a tool to develop the intuition and to make a bridge between the gods and men. Lionel[4] claims the trumps developed from the *Kybalion*, the Egyptian book of magic: 'Everything is spirit. Everything vibrates. Everything is dual. Everything revolves in the rhythm of time. Every cause produces an effect. What is below equals what is above. The masculine and feminine principles are in all things.' Others have claimed it was a remnant of the ancient Egyptian book of *Thoth*, and Aleister Crowley named his Tarot pack after this book. (Thoth was the god of magic.) Others said it was the gypsies' gift to Europe, although they arrived a century after the cards were first seen there. Others said it was the crusaders who brought the cards back from the Middle East. (But the last crusade was in 1291 and the cards didn't appear until a hundred years later.)

The gypsies were originally Hindustani and were driven from India by the Islamic conqueror of much of central Asia, Timur Lenk, in the fifteenth century. There are records of them in Hamburg in 1417, Rome in 1422 and Barcelona and Paris in 1427. Rakoczi says that as the Pagan cults were being destroyed by the Christians their priests (sic) put their knowledge into the hands of the gypsies who undertook to travel with it, hide it, and only pass it on to the worthy. Thus they were guardians of the wisdom of Chaldea, Egypt, the Druids, yoga teachings of the East, Gnostics, Cathars, Albigensians, Bogomils and Patarini. *Tahoti* is a gypsy word meaning the Royal Way, like *Raja Yoga* in Hindi. The gypsies claim the Tarot came from Thoth and so was his sacred book. The gypsies worked magically with the witches of Europe who entrusted their secrets to them during the burning times. (As wandering peoples, the gypsies escaped the worst excesses of the witchcraze.)

In gypsy lore men are initiated by the sun and women by the moon, and in every tribe there is a gypsy mother, who is a wise woman and to whom each man swears an oath of loyalty taken at her feet.

At the same time that the religious repression of Pagans was becoming a gathering force, from the eleventh to thirteenth centuries, trade routes were opening up in both the Near and Far East. (Marco Polo and his family, for instance, traded with Kublai Khan in Peking in 1266.) Mongols were a people tolerant of all religions and Peking became an international meeting place for Buddhists, Confucians, Taoists, Shamanists,

Moslems, Jews, Nestorian Christians and Gnostics. Trade opened up into Scandinavia, Russia and other Northern countries. There was a huge cultural interchange and many ideas were cross-fertilised as traders were followed by priests of the many religions. At the same time many classical Greek and Persian texts were being translated, particularly in the scholastic centres of Toledo in Spain and Montpellier in France. The Norman conquest of 1066 opened up the Celtic kingdoms whose teachings also spread and mixed with European thought. Bernard Sylvester wrote *de Mundi Universitate* in 1145–53 and it was a great success. He spoke of the Mother Goddess fecunding nature, and the power of the moon and stars. The Gnostics or Cathars flourished in Southern France and Northern Italy during the twelfth and thirteenth centuries, they were also known as the Albigensians after their centre in Albi near Toulouse in France. They had a dualistic belief, like the Taoists, and the 22 trumps of the Major Arcana can be read as a Gnostic journey. Although they were broadly Christian, many of their beliefs were clearly pagan in origin. They were persecuted by the Inquisition and perished, their lands confiscated.

The first Tarot cards were recorded in the middle of the fourteenth century. Writing in 1377 a monk, Brefield Switz, described card games, and in 1379 a Belgian, Duke Brabant, records the purchase of a pack of cards. From that time onwards, references to card games are found throughout Europe where they were eventually banned (Paris in 1397, Stuttgart in 1440) by the church which was fearful of their pagan symbolism.

The earliest known packs of cards were Chinese and Korean. Made sometime in the eleventh century, they had four and eight suits, respectively. It is possible that the trumps evolved separately from the suits. The four suits are the basis of our modern playing cards.

The oldest Tarot pack as we know it today is the Bembo pack which was painted for the Visconti family of Milan in 1415. It was used to play a game called Tarocchi and had four suits of 14 cards and 22 trump cards. Then came the Marseilles deck which was created sometime during the Renaissance. The most common deck is the Rider-Waite deck, drawn by Pamela Coleman-Smith in 1910 under the guidance of A E Waite, both of whom were members of the Golden Dawn esoteric movement. (See the Bibliography Tarot section.)

THE MAJOR ARCANA

'An imprisoned person, with no other book than the Tarot, if he knew how to use it, could in a few years acquire universal knowledge and would be able to speak on all subjects with unequalled learning and inexhaustible eloquence.' (Eliphas Levi)[5]

THE FOOL

THE FOOL is the wild card of the major arcana, as it is in an ordinary card deck. It has no number but is generally seen to begin the journey to the self that the Tarot explains. THE FOOL can be taken in two ways, depending upon the level of awareness of the querent. It can mean a stupid, rash person, one who heeds no one, who rushes in where angels fear to tread and leaves a trail of destruction wherever he or she goes. It can signify that the querent is about to make, or has made, a stupid decision for which she or he will pay with humiliation at the least and disaster at the worst. If trouble cards fall around THE FOOL, especially the TOWER, the DEVIL and, in some instances, the MOON, the outcome will be negative. If the surrounding cards are positive, for example the WHEEL OF FORTUNE, STRENGTH, THE SUN and THE STAR, then all will be well. A leap into the unknown, trusting your intuition, will bring rewards.

On a deeper level THE FOOL is about trusting your inner impulses, the pull of your soul, taking your road in life. All esoteric traditions talk of the gullible neophyte who in some way is 'tricked' or 'duped' into treading the path to wisdom. The seeker after truth has to leave life as she has known it and travel the lonely path to self-realisation. If this card comes up you are beginning a sacred journey. It may be an inner or an outer journey but it will be taken alone, and you will have little but your instincts to guide you.

1 THE MAGICIAN
Astrological symbolism: **The Moon**[6]

This is the first numbered card. I call THE MAGICIAN the trickster. In mediaeval times he was the magician who travelled around the countryside. The magus and the mountebank, the magician can be a hustler, someone who knows how to wheel and deal, to manipulate the forces a little. She can make things appear and disappear, do optical illusions, card tricks. But THE MAGICIAN is also the messenger of the gods who shows us that everyday life is all illusion, Maya, a trick of the light. She promises real treasures, not the tawdry prizes on offer in everyday life. When this card comes up it usually means news is coming. A messenger or message arrives which helps clarify a situation, removes the veils from a problem, reveals the truth. On a deeper level, THE MAGICIAN speaks of the need to pierce the veils of illusion to see the reasons behind things, to try to understand the nature of reality and to transmit spiritual energies, bringing the spiritual into everyday life.

2 THE HIGH PRIESTESS
Astrological symbolism: **The Moon**

THE HIGH PRIESTESS is the sibyl aspect of the Great Mother. Wise beyond all knowledge, all-knowing, all-seeing; the essential feminine. Deep, mysterious, unfathomable, elusive, fluid, profound. She is the wisdom of ages, the holder of esoteric truths, the Divine Mistress. In older packs she is also called the PAPESS, the female counterpart to THE POPE, but I think this gives her power of too temporal a kind. She traces back the Egyptian high priestesses, the holders of ancient lore, the pivot around which society moved. She read the oracles, and may have been a sibyl, but more likely was the priestess in charge. If this comes up in a reading it means it is time to deepen your experience, time to connect with what is deep and meaningful in your life. Possibly a time for withdrawal and meditation, or for inner silence and contemplation. Dreams will be important and you should heed their mes-

sages. Write poetry, dance, paint, play music and be open to
the messages of your deepest self.

The next three cards deal with temporal life, the challenges
that a seeker after truth has to overcome before she can move
along the path.

3 THE EMPRESS
Astrological symbolism: **Venus**

THE EMPRESS is Earth Mother, fecundity, fertility, abundance
and pleasure of all that the earth gives us. Sensual delights,
physicality, sexuality, pregnancy of babies and ideas, creativity
on all levels. She is also THE EMPRESS, in that she is consort to
the King. As such she is the female figurehead, a woman of
power and authority who has not bartered her femaleness to
attain and hold on to that power, and may be a woman who
uses seduction to gain power. That is, she has not become
'masculine' and 'hard', but has used womanly ways to get
power. A woman who is a physical mother and mainly identifies herself as such, or a dancer, an athlete, a student of Hatha
yoga, a masseuse. THE EMPRESS may signify the querent will
experience a better relationship with her body, or needs to
develop one. A card for those with eating problems to meditate
on, to envisage the Earth Mother aspect of the Goddess. On
a deeper level it means coming to terms with the physical
world, neither dismissing nor idealising it, but becoming more
at ease with food, sexuality, money and power.

4 THE EMPEROR
Astrological symbolism: **Mars**

THE EMPEROR is the leader, the wise ruler, masculine authority,
rule by the law and at times by the sword, for THE EMPEROR
was always a warrior as well as a statesman. Sadly, such
positive masculine archetypes are hard to find, but he is Arthur
king of Britain, wise and kindly ruler, who has knights to
protect the vulnerable from abuse. He is that part of ourselves
which has natural authority, which is wise and courageous,
our ambitions and goals. Often, however, THE EMPEROR represents the forces of patriarchy oppressing women. He is the

rapist, the bully, the invading army, the 'might is right' mentality. He is big business ripping off developing countries, polluting the land, destroying free thinkers. When this card comes up, especially if it is near THE HIEROPHANT or JUSTICE cards, watch out for big brother, the police, social security, the tax man, any bullies in uniforms, or people who rule by force. THE EMPEROR generally means an opponent bigger than you, and unless there are positive cards around such as STRENGTH or THE SUN, back off before the people who threaten you do you harm. The card may also mean you are oppressing others, throwing your weight around. It can mean a powerful and wealthy man will feature in your life. THE EMPEROR teaches us about power, both our own and that of other people.

5 THE HIEROPHANT OR POPE
Astrological symbolism: **Saturn/Capricorn**

THE HIEROPHANT is another difficult card. He is the high priest, Merlin the magician, guardian of the Tradition, Grand Master, Gypsy Prince, and so in a real sense the masculine counterpart of the HIGH PRIESTESS. But where is he? Well hidden unfortunately. In contemporary society, priests are not respected. Having abused their power for centuries, the churches are not associated with the teaching of spiritual truths but with hypocrisy, cant, prejudice and ignorance. Like the bullying EMPEROR, THE POPE, with his hatred of women and all things female, represents a terrible distortion of the archetype of masculine spirituality. So usually THE POPE is a bad card for women. It represents the system, unfeeling, unbending bureaucracy, male cruelty especially through religion, dogma and rules. It can mean brushes with the police, especially if the JUSTICE card is around, also abuse by councillors, politicians and minor officials. The card may also relate to women's struggles within the male religious hierarchy to be allowed to perform religious functions. On a deeper level it concerns the quest for spiritual knowledge through study, practice and training, in contrast to the HIGH PRIESTESS' knowledge which is more intuitive and contemplative.

As with the EMPEROR card, THE HIEROPHANT originally represented the sacred masculine; the EMPEROR was temporal power,

THE HIEROPHANT, spiritual or religious influence. After 2000 years of bloody patriarchy, however, it is really hard to find positive representations of the masculine. This is perhaps work for men in the future, but as we deal with what is the present reality this card is usually difficult for women.

The next two cards concern choice, for when the lessons of power have been learned we then come face to face with the choices we have to make about our lives and our value systems.

6 THE LOVERS
Astrological symbolism: **Gemini**

THE LOVERS is a card people wax lyrical about, but in spite of its affiliation to love it usually doesn't mean love in the ordinary sense. What it is concerned with is choice and integration of the many sides of ourselves. Love, or, rather, falling in love, is usually about meeting our opposite, that which complements ourselves, and then trying to integrate that person into our lives. It so often involves adjustment and compromise which is painful and can be disturbing to the status quo. Love integrates and orders, and teaches us humility and compassion. Sacred love heals; profane love degrades. It is we who must choose which path we will follow. Chastity invites us to make our love sacred and to have no other motives but the highest. When you throw this card a new love may come into your life or events will cause you to look at your conduct and how you relate both to yourself and others. On a deeper level THE LOVERS teaches us to be heart-centred, aiming to love without ties, without expectations, learning about unconditional love.

7 THE CHARIOT
Astrological symbolism: **Cancer**

THE CHARIOT is the card of the hero, the young Amazon, full of health, strength and, most of all, energy. This card has tremendous energy, exuberance of life, love of the outdoors, physical challenges, competitions, quests. This is the card of the human rights worker, the defender of the poor and helpless. The woman who speaks out against injustice and then acts, for this is a card of action, movement. The Greenpeace warriors, rappelling dykes, Band-Aid musicians. It is usually a card of that youthful enthusiasm which is forceful and singleminded, but often a little intemperate, which can be rash, heedless, dismissing those with less courage or weaker convictions. The lesson for those with THE CHARIOT is to learn that this energy which flows through you, which you manifest, comes from a higher source than yourself. You are an instrument and channel for these energies, but not their originator. The downfall of THE CHARIOT is in imagining that she wields these forces; pride comes before a fall.

On a higher level THE CHARIOT is about integration of the 'masculine' energies of action and initiation with the 'feminine' energies of compassion and love. The charioteer is usually shown driving two horses representing these two poles. Its lesson is about balance and harmony, neither too much of one or the other.

THE CHARIOT ends the first seven cards. Seven is a sacred number, the number of completion and accomplishment. With the first seven cards we have begun our journey and encountered the everyday obstacles to growth and the visions of the prize (the HIGH PRIESTESS and THE MAGICIAN) if we continue on the path. The next seven cards take us further inwards.

8 JUSTICE[7]
Astrological symbolism: **Libra**

As its name suggests, JUSTICE is about equilibrium, the weighing of pros and cons and the attempt to find the middle path, a balance. On a mundane level this card can mean the police, trouble with the law, a need to be honest about an issue. (See if the surrounding cards are positive or negative to judge the outcome.) Perhaps the querent is being unfairly treated or needs a more balanced viewpoint over an issue. The card may also mean the querent is balanced in herself, has reached a state of equilibrium, or that this state is required. There are issues around fairness, being impartial and distancing oneself from a matter to gain a perspective on it. The JUSTICE card speaks of taking responsibility for past choices and forgiving oneself for errors. It also means taking control. This is an active, not a passive, card; if your life is one-sided it means taking action to right the imbalance. On a deeper level, this card speaks about the laws of Karma, you reap what you sow. All actions have their reactions and we are responsible for the things that happen to us.

9 THE HERMIT
Astrological symbolism: **Virgo**

After the weighing up of JUSTICE comes the introversion of THE HERMIT. A deeper turn of the spiral of wisdom, following on from THE MAGICIAN, this is a wisdom card, wisdom attained through aesthetic practice. Meditation, fasting, study of occult laws, solitude and poverty. When this card comes up in a spread (see illustration on p. 196), it usually means the querent needs some time apart from the world. She needs solitude or a deepening of her life. It may mean she is about to undertake a course of study, but it does mean she will experience solitude and a separateness from day-to-day living. It does not necessarily mean she will withdraw physically, more that her energy and attention will be focused inwards, feeding her spiritual self. It often means a time of celibacy. This card comes up in major life transitions when the querent needs to digest and assimilate her experience, to make sense of the changes which have occurred. On a deeper level this card can represent the dark night of the soul, where the seeker feels alone and abandoned and beyond the reach of anyone, where she has to heal herself from her innermost core.

10 THE WHEEL OF FORTUNE
Astrological symbolism: **Jupiter**

At the half-way point stands THE WHEEL OF FORTUNE. Luck, fate, chance happenings, surprises and upsets come with this card. Generally it means good news, a door opens, and opportunity comes along, changes are on the way. Forces larger than the querent are in operation. Roll with the punches, go along with new influences which come into your life. If travel is a possibility, then travel, change your outlook, open up, let go of old, outworn points of view, habits and patterns. On a deeper level the wheel is the wheel of Karma and the aim is to move from the periphery of the wheel where all is movement and change to the still centre of non-attachment and freedom. Often those who are on some path have lives full of 'karmic' happenings. Things, people and places come and go, often with alarming rapidity, they learn that outside changes, however violent, are ephemeral to the constant, unswerving nature of the soul or spirit. Only that is constant, and only that can give a sense of security we all crave. But we usually learn this lesson through repeated shocks; by having those things we value taken away from us we learn their true worth; we learn what we cannot live without and what are non-essential.

11 STRENGTH – THE ENCHANTRESS
Astrological symbolism: Leo

STRENGTH is the power of the feminine which tames the instincts. Befriending the natural world she lives in harmony with it, but is not of it. A nature-witch, a gardener, a healer, a worker with animals, a weather-witch. Following on from THE EMPRESS, STRENGTH teaches about the struggle most of us have with our instinctual natures. How we learn to deal with matter, whether money, food, any kind of resource. It is with STRENGTH we find the wisdom to overcome our obsessions and learn to direct our energy into life-nourishing activities, not self-destructive ones. Here we learn the lessons of passion and balance it with the aestheticism of THE HERMIT to find a middle ground where both are present but neither to the exclusion of the other. The spiritual power (love) of THE ENCHANTRESS overcomes the mighty lion (king of the jungle), but neither is subdued; they are together but there has been no fight, only a realisation that they are interdependent, one cannot survive without the other. This is the lesson nature teaches us; we can conquer it but if so we will be the loser, we can co-operate with it and if we do we will both be victorious.

12 THE HANGED MAN
Astrological symbolism: **Saturn**

A stage further on, a progression on from THE HERMIT, THE HANGED MAN is total powerlessness and isolation. The world has gone mad, turned upside down, what once made sense is now insane. There are no points of reference; you have been swept off your feet and now find yourself suspended, in limbo, waiting to see what will emerge. Often this card means a problem or a situation needs to be looked at from a completely different perspective. Turn everything upside down and then wait: the answer will come. As long as you hang on to your cherished illusions you will remain confused; let them all go and allow a different light to shine through. You may have to make a sacrifice to move forward; those things you once valued will be seen as valueless. It is a time of waiting, listening to the sound of silence, suspension of normal activity, a need to gracefully accept your fate. This is a time of profound spiritual experience, all you can do is try to listen to the voice of your spirit.

13 DEATH
Astrological symbolism: **Scorpio**

DEATH always comes as a shock. The card only rarely means physical death, unless there are bad cards (big change or challenge) around, THE TOWER, for example, or a lot of SWORDS. Generally the death referred to is the death we have all experienced in our everyday lives. The death of a relationship, a friendship, a job, a home, an identity, a bad habit, the ending of some important part of our lives, the death of an illusion. Death follows on from THE HANGED MAN in that once the seeker has discarded that which is not essential those parts of herself will die. Older esoteric texts talk of the 'lower self' dying, which does not mean that they are killed but that through lack of attention they die back like plants in the autumn. If we stop feeding our destructive natures and pour energy into that which is creative in our lives, those negative traits will eventually die from lack of attention. But the key is to focus on what is good, true and beautiful rather than to battle with our demons directly. DEATH teaches us that life is cyclical, and before anything can be born, something has to die. This is the lesson of nature the gardener learns; each thing has its season.

14 TEMPERANCE
Astrological symbolism: **Jupiter**

Aleister Crowley called THE TEMPERANCE card art, and it is indeed a card of the artist. The creative impulse comes from a deep, ineffable source, a fountain which can never run dry but which can be blocked. After the DEATH card a space is created for something to be born. Spiritual energies rush in, there is a rebirth, an outpouring of energies, a creative surge. The querent will feel a renewal, an optimism, a strengthening of faith, a new hopefulness. Projects will flourish, inspiration will flow, dreams will be teachers, your creativity will blossom. Listen to the voice of the unconscious: draw, paint, dance, write, dream. Consciously draw on the fountain of life, be aware it can never empty. Your doubts and depressions can block its flow but its source is eternal. It is a healing and inspiring time, an end to depression and despair. For workers in magic, the card shows a high energy time. Do spells and rituals, allow your healing energies to flow, deepen your meditations.

We have now passed through the second set of seven cards. The seeker has now begun her search in earnest, has confronted some of her demons and has been shown the rewards which come from her struggles. The last seven cards deepen her experience.

15 THE DEVIL
Astrological symbolism: **Capricorn**

With THE DEVIL the spiritual uplift and healing energies of TEMPERANCE are now thoroughly put to the test. With THE DEVIL we are confronted with our shadow, the dark, unpleasant sides to our nature. THE DEVIL represents all the temporal things which tempt us away from the good: sex, money and power. Seductive and often insatiable, these vices represent the major stumbling blocks for most disciples. Sex without love, the love of money and the lust for power all lead us directly back to THE DEVIL. He holds us captive, in bondage to him. Because these drives can never be satisfied. If you are on the treadmill after money, for example, there is never enough; a fix will only last so long and then, as an addict, you have to start hunting for it again. The same is true of sex without love, or power. These are impossible dreams and lead us further and further from the truth. Addictions are found with THE DEVIL; just another drink, one last cigarette, just another chocolate, in a never-ending cycle of craving, momentary satisfaction and then more craving. What THE DEVIL hates is peace, solitude, stillness. He keeps the mind so fixed on the next fix that we do not have time to question the sanity of our actions. The vice is all. Unlike THE DEATH card which causes fear, everyone recognises and identifies with THE DEVIL. THE DEVIL is what is known in esoteric parlance as the DWELLER ON THE THRESHOLD. He is the nightmare that has to be confronted before we can become initiates.

Mary Swale tells me that THE DEVIL is an earlier representation of Lilith (see chapter 3). She is shown in a bas relief, dated around 2000 BCE, in exactly the same pose as THE DEVIL card. She may, then, represent the wild, untamed, savage woman, which would be seen as devilish within patriarchy.[8]

16 THE TOWER
Astrological symbolism: **Uranus**

THE TOWER destroys redundant structures in a person's life. If we confront THE DEVIL, the house of cards we have constructed as a personality collapses. Often this is experienced as a bolt from the blue, a flash of lightning which destroys everything. If we have built on sand, THE TOWER destroys our house, but we, the soul, remain untouched. Often such changes occur around the age of 40, when we have to come to terms with our lives and often experience a frantic urge to recapture our lost youth. The realisation that we are not who we imagined ourselves to be comes as a great shock, and many people are deeply disturbed and unsettled by this realisation. We may experience THE TOWER as the world doing things to us; layoffs, divorce, bereavement. Illness may suddenly happen out of nowhere, and completely disrupt our world. The only thing to do when THE TOWER appears is to give in gracefully. The lesson is to let go, and allow whatever is superfluous to drop away from your life. These changes may appear to have no rhyme or reason, no sense; all we can do is to trust that forces which we cannot understand are at work and that all will be revealed at a later date.

17 THE STAR
Astrological symbolism: **Aquarius**

After the nightmare, there is hope. THE STAR promises health, light, peace, stillness, clarity. Its cool energies refresh the weary traveller, and its clear light guides them on their journey. THE STAR is purity, deep, clear female energy, calm and emptiness. Having cleansed herself of evil habits a space is created and energy of the spirit rushes in and fills her. She is renewed and replenished. In a reading, THE STAR speaks of restoration of health after illness, of hope after despair and of energy after depression.

18 THE MOON
Astrological symbolism: **The Moon**

The card, like the moon herself, has a dual nature. Ordinarily, THE MOON signifies illusion, deception, distortion, confusion, and sometimes hysteria and unwanted psychic phenomena such as hauntings. For someone who is ungrounded, THE MOON can mean she is living too much in dreams, or she is dabbling with occult energies unwisely. It may also indicate people who are childish, regressed, who need to grow up and face their responsibilities. For people who work with magical energies, THE MOON suggests they should be aware they are extra sensitive at this time and perhaps not as grounded as they imagine. This is a good time for doing magical work, but extra care is needed to protect yourself from outside energies. Listen to your dreams, watch hunches and intuitions, pay attention more to what is going on in your environment. Keep your eyes and ears open. THE MOON also represents the glamour of magical work; you may develop a magical persona, which leads you to imagine you are more powerful than you truly are. Then you become lost in the illusion of the work and forget the work itself.

19 THE SUN
Astrological symbolism: **The Sun**

THE SUN is rebirth, the heart of a child and the strength of the eternal. Something new and significant is happening, the seeds have finally taken root and are beginning to sprout. THE SUN has an expansive, warm, optimistic, joyful feeling. It promises good times, companionship, confidence, new forms of expression, great creative outflow and an expansion of consciousness. The seeker has passed through the fire and is now bathed in light.

20 JUDGEMENT
Astrological symbolism: **Saturn**

After re-birth comes the evaluation. THE SUN breaks down the artificial barriers between the inner and outer worlds and JUDGEMENT calls the seeker to take up the challenge to a more meaningful life. A crossroads has been reached; the old self has fallen away and the new emerges. It is an ending in the life of the neophyte; a cycle comes to a close; it is weighed up for judgement and then life carries on.

21 THE WORLD
Astrological symbolism: **Sagittarius**

THE WORLD represents the turning of the wheel, movement, change, new beginnings, new people, new places, new experiences. The querent is at the centre of her universe and has the four elements around her; she carries the wand of power and dances the dance of life. THE WORLD is cosmos, truth, essence. The feminine principle waves her baton triumphantly. A cycle has been completed, the wheel turns once more.

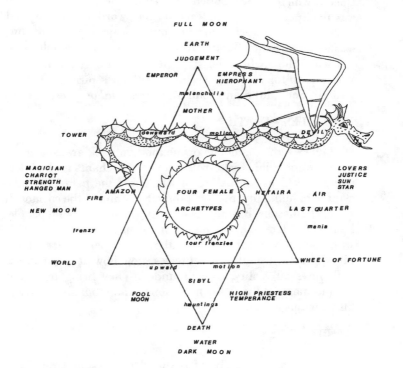

THE MINOR ARCANA

The Minor Arcana (the lesser secrets of the Tarot) consists of 56 cards, four suits of 14 cards each. The cards are a direct descendent of modern playing cards, and may have evolved separately from the Major Arcana. Because there are so many meanings to learn, the best way of approaching the cards is by understanding the essence of the four suits and then to look at the numerology of the cards. Each of the four suits represents one of the four elements, earth, air, fire and water.[9] The system of four traces back through history. The four suits may be traced back to the Four Grail Hallows, or the Four Treasures of Ireland. (See R S Loomis, *Arthurian Literature in the Middle Ages*, 1959.) The cup was the cauldron of Dagda, which never emptied and fed all the people, the club was the Spear of Lug the warrior; the sword was the Sword of Nuada, so powerful no one could escape it if it was unleashed. The pentacle came from the stone of Fal which cried out when the lawful ruler stepped on it. The Arthurian cycle was a quest for wisdom, psychic growth and spiritual emancipation. (See Caitlin and John Matthews, *Hallowquest*, 1990.)

PENTACLES – EARTH

PENTACLES – the diamonds of the modern pack are concerned with the material world, with money, merchants and tradesmen, as well as sensuality. In witchcraft the pentacle is the symbol of humanity, the five-pointed star and of the cosmos. It relates to masons, businessmen, crafts people, working people. Pentacles relate to autumn and the planet Saturn. Concerned with the function of sensation they show persistence, durability, practical solutions. Pentacles show how at ease you are with physical reality, how grounded. They bring up issues around material living, such as money and food, and how you fill your sensual needs.

WANDS – FIRE

The WANDS are the clubs of the modern pack and represent the element fire. WANDS can be the fairy wand, the Bishop's crozier, the shepherd's crook, the caduceus, the pastor's cane. They signify enterprise, growth, progress, advancement, invention, energy, enterprise and glory. They relate to summer, the choleric temperament, the planet Jupiter and the Sun.[9] WANDS usually show upright, fair and honest people. Relating to the intuitive function, they show powerful energies which can be directed anywhere, also willpower and how you project yourself. Wands are batons of commandment and have authority. Fire also represents the growth of the self, learning who you are.

SWORDS – AIR

SWORDS are generally bad news and indicate discord, fights, arguments, misfortune. They symbolise the double power of defence and attack. They also relate to courage, boldness, force and ambition. It is the suit of leaders and warriors. It is spring and the planets are Mercury and Mars. They are concerned with thinking, reasoning, analysing, verbal communication. Also gossip, slander, rumour and hearsay.

CUPS – WATER

CUPS are concerned with love, the emotions and happiness. The cup was the symbol of the Holy Grail and the heart. Usually a CUPS card shows joy, passion, deep feeling and a humane person. For the Egyptians the heart was the seat of the soul and in many traditions it contains the drink of immortality. It shows aristocrats and the clergy and feeling, compassionate people, sympathy and romance. It shows how a person relates to her emotional needs. CUPS relate to winter and to the Moon and Venus.

ACES, ONE, TWO, THREE

Aces contain the essence or root of the suits and are usually good cards:
Ace of PENTACLES often indicates money coming, material things.
Ace of WANDS shows a renewal of energy, new projects, intuitions.
Ace of SWORDS indicates clarity of thought, cutting through problems and situations, decisive action.
Ace of CUPS implies emotional fulfilment, love, happiness, good times of the heart.
Twos can show polarity, balance, developments, trying out what was started with the ace.
Two of PENTACLES implies juggling money and resources, perhaps two jobs.
Two of WANDS indicates testing out your strength, seeing how far you can go.

Two of SWORDS shows a temporary peace, stasis, a refusal to look at problems.

Two of CUPS shows love, union, a meeting of hearts, a new friend or lover.

Threes usually represent conflict, a third party. This can make things dynamic but may also rock the boat.

Three of PENTACLES indicates the beginning of hard work, getting your hands dirty, refining your skills.

Three of WANDS implies abundance, virtue, forward planning.

Three of SWORDS denotes sorrow, hurt by rumour, gossip, a third person joining and ousting you, power struggles.

Three of CUPS indicates partying, celebration, good times, the company of women, abundance.

After three we have passed the wobbly beginning phase and now move on to actualisation.

FOUR, FIVE AND SIX

Fours represent attainment, solution to problems, stability, becoming established. There is not much movement in the fours.

Four of PENTACLES implies hanging on to what you've got, being mean and materialistic, not sharing or letting go, by so doing you block anything new from coming in.

Four of WANDS shows a respite from work to party, celebration of how far you have already come.

Four of SWORDS denotes enforced rest, perhaps being ousted, made redundant, plotting the future.

Four of CUPS implies emotional boredom, repletion, an inability to foresee what is coming in, turned in on oneself.

Fives are dynamic and usually represent conflict of some kind. What has been worked for and then perhaps not cared for, or valued, is now taken away.

Five of PENTACLES shows material poverty, ruin, the spectre of bankruptcy, worry about money.

Five of WANDS indicates fights, with yourself or others, chasing your own tail, energy wasted in useless argument.

Five of SWORDS denotes a rip-off, theft of ideas, sneaky behaviour, defeat in argument.

Five of CUPS implies emotional loss, misery, sadness, disappointment, depression.

Sixes imply back to basics. Having lost, you now repair the damage and, somewhat chastened, you learn the lesson of the suit.

Six of PENTACLES denotes charity, asking for loans, favours, handouts, supporting or being supported by others financially.

Six of WANDS shows a victory, a leader arises, the way opens up before you; you are on the right road.

Six of CUPS indicates innocence, childhood memories, childish love, the gentle beginnings of relationship, simple pleasures.

Six of SWORDS shows retreat from trauma, emotional turmoil, defeat, cutting and running. A high price is paid for peace of mind. Disappointment, loss, sadness, defeat.

SEVEN, EIGHT AND NINE

Seven, eight and nine show that now we have become re-established we have to build again, but this time from a more mature perspective, dealing with the outside world, taking our responsibilities seriously.

Seven of PENTACLES shows that having sown the seeds of your project, you must now wait to see if they will take, waiting for signs of green shoots, the fruit of your labours.

Seven of WANDS denotes being overwhelmed by responsibility, you keep people at a distance, it's all too much.

Seven of SWORDS implies unstable effort, stealing someone else's ideas, futile activity, no good will come of it.

Seven of CUPS denotes too many choices, self-delusion, the glamours, lost in a fog of indecision and illusion.

Eight of PENTACLES denotes refining your skills, taking classes, studying craft and technique, putting your wares on display.

Eight of WANDS implies new ideas rush in, connections are made, intuition is working well; listen to hunches, follow up leads.

Eight of SWORDS indicates things are getting worse, you feel trapped, bound and gagged, you are in an impossible situation, there seems to be no way out, passivity.

Eight of CUPS gives a solitary journey, leaving loved ones

behind and all that is familiar, and trudging off with only the Moon to guide you. Walking away from your problems.

Nine of PENTACLES implies harmony, material well-being, great creativity, beauty, natural surroundings.

Nine of WANDS indicates that you have overextended yourself, you feel battered and bruised by opposition to your plans, but you have survived, you know how strong you are.

Nine of SWORDS shows still worse, the stuff of nightmares, great fear, perpetual worry, bad dreams, unrealistic fears; light is needed for clarity and perspective; look for help. Despair.

Nine of CUPS implies contentment, but is there a smugness here, an 'I'm all right, Jack' attitude?

TENS

Tens represent the ending of the struggle and a resolution of the issue, for good or ill.

Ten of PENTACLES shows wealth, material security, contentment, the family, the founding of collectives, groups, organisations.

Ten of WANDS indicates the burden has fallen all to you, your individualistic way of relating has meant you are alone carrying everything. Oppression.

Ten of SWORDS represents utter defeat, ruin, usually by gossip or slander. Others destroy you with words or mind games. Your divisive tactics have failed and you are thrown to the wolves.

Ten of CUPS shows a happy ending of any matter, good life, loving people around you, possibly children, emotional contentment and fulfilment.

THE COURT CARDS

These cards more often than not relate to types of people who may come into your life or with whom there are outstanding issues.

Pages are young people, new projects, beginnings.

PAGE OF PENTACLES implies a new material project has been started. It augurs well, begin now; you are finding out new things about the material world.

PAGE OF WANDS implies a release of new energies, an end to sickness or depression, a positive looking forward to the future.

PAGE OF SWORDS denotes wielding new ideas, bursting with energy; watch for impatience and bad temper.

PAGE OF CUPS shows something is emerging in your emotional life, new friends, or simply a new maturity about the way you relate to people.

Knights are more mature people, in the middle stages of life, they are often searching or questing and are usually on the move.

KNIGHT OF PENTACLES denotes hard work, diligence, perseverance. Apply yourself whole-heartedly to the project in hand and rewards will come in their own time.

KNIGHT OF WANDS shows you are on your white charger and ready for action. Seize the moment, follow your intuitions and follow your star.

KNIGHT OF SWORDS warns to be careful! You are too impatient and quick tempered, you will get into fights unless you slow down; you may be being reckless; watch out for accidents.

KNIGHT OF CUPS indicates the gift of love is brought to you through a person or a project, calmness, centredness; you experience a deepening of your feelings.

Queens are usually powerful women who operate on their own terms and are used to being authoritative, of having respect shown to them and being in control. They are leaders.

QUEEN OF PENTACLES is the lower Arcana counterpart to the EMPRESS. The card denotes fertility, creativity, maybe a biological mother, a family-orientated, nature-loving woman. Women who work with their hands, with fashion, art and money.

QUEEN OF WANDS shows a fire witch at home with nature, powerful, bright, strong, she inspires those around her, others marvel at her energy, her enthusiasm, her resilience, physical dynamism, humour.

QUEEN OF SWORDS implies an intellectual queen, a woman who has a razor-sharp mind, but who might be a bit lacking in compassion and warmth. A cool, aloof, clear, logical, thoughtful woman.

QUEEN OF CUPS is related to THE HIGH PRIESTESS card. THE QUEEN OF CUPS denotes a loving, creative, often psychic, woman.

Emotionally secure she nourishes those around her, rescues the lost and bewildered.

Kings may be men in the life of the querent or represent women at the top of their fields who, though they may have been ruthless to get where they are, are nevertheless instinctual leaders, potent people.

KING OF PENTACLES represents a rich person who has a firm command of the material world, someone who works with money or just amasses it. A sensualist who loves good food, good wine and good sex, and gets these effortlessly. Negatively, a materialist who cares for nothing other than material things, a coarse, brutish person.

KING OF WANDS denotes a dynamic, innovative person who loves power for its own sake and not for the material things it brings. An intuitive worker, creative person, an artist, writer, poet. Negatively, a megalomaniac who insists on absolute control, extrovert, brash, loud and bullying.

KING OF SWORDS shows an intellectual giant, a scholar, a thinker, a communicator, someone working in the media or with words. Often emotionally detached but kindly. Negatively, using words to wound and bully. Valuing the intellect above everything else, seeing feelings as both threatening and unnecessary. Cold and ruthless.

KING OF CUPS implies a man full of feeling, who is at home with his emotions. A person who works in the world of feeling, healers, psychotherapists, those working with the disadvantaged, the down and out, the oppressed. Negatively, an emotional manipulator, drama queen, an emotional vampire.

THE RITUAL OF READING THE CARDS

The most important part of a Tarot reading is the relationship between the reader and the querent. The reading must meet the needs of the querent, otherwise it serves no purpose other than to fatten the ego of the reader. My personal approach is to be as pragmatic as possible, the process is mysterious enough without the reader making prophetic announcements or giving a mystical side-show. Try to make your reading a dialogue between you and the querent, particularly if she cannot relate to your interpretations; this rarely means the reader is wrong, just that the language she is using is the wrong one. Be skilful. As you become familiar with the cards your own rituals around them will develop. Here in brief detail are some of mine.

If possible, get someone to give you your first pack, or make a present of a pack to someone you know is interested. Wrap your own cards in a silk scarf, black, purple or a colour with which you have a particular resonance, an auric colour of yours. You might also wish to keep them in a wooden box; one made of sandalwood is ideal. Don't let the curious handle your cards, unless you are experienced in 'wiping out' other people's energies. You may wish to consecrate your pack; if so, do this on a water moon, asking for guidance and clarity.

Before you sit down with the querent, centre yourself and try to empty your consciousness of your preoccupations, thoughts and feelings. Become as empty as you can (see Chapter 11 on psychic skills and healing) and then fill yourself with light and love. Spread out your silk square on a low table or the floor and go through the cards one by one, touching and looking at them. This can be done quickly but I find it helps to clear the cards and also reconnects me with each one. Like saying 'Hello.' Then you shuffle the cards, holding the querent in your mind. Shuffle for as long as you feel you need to; the cards will get a 'cooked' feeling as you get used to handling them. Then hand them to the querent and ask her to shuffle them. Tell her to take as long as she wishes, and if she has a particular question to concentrate on that question while she is shuffling. When she has finished, take the cards, and with your left hand cut them three times and then lay them out, turning them over as you go.

The spread

The spread I use is adapted from *A Feminist Tarot*.[10] I like it because it is a circle with a cross in the centre and seems to answer most needs.

The first card laid down is the **significator**, which represents the *querent* (questioner). The second card represents **factors** (or people) who *help* the querent. The third card shows **factors** (or people) who might *hinder* or *oppose* the

TAROT SPREAD

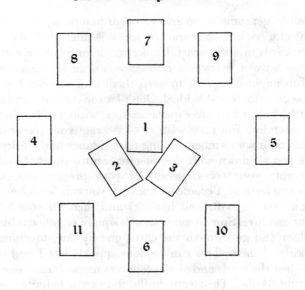

1 significator
2 factors helping
3 factors hindering
4 the past
5 immediate future
6 root-foundation
7 possible future
8 your attitude
9 hopes and fears
10 environment
11 the outcome

querent. The fourth card shows the **immediate past**. The fifth card shows the **immediate future**. The sixth card shows the **foundations** or **root cause** of the *issue* or *problem*. The seventh card shows the **possible future**, or **long-term prospects** concerning the *question*. The eighth card shows how the querent **feels** about her *situation*, her **attitude**. The ninth card shows the **hopes** and **fears** of the querent. The tenth card shows the querent's **environment**, her **personal life, friends** and **colleagues**. The final card, the eleventh, shows the **outcome** of the *issue*, or a **factor** which will **change** the **outcome** of the *question* or *issues*.

Lay the cards out and look at them as a whole. See patterns, connections, themes repeated, there may be lots of one suit, or similar numbers coming up. Generally a spread will have a flavour. But take your time, stay centred, and eventually the cards will speak to you.

A mistake beginner readers often make is to go on too long. I can never do readings for more than an hour, more like 30 to 40 minutes. Stop when you get tired and start to repeat yourself. Be firm and say to the querent, if necessary, that you can only focus for an hour at a time.

After the reading wrap up your cards and put them away. Light a candle briefly and perhaps burn a bit of incense to clear the air.

I also use the cards as a meditation for myself. When I do a reading I keep the cards laid out by my altar, or use any quiet spot so that each time I pass by the reading I quickly register the symbols and see them unfolding daily.

The cards mirror forces working in the life of the querent. They are a learning, self-discovery tool. They do not *do* anything other than instruct. They are your own esoteric, magical storehouse of knowledge.

13

HERBAL LORE

A WISE WOMAN'S GARDEN

Whether she lives in city or town or deep in the countryside, plant life is central to the witch. In the same way that witches are always supposed to have cats or dogs, and other familiars, all witches have their garden, whether in a physical or metaphorical sense. Rolling acres or plant pots, the living, breathing greenness of plants nourishes the spirit, soaks up negative energies and fills your everyday world with life. Tending a garden or allotment is the way many city dwellers, particularly crones, can deal with the insanity and pace of the concrete jungle. Country dwellers may garden or farm on a larger scale, or be lucky enough to watch the miracle of the changing seasons, the birth, flowering and fruiting of the yearly round and the decaying and death of the silent winter months.

Just as a woman's life is lived in the round, with the monthly waxing and waning of her cycle, so is the witch's calendar inextricably bound up with the rise and fall of the year. 'Plants hold the secrets of our witch foremothers, buried so deep only the wise can find them.'

Herbs heal, everyone knows this; that herbs also teach is a better-kept secret. Deep within each herb is a legend, a whisper of a story which, if grasped and followed, will not only take you deep within the plant's psyche but into your own innermost regions. Plants will tell you what you ask them, but will steadfastly refuse to speak to the unwary, the foolish, and the weak.

My psychic work with herbs began by accident. Early in my career as a herbalist I was giving workshops to women who wanted to know more about healing plants. At the same time I was teaching a lot of adult education classes on herbal medicine. One summer's morning the women's group assembled and my heart sank at the thought of yet another didactic day-long session. I was tired of the way I was teaching. I had gone out early that morning and picked armfuls of fresh herbs from the canal side, and the contrast between the green, living plants and the dry-as-dust facts I had learned could not have been greater. I had been learning psychic skills with a friend of mine, Susan Marionchild, and that week we had been working with psychometry (divination from objects). These three elements combined in a flash; my heart felt the need to do something different, there was the physical reality of the plants and the thoughtform or memory of work I had been doing. And I decided to work intuitively with plants. So the group and I spent the first day of the first workshop tuning into the plants. The results were amazing. Not only did a commonality of experience emerge but the depth and colour of the messages we picked up made me realise I was on to something. Most of the women were trained psychics so we all worked at a deep and intense level and worlds opened up to us. I found my plant teacher and together she and I systematically went through about 50 of the most commonly used herbs. I mixed the psychic work with pathworkings of guided imagery as I felt this would be appropriate. At that time, I was also studying psychosynthesis and I incorporated many of Roberto Assagioli's techniques into my work. I found his techniques blended perfectly with the psychic work we were doing.[1]

Combining psychic work with astrological lore, I found there was a wheel of the year, a meditation continuum that working with plants represented. Each plant is ruled by a sign of the zodiac and has qualities associated with that sign; the days of the week are also ruled by the signs, the moon moves through the 12 signs in the course of a lunar month and once a year the moon is full in that sign, bringing more of that particular planetary energy to bear on the plant. The sap or vital energy of a plant rises and falls according to the phases of the moon; as it is highest at the full moon this is the perfect time for harvesting. Coloured by the planetary energy of the sign of the zodiac the moon is in, and the quality of the plant, its essence varies, ebbs and flows, waxes and wanes. A plant coming under the sign of Venus, for instance, will be at its most potent in the months of Venus (May and September) and also when the moon is in Taurus and Libra (which are ruled by Venus) and Friday which is the day of Venus and the first hour after sunrise which is the hour of Venus. If the moon is full in May or September, the power is increased still further. Thus there is a web that weaves itself through time, place and plant which mirrors and reflects the celestial clock as the sun and moon make their respective journeys through the heavens.

There exists, then, an elegant symmetry in the dance between plant and planet. Webster's Dictionary (seventh edition) gives us plant coming from the Latin *plantare* to fix in place, whereas planet derives from the Greek *planes* meaning wanderer. The fixed and the wanderer, the rooted and the rootless, plant and planet are woven in a witch's world tapestry. The Goddess spins and reaps and creates poetry with both plant and planet. Cerridwen boiled up a cauldron of inspiration and knowledge which was simmered for a year and a day. Season by season she added magical plants gathered in their appropriate planetary hours. The boy set to stir the cauldron was splashed by three drops of this magical liquid and putting his burned fingers into his mouth he at once 'understood the nature of all things past, present and future'.[2]

Plant lore is pivotal to any study of natural magic. The wheel of the year cannot be studied without the growing year. I always pick my plants in the week leading up to the full moon and on the day and hour of their planetary rulers. If I made medicines or incenses they would be made on the day of the full moon and left to work until the day of the following full moon. It is spell work and a meditation. For me, the full moon is a sacred time and picking herbs and preparing medicine is a sacred act. Each month as I work I hold the awareness that ill and suffering people will be taking these plant essences, burning this incense, and the way I prepare them, lovingly or hurriedly, facilitates or hinders this process. The witch's world is a world of the Goddess immanent. Each action, each thought, contributes to the weave of goodness or badness. My actions count, but the intention behind my actions counts for even more. Motive matters. When working with plants I am always guided back to the sacred, the good, the true and the beautiful. May this be true for you. Blessed Be!

In my book, *A Woman's Book of Herbs*,[3] I discuss at length the psychic properties of some common herbs and readers may wish to refer to this book for more information on the subject. Here I feel it would be appropriate to include some flower meditations so readers can work on their own.

Meditation to meet the wise woman

This meditation takes you to meet your plant guide or teacher who will answer your questions, guide your study and suggest areas of work in your learning about the plant world.

Allow yourself at least 20 minutes for this meditation. Go to a place where you will not be disturbed, and unplug the phone. It is a good idea to pre-record the meditation on a tape recorder and then play it back to yourself, or, if you are a group, elect one member to guide the rest.

Make yourself comfortable, lie or sit down, loosen tight clothing, be warm enough as your body heat will drop after a while.

Relax, take a few deep breaths, with each out-breath feel yourself breathing out tension, relaxing down, down into the ground. Relax your feet. Feel the muscles of the feet become heavy and let go of any tension there. Relax the calves, breathe out any tension in the calves. Relax the knees, feel them grow heavy. Relax the thighs, relax the buttocks. Feel the floor (or chair) support them, let go. Relax the genitals and the belly. Breathe away tension, feel them become soft and empty. Relax the spine. Feel the tension draining away. Allow your spine to become heavy, to sink into the floor. Relax your abdomen, feel it become soft, breathe out any tension there. Relax your chest. Be aware of your breathing; with each breathing in breathe in light and with each out-breath

breathe out tension. Relax your shoulders, let them go heavy and sink into the floor. Feel the weight glide off them. Relax your upper arms and then your lower arms and hands, feel tension washing out of your arms, through your fingers and into the floor. Relax your neck, relax your throat, feel them become soft. Relax your face, relax your jaw muscles, relax your eyes, feel them turn inward. Relax your scalp muscles . . . Imagine you are walking in a wood. It is a bright summer's day, the sunlight dapples through the trees overhead and there is a warm and balmy breeze. Be aware of your surroundings. See the plants growing on the ground around you, notice the trees and any birds and animals nearby. Begin to walk, treading a well-worn path which leads you deeper and deeper in the forest . . . As you walk, pay close attention to your surroundings, notice what is around you . . . As you move deeper and deeper into the forest the trees begin to grow closer and closer together; it becomes darker. But you are not afraid; this is a welcome darkness; you feel safe and protected . . . Suddenly you come across a clearing in the forest and in the centre of the clearing is a hut. Make the choice to approach the hut, someone will come out to greet you . . . Allow her to take you inside, go with her where she takes you . . . Speak to her, ask her any questions you have . . . She will teach you about plants . . . (Allow 10 to 15 minutes to hear what she has to say to you) . . . Then realise it is time to leave, but be aware that you can return any time you wish. Say goodbye now, and slowly walk back along the path until you reach the place you started at . . . Then gradually come back into the room. Open your eyes, re-orientate yourself and write down your experiences.

Your plant teacher will teach you about the physical uses of plants, their magical and emotional properties, their plant lore and everyday uses. As you develop a relationship with her you will also go on a journey deep into yourself.

Remember, you! mugwort: what you revealed.
what you arranged: at the Magic Proclamation.
'Una' you are called: oldest of herbs.
you have power against three: and against thirty.
you have power against poison: and against infection.
you have power against the hostile one: that about the
land travels.[4]

How do witches use plants? *Witches Heal*, as Billie Potts says
in the title of her book, but we do more than attend to
the physical body. Plants have been used in spells and in the
making of amulets; they are used in ritual and in festivals, as
teaching plants and as power objects.[5] The most poisonous of
plants will, if the right dose is taken, take the seeker on a
wild journey to spirit kingdoms and the lands of the shades.
Great care must be taken. **Rather than ingest the plant, you
can work psychically with it**; it will still have a powerful
effect but you are unlikely to become intoxicated. At Samhain
on the first year we were working psychically with plants, I
decided we would work with the 'heavies,' that is, plants
traditionally associated with witchcraft: flying plants, poisoning plants, Hecate's tool kit. **NEVER EVER INGEST THESE
PLANTS**. I chose thorn apple, a well-known hallucinogenic,
lobelia, a very deep relaxant, and skullcap, a sedative. By
the end of the day, I was flying, literally, and experienced the
dream-nightmare world that Castañeda describes working
with *el diablo* (thorn apple/datura).[6] My friend and I sat out
on her flat roof and I became aware of or 'saw' the threads
which hold the world together. I felt I could hook onto the
threads and fly, but did not try to do this as I wasn't sure I
wouldn't go crashing to the ground. Years later I read Castañeda's account of the sisters flying and was struck by the
similarity of the experience.[7] Our reveries were broken by the
front doorbell. In walked my friend's ex-lover, the worse for
drink, and hell-bent on seeing her, while she clearly did not
want to see him. The situation degenerated into farce as,
failing to reason with him, I threatened to call the police. The
telephone presented an insurmountable object to me so the
ex-lover in exasperation dialled the number. The police duly
arrived minutes after the spurned lover had left and looked

on us all with deep and menacing suspicion. Still flying I managed to persuade them to leave without arresting any of us, and we collapsed into tears and giggles. Such hilarious and surreal events often happen with magic, as the inner experience is reflected by the outer. We also felt somewhat chastised; these energies are powerful, dangerous and have the potential for violence. Afterwards we were more careful. Thorn apple is not called *el diablo* for nothing.

Thorn apple is one of the ingredients of a witch's flying ointments, along with belladonna. They are hallucinogens of the first order and **taken in too high a dosage can kill**. Thorn apple did make it clear to me what mediaeval witches had meant about flying and why they had done it in groups. I imagine it would be terrifying flying alone.

In his apprenticeship with Don Juan, Carlos Castañeda is taken to several meetings with *el diablo* and, questioning his teacher, Don Juan speaks about the plant: 'She distorts men. She gives them a taste of power too soon without fortifying their hearts and makes them domineering and unpredictable. She makes them weak in the middle of their great power.'[8] To the Yaqui Indians of Mexico, power plants are a terrifying reality, a huge power source that can be tamed (if you are right for them) and used for power, an ally:

> An 'ally,' he said, is a power a man can bring into his life to help him, advise him, and give him the strength necessary to perform acts, whether big or small, right or wrong. This ally is necessary to enhance a man's life, guide his acts, and further his knowledge. In fact, an ally is the indispensable aid to knowing.[9]

Plants teach, hold the wisdom of our foremothers buried so only the wise can find them.

Plants hold power, and' they are also prophets, as lobelia taught me.

Working with lobelia, an American herb (*lobelia inflata*), I was given a revelatory flash which pushed me into ordering my notes for a book and gave me a vision about the future. (I first wrote about this in the journal *Panakeia* in 1982 (No. 2, p. 19).

The following meditation can be used for preliminary work with plants, best done with a friend or in a group so you can compare experiences.

Meditation

Take about 20 minutes. Sit in a comfortable place where you will not be disturbed. Go through a short relaxation (see Chapter 13, p. 201 above) and take the plant, fresh or dried, in your hands. Turn your attention inwards and on to the plant. Feel your psyche merging with that of the plant, gradually penetrating its essence . . . Wait and a guide will come to you . . . If you feel good about her or him, then follow where she leads. Remember you can come back whenever you wish, and go as fast or as slow as you choose. If you are working with the more powerful plants it is best to have a friend with you for reassurance should you need it.

I found it best to use, say, two plants of a similar nature, for example, those ruled by Venus, and then two of a contrary nature (Mars) to compare and contrast their energies. Keep notes and share what you pick up.

Plant lore

Hecate, queen of the witches, had many flowers dedicated to her: mandrake, deadly nightshade, aconite, azalea, cyclamen, mint. She instructed her two daughters, Medea and Circe, in the use of herbs. A witch traditionally made her broomstick handles from ash so that they could not drown, with birch twigs for the brush, and bound them with willow. Hecate grew hemlock and henbane in her garden. She also favoured cinquefoil, vervain, endive and bryony, but did not like yellow or greenish flowers. Foxgloves were called witches' bells, mullein, hags' tapers. Elder was believed to keep away witches as was rowan. As the rhyme says, 'Rowan tree and red thread, put the witches to their speed.'

There are seven herbs that nothing supernatural can injure. St John's wort, vervain, speedwell, eyebright, mallow, self heal and yarrow. They should be gathered near the full moon on a bright sunny day. Four-leafed clover will help you see through glamour.

When Demeter was wandering the earth, looking for abducted Persephone, poppies sprang up under her feet to lighten her on her way in the darkness. She ate their seeds and fell into a weary sleep. After the slaughter in France during the First World War, poppies sprang up, carpeting the ravaged land, as if to symbolise the rivers of blood and renewal after physical death.

THE TREE ALPHABET

Immortalised by Robert Graves in the White Goddess, the Tree Alphabet is said to be a genuine relic of Druidism and tree-magic found in the Irish Celtic tradition. Each of the 13 trees represents one of the lunar months of the year, of 28 days in length, with one day left over. The year and a day of the witches. Working through each month, Graves relates the tree to traditions of the White Goddess.[10] Thus, birch twigs are used to beat out evil spirits and beat the bounds, that is, mark out the boundaries of fields and temples. No one should fell an alder tree, lest their house burn down. Traditionally used for milk pails, alder has the name of *Comet lachta* (guarding of milk). The green dye of alder flowers coloured the clothes of the fairies and would have also hidden wise folk hiding from persecutors in deep woodland and forest. Willow is sacred to Hecate and its word root is the same as that of witch, Wicca and wicked, meaning to bend. Sacred to the moon goddess this water-loving tree yields salicylic acid which calms aching joints formerly thought to be a witch's curse.

Hawthorn trees were felled at great peril; a man could lose his home and his family by such an act. Hawthorn presides over the unlucky month of May, a month of mourning and chastity. The vine, although not native to the Celts, is a tree of joy, exhilaration and wrath.

The thirteenth tree is elder, a very special tree. It has a long association with death, elder leaf-shaped funerary flints were found in megalithic long barrows.

Every sacred grove was planted with oak trees. An ancient druidic chant runs, 'in a wide circle the oak tree moved round.' Until the reign of Elizabeth the First it was forbidden to cut down oak trees as they were seen to be the heart of England.

Groves of hazel and elm were often used by the Saxons for their temples. The hazel was one of Thor's trees; the first Christian church in England, built in Glastonbury, was made from hazel trees, and Patrick used hazel rods to drive the snakes (female wisdom) out of Ireland. Hazel rods are used in divining and for finding buried treasure.

Trees living as long as they do hold deep mystery and a timeless wisdom. Care for them!

THE LADY FLOWERS

Continuing through Goddess lore about plants we are drawn to the lady flowers. Ostensibly named after Our Lady (the Virgin Mary) they are in fact Goddess flowers, co-opted by the church. The lady flowers are Goddess flowers, in her maiden or mother aspect: lady's smock (cuckoo flower), our lady's mantle (morning glory), our lady's ribbons (ribbon grass), our lady's laces (dodder), our lady's nightcap (Canterbury Bell), our lady's thimble (campanula), our lady's tresses (quaking grass), our lady's bedstraw, our lady's cushion (thrift), our lady's candlestick (oxlip), our lady's taper (mullein), our lady's slipper. Gardeners would do well to save a corner for her plants and give rein to her flowering. As our lands become more and more clogged with pollution and poisons, witches need to grow and sow all manner of the Goddess and Fairy plants.

FAIRY FLOWERS

In Ireland primroses were scattered or grown before a door to keep fairies away, but in Somerset they belong to fairies. It is bad luck to dig up a fairy ring, but to weed and care for one ensures an easy death. Cowslips will help you find fairy treasure and so will forget-me-nots. Other fairy flowers are red campion and periwinkles, while the juice of foxglove leaves will cure a fairy-struck child, which is the touch of a wand by an angry fairy if you knocked over a foxglove, cow parsley or dock she was hiding in. (Fairy illnesses are stitch, itch, cramp and blight.) Fairy bells were wood sorrel, fairy cap was foxglove, fairy cheese, mallow, fairy flax, ground flax, fairy horse, ragwort, fairy tables, toadstools and fairy cup, cowslip. Any respectable fairy garden, planted to entice them and make them stay, would have most of the following plants: foxgloves, bluebells, cow parsley, violets, primroses, anemones, wood sorrel, cranesbill, ragged robin, campion, snowdrops, celandine and periwinkle.

Remember the saying: 'More in the garden grows than the gardener sows.'

Witches keep gardens as they keep cats; beware the woman who can keep neither.

A WITCH'S GARDEN

I was lucky enough to work with some of the women who created the Witch's Garden and thought that other witchgardeners might like to share my delight in seeing their creation.

In the 1984 Liverpool Garden Festival, one of the gardens had to be blessed by the local bishop. It had already caused great consternation amongst the local clergy. It was, as you may have already guessed, a witch's garden. To be fair, in Liverpool at that time there had been an outbreak of Satanic lunacy, which had had absolutely nothing to do with the witch's garden. Unfortunately the clergy were unable to tell the difference between Satanism and witchcraft, and theirs was probably a knee-jerk response to the word 'witch.' After all, the last English witch to be hanged was as late as 1712 and that is really a very short time ago. The witch garden with its sculptures, spider's web and brightly coloured plants contrasted wildly with the Christian 'Garden of Hope', which was dark, colourless and full of terrifying statuary of writhing, anorexic men dying on crosses. On the one hand there was a garden full of death, torment and suffering men, and on the other a garden, full of light, beauty, creativity and women. There was no need to ask which was witch!

As with all women's projects, the garden was high on enthusiasm and willing hands and low on cash. Liz Brandon-Jones, who designed the original garden, and whose beautiful illustration is to be found opposite, said although many potential sponsors were delighted by the idea, they were afraid of reprisals or of bad publicity. But the Goddess' work was done and was a delight as the warm sun shone on it on the opening day. Even the Queen asked to see it.

The theme of a witch garden was chosen because the 'witch was an important & revered member of the community. The Garden & its contents were the raw materials of her trade. She harnessed the power of her garden, its land, superstition & myth to her own end.'[11] The theme was thoroughly researched from both modern and historical sources and the local Pendle Witches of Lancashire were called on to provide a local flavour for the garden. It was based on the three goddesses of Fate, Clotho who spun a life-thread for each human at birth, Lachesis who determined the length of the thread and Atropos who cut the thread, using nightshade berries to do this.

The design was based on Hecate the triple Goddess of the Moon and Queen of the Witches. The beautiful statue of Hecate, sculpted by a local woman sculptor, had three faces, reflecting the waxing, waning and full moon. One of each of her three faces pointed to one of the three gardens. She sat inside a magic circle which was decorated with runes and an intricate paving pattern. Entering the garden through the path of life and moving through the garden of Clotho the Spider's web pergola, made from thick rope, represented the web of life which Clotho spun.

Clotho's garden led into the garden of Lachesis, the full moon garden. It was planted with plants of vibrant colour, coloured glass and a sunburst canopy (looking like the sun) to reflect the vivid light of the full moon. The canopy was

210

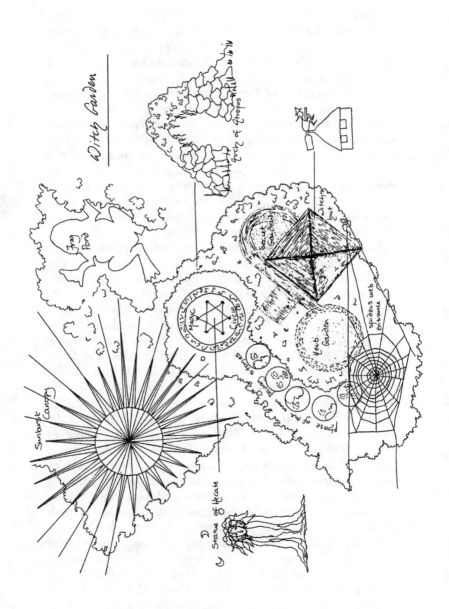

- 18 -

LIVERPOOL LANDSCAPES: HERBAL HOROSCOPE
WITCH GARDEN   WOODEN WHEEL 6 metre DIAMETER, DIVIDED INTO TWELVE.
EACH COMPARTMENT IS 1·5m x 1·25 m. (CENTRE FILLED WITH GRAVEL
(SEE ENCLOSED LIST FOR MORE DETAILS ON SPECIES REQUIRED.)

N.B: ZODIAC SIGNS UNDER THE SAME RULING PLANET CAN SHARE THE SAME
PLANTS. E.g. PISCES & SAGITTARIUS CAN BOTH BE RULED BY JUPITER.

SCALE 1:50

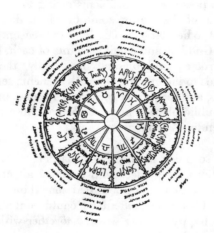

made from brightly coloured sailcloth painted in warm colours.

The final phase of the moon was represented by the third part of the garden. Walking through the arch of Atropos, which was constructed by stone boulders, you passed into a dark and shaded area dominated by the frog pond planted with dark and sinister plants showing the decline and decay of life.

There was also a hut and garden of the witch herself, full of the herbs and mystical plants used in her trade. These she gathered under the cover of night, not only for reasons of self-concealment, but also because she believed that plants had to be plucked in certain phases of the moon. On the top of the hut was the witch weather vane; the hut itself was made from timber and was donated to a children's home after the festival was over. The exquisite wooden paving stones were made from cutting transverse circular sections from a large tree and carving on them various phases of the moon. Wattle fencing surrounded the garden's perimeter.

Marie McGoldrick was in charge of the herbal horoscope and the medicinal beds, see previous page. Helped by local women growers and artists, Marie built up a floral zodiac reflecting the planetary rulerships of herbs. The medicinal garden also presented its problems owing to the difficulty in finding some of the plants, some of which died off because they needed to be planted so early in the season. But with the help of the Goddess and small amounts of cash, both gardens were constructed and planted out. Sadly, there were not enough funds to include the women's ailments section and the love potions, and the poison garden was seen to be too danger-ous for a public place. The herbs Marie chose can be found in the appendix. As she wrote:

> There is so much in the Witch Garden; plants, art work, constructions, with ideas and symbols all created by the women, and they, too, identified something of themselves in it . . . I am very glad that I could contribute my part and very happy to have worked together with the women on the Witch Garden.[12]

When the garden festival ended, Marie organised the moving of plants from the Witch Garden to Manchester. There, together with a student of Art and Drama at Manchester Polytechnic, Chet Alexander, she organised the planting of a Herbal Medicine Wheel. (See diagram opposite.) 'A Medicine Wheel is used to create a circle of healing, where a person may, by sitting in peace, contribute to, or draw, inner strength from the circle.'[13] They obtained permission to plant the Wheel in Withenshaw Park in Manchester, and the plants were moved from Liverpool to Manchester.

Each section of the Wheel had a stone collected from the estuary of the River Wirral. Marie says: 'Great care was taken to choose the right stone for each section. I remember the Moon stone was a beautiful white stone and the Mother stone,

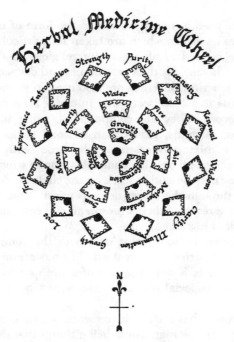

9 yards diameter – outside circle

proudly chosen by Liz Coyne, was red sandstone with soft round ripples.'[14]

With the minimum of money but with many willing hands the garden was finally finished:

> It looked really good, the wheel was cut out from lush green turf and the herbs and stones placed in their positions. Everyone was happy, the Medicine Wheel was created and the Witch Garden plants had a new home. It was wonderful to sit on the Creation Stone in the centre of the wheel.[15]

See Appendix B, p. 219 for the layout of the wheel.

INCENSES

Plants are used in ritual, usually in the form of incenses and sometimes as drinks which are taken for particular effects.

Incense is used in all the major religions of the world to provide a 'flavour' for their ceremonies and deepen the experience of their rites. Incenses are also used in ritual by witches and pagans to set the scene and to create an atmosphere for magical work. They are compounded, using the planetary rulerships, of gums, resins, herbs, wood barks, seeds, etc. With the admixture of essential oils, these heady compounds facilitate magic by opening channels through which the spirits rush. They may be said to work on the chakras, on the etheric body, or through the senses or deep mind. That they work is evident as a result of their widespread and continued use; how they work is less clear.

The Egyptians took great care with the compounding of incenses and perfected a great art. The most famous of Egyptian incenses is Kyphi, the manufacture of which was surrounded by a special rite. Leo Vinci writes, quoting Plutarch:

> The incense has sixteen ingredients, which is a square out of a square, the ingredients being things that delight in the night. It has the power to lull people to sleep, brighten the dreams, loosen the tensions of daily anxiety, by bringing calm and quiet to all who breathed it.[16]

Although various authors have provided different recipes the main ingredient is always frankincense. Said to be a tree guarded by winged serpents native to Somalia, only certain families had the right to harvest the resin, and the picker had to be purified before (s)he was permitted to gather it.

India was also famous for its perfumes, especially sweet-smelling gums and resins. Sandalwood, probably one of the most well-known scented woods, is used to purify an atmosphere and aids psychic work. In ancient Greece, cedar and myrtle woods were burnt in houses to give off fragrant smoke. Incense was believed to have come to Greece through the cult of Aphrodite from Phoenicia through Cyprus, where it was used in her temples.

Burning herbs and oils releases their magical properties and set the scene for magical work. It is best to make your own incense, and nowadays the ingredients are fairly easy to come by. Here is a standard recipe which can be altered according to the seasons and effect required:

> 2 parts musk
> 3 parts powdered orris root
> 10 parts sandalwood
> 3 parts patchouli leaves
> 3 parts benzoin
> 5 parts cinnamon
> 5 parts powdered myrrh
> 10 parts frankincense.

Mix together and sprinkle on to a charcoal disc. It can be burned at any time.

Plant lore is almost limitless. Look at the bibliography to follow up ideas which attract you.

APPENDIX A

MEDICINAL PLANT LIST

Nervous system

Brooklime	*Veronica beccabunga*
Coltsfoot	*Tussilago farfara*
Common mallow	*Malva sylvestris*
Mullein	*Verbascum thapsus*
Feverfew	*Chrysanthemum parthenium*
Primrose	*Primula vulgaris*
Wild parsnip	*Pastanica*

Heart and circulation

Bugle	*Ajuga reptans*
Dyers greenweed	*Genista tinctoria*
Golden rod	*Solidago virgaurea*
Figwort	*Scrophularia nodosa*
Yarrow	*Achillea millefolium*

Chest and throat

Coltsfoot	*Tussilago farfara*
Elecampane	*Inula helenium*
Mullein	*Verbascum thapsus*
Sweet violet	*Viola odorata*
Comfrey	*Symphytum officinale*
Water mint	*Mentha aquatica*

Stomach and bowels

Herb Robert	*Geranium robertianum*
Herb Bennet	*Guem urbanum*
Dandelion	*Taraxacum officinale*
Angelica	*Angelica archangelica*
Wild carrot	*Daucus carota*
Water mint	*Mentha aquatica*
Ground ivy	*Glechoma hederacea*
Valerian	*Valeriana officinalis*
Yarrow	*Achillea millefolium*
Bistort	*Polygonum bistorta*

Skin, wounds and bruises

Great plantain	*Plantago major*
Figwort	*Scrophularia nodosa*
Burdock	*Arctium lappa*
Butterbur	*Petasites hybridus*
Bistort	*Polygonum bistorta*
Foxglove	*Digitalis purpurea*
Common mallow	*Malva sylvestris*
Red clover	*Trifolium pratense*

Painful joints

Lords and ladies	*Arum maculatum*
Burdock	*Arctium lappa*
Borage	*Borago officinalis*
Primrose	*Primula vulgaris*
Meadowsweet	*Filipendula ulmaria*

Urinary

Wild carrot	*Daucus carota*
Garlic mustard	*Allaria petiolata*
Alexanders	*Smynium olusatrum*
Common agrimony	*Agrimonium eupatorium*
St John's wort	*Hypericum perfoliatum*
Cowslip	*Primula veris*

| Witch grass | *Agropyrens repens* |
| Devil bit scabious | *Succisa pratensis* |

Women's ailments

Lemon balm	*Melissa officinalis*
Black cohosh	*Cimicifuga racemosa*
Catmint	*Nepeta cataria*
Mugwort	*Artemisia vulgaris*
Raspberry	*Rubus ideas*
Yarrow	*Achillea millefolium*

Love potions

Damiana	*Turnera diffusa*
Jasmin	*Jasminum officinalis*
Sandalwood	*Santalum album*
Myrtle	*Myrica gale*

Poison garden

Thorn apple	*Datura stramonium*
Aconite	*Aconitum napellus*
Cinquefoil	*Potentilla reptans*
Deadly nightshade	*Atropa belladonna*
Henbane	*Hyoscyamus niger*
Mandrake	*Atropa mandragora*
Hellebore	*Veratrum album*

APPENDIX B

LAYOUT OF THE MEDICINE WHEEL

Creation stone

Centre circle

growth	Penettya
transformation	dyer's greenweed
decay	periwinkle and yew

Inner circle

water	sage, bear's breech, horehound
fire	nettles, horseradish, great celandine
air	hazel, pennyroyal, valerian
Mother Goddess	lady's mantle, mugwort, willow
Sun	St John's wort, chamomile, lovage
Moon	privet, geranium, honesty
Earth	yarrow, plantain, comfrey

Outer circle

purity	flax, heartsease, comfrey
cleansing	marshmallow, sorrel, coltsfoot
renewal	sage, lemon balm, dandelion
wisdom	columbine, feverfew, nettles
clarity	yarrow, foxglove, lady's mantle
illumination	horehound, valerian, meadowsweet
growth	bear's breech, iris, geranium
love	St John's wort, celandine, garlic, mustard
trust	white horehound, cowslip, mugwort
experience	figwort, catmint, daisy
introspection	heather, mint, garlic
strength	sage, dandelion, betony

APPENDIX C - CORRESPONDENCES

Correspondences are used when making up your own spells and rituals. If you want to do some work on love, for example, look under water, also the planets Venus and the Moon. Similarly for studying, look to air and Mercury. The oils are for anointing your body and candles are used for making incenses. So choose the mood or feeling most appropriate to your spell or ritual. For magical work harmonise the planets, the elements, incenses, oils, candles, and days of the week.

THE FOUR ELEMENTS

EARTH

Direction: North
Astrological signs: Taurus, Virgo, Capricorn
Planet: Saturn
Rules: the physical body, the earth, all growing things, animals, the material world. Physical cycles of birth and death. Money, fertility, sensuality.
Season: winter
Colours: black, green and white
Tool: pentacle
Feelings: stability, melancholy
All earth and fertility goddesses: Demeter, Ceres, Rhea, Rhiannon, Gaia.

WATER

Direction: West
Astrological signs: Cancer, Scorpio, Pisces
Planets: Moon and Venus
Rules: feelings, dreams, love, sorrow, lakes, the sea, all water, fluidity, unboundedness, psychic skills. Love, fertility (with Earth), family (mother-centred).
Season: autumn
Colours: blue, blue-green, grey, indigo, sea green
Tool: cup
Feelings: love, fear
All sea and love goddesses: Aphrodite, Isis, Mari.

FIRE

Direction: South
Astrological signs: Aries, Leo, Sagittarius
Planets: Sun and Mars
Rules: energy, action, courage, impulsiveness, grand schemes, fires, purification, sexual passion, deserts, volcanoes.
Season: summer
Colours: red, gold, crimson, orange
Tool: wand
Feelings: passion, anger
All fire goddesses, Brigit, Hestia, Vesta.

AIR

Direction: East
Astrological signs: Gemini, Libra, Aquarius
Planets: Mercury, Jupiter (as a planet of learning and philosophy).
Rules: thought, communication, energy, speed, theory, learning. Mountains, plains, high towers, wind and breath.
Season: spring
Colours: yellow, white, silver, blue-grey
Tool: sword
Feelings: joy, worry
All air goddesses: Urania, Arianrhod, Aradia, Nuit.

THE PLANETS

SUN

Astrological sign: Leo
Day: Sunday
Colours: gold, yellow
Incenses: solar, juniper, rosemary, marigold, chamomile, cloves, frankincense, cinnamon, cloves, angelica, musk, amber, myrrh, orange, lemon
Jewel: topaz
Rules: the heart, success, leadership, courage, expansion, optimism, creativity, growth, children
Key words: authority, bright, honour, warm, regal

MOON

Astrological sign: Cancer
Day: Monday
Colours general: white, silver; new moon: silver; full moon: red; dark moon: black.
Incenses: jasmine, poppy, myrtle, ylang ylang, white sandalwood
Jewels: moonstone, pearl, crystal
Rules: the reproductive cycle, fertility, psychic skills, dreams, creativity, birth
New moon: maiden, beginnings, initiation, birth, virginity; full moon: mother, fecundity, creativity, sexuality, maturity; dark moon: crone, old age, death, wisdom, solitude, endings.
Key words: fluidity, change, dreamy, nocturnal, moist, womanly.

MERCURY

Astrological signs: Gemini and Virgo
Day: Wednesday
Colours: metallic, changeable colours
Incenses: lavender, valerian, mandrake, liquorice, aniseed, mace, sandalwood (some give this to Mercury rather than the Moon).

Jewels: agate, topaz
Rules: ideas, communication by speech or writing, quickness, thievery, deception, humour.
Key words: busy, dual, alert, adaptive, nervous, speedy.

VENUS

Astrological signs: Taurus, Libra
Day: Friday
Colour: green
Incenses: red sandalwood, almond oil, bergamot, jasmine, rose, pennyroyal, violet, verbena, strawberry, apple, mint, mugwort, elder, thyme, lily of the valley.
Jewels: emerald, coral, lapis lazuli
Rules: love, sexual passion, friendship, harmony, beauty, creativity, sweetness, pleasure, indulgence.
Key words: amorous, elegant, frivolous, peaceful, loving.

MARS

Astrological signs: Aries, Scorpio
Day: Tuesday
Colour: red
Incenses: ginger, pepper, wormwood, all hallucinogens, garlic, sarsaparilla, patchouli, cannabis, nettle, tobacco, myrrh, hops, hawthorn.
Jewels: bloodstone, garnet, ruby.
Rules: warfare, strife, energy, sport, courage, recklessness, aggression, passion, desire.
Key words: struggle, anger, energy, courage, discord.

JUPITER

Astrological signs: Sagittarius, Pisces
Day: Thursday
Colours: magenta, purple
Incenses: dandelion, agrimony, borage, limeflowers, sage, melissa, red clover, meadowsweet, hyssop, orris root.
Jewels: amethyst, turquoise

Rules: honour, riches, power, fame, success, leadership, the
law, higher education, philosophy.
Key words: benevolent, luxurious, prosperous, generous,
rich, excessive.

SATURN

Astrological signs: Capricorn, Aquarius
Day: Saturday
Colour: black
Incenses: aconite, comfrey, mullein, hemlock, henbane,
mandrake, horsetail, nightshade, all bad-smelling herbs.
Jewel: onyx
Rules: time, restriction, loneliness, old age, sorrow,
limitation, death, obstacles.
Key words: austere, conservative, prudent, cautious, mean,
sober, profound, miserable.

INCENSES

To make your own planetary or elemental incenses, mix
herbs and oils of the planet or element together and
compound on the planetary day. For example, a Solar
incense, made on Sunday, might contain: marigold flowers,
rosemary, juniper berries, orange peel, saffron, orris root and
chamomile oil.

CANDLES

Choose the candles you burn according to their colour:
White: peace, purifying
Yellow: money, health, attraction
Orange: happiness, health
Purple: concentration
Blue: cleansing
Green: health, purifying, happiness
Pink: love, sexual attraction
Red: courage, anger, passion
Brown: to dispel sorrow, for growing plants
Black: hexing, returning bad vibes
Silver: clairvoyance, astral travelling, spell-making

ANOINTING OILS

Use these essential oils to anoint your candles before lighting them and to anoint your body. They work on the deep mind. Try to buy them as undiluted as possible. Don't use synthetic oils.

Carnation: for developing spiritual life, purifying and elevating.

Geranium: active, daring, to get what you want

Frankincense: spiritual power, meditation, clairvoyance

Heliotrope: heady, narcotic, aphrodisiac

Honeysuckle: thinkers, communicators, dreamy

Hyacinth: rash, quixotic, unstable, airy

Jasmine: heady, aphrodisiac, lucky, for success

Lavender: calming, soothing, expanding

Lily of the Valley: shy, retiring, delicate, sensitive

Musk: strong willed, sensual, erotic, intense

Myrrh: magical, uplifting, psychic, sweet smelling, heady

Patchouli: passionate, obsessive, heady, narcotic

Rose: sensual, loving, harmonious, old fashioned, safe

Rosemary: bold, courageous, energetic, unusual. protective

Sandalwood: erotic, sensual, clairvoyant, harmonising

Verbena: strong, resilient, far-seeing

Violet: delicate, sweet, harmonious, balanced

Ylang Ylang: heady, narcotic, sensual, erotic

This is a short list, there are many more. I write about the magical use of plants in *A Woman's Book of Herbs* (published by the Women's Press in 1992).

NOTES

CHAPTER 2

1 The Kundalini is energy found deep within the body and it can be tapped and used in magic.

CHAPTER 3

1 Frank Boas, writing in Johann Jacob Bachofen, *Myth, Religion, and Mother Right*, 1967, p. xxiii. [First edition 1926.]

2 Ibid; also Jan Harrison, *Prologomena to the Study of Greek Religion*, 1921.

3 Johann Jacob Bachofen, op. cit., p. 75.

4 Ibid, p. 75.

5 Ibid, p. 71.

6 Ibid, p. 80.

7 Ibid, p. 82.

8 Ibid, p. 87.

9 Ibid, p. 137.

10 Strabo, *Geography*, edited and translated by H L Jones, 1917–32, 8 vols, 7: p. 297.

11 Carl Jung and Carol Kerenyi, *The Science of Mythology, Essays on the Myth of the Divine Child and the Mysteries of Eleusis*, 1985, p. 128.

12 Carl Jung, *Psychological Reflections*, 1961, p. 159.

13 Carol Kerenyi, *Eleusis*, 1967, p. 92.

14 Carl Jung, from C Jung and C Kerenyi, *Essays on the Science of Mythology*, 1950, p. 245.

15 Carol Kerenyi, op. cit., p. 9.

16 Ibid, p. 130.

17 Ibid, p. 106.

18 Jane Harrison, op. cit., p. 269.

19 Carol Kerenyi, op. cit., p. 138.

20 Erich Neumann, *The Great Mother, An Analysis of the Archetype*, 1963, p. 318.

21 Ibid, p. 318.

22 Ibid, p. 319. Sophocles, *Oedipus at Colonus*, trans. Robert Fitzgerald, Faber and Faber, 1957, pp. 26–7

23 Ibid, p. 319.

24 *Hymn to Demeter from Hesiod, the Homeric Hymns and Homerica*, 1920, p. 322.

25 Carol Kerenyi, op. cit., p. 141.

26 Carl Jung, op. cit., p. 225.

27 C. Kerenyi, op. cit., p. 17. Quoting *Eunapios Vitae Sophistarum* VII.3. Eunapios was initiated into the cult by the last legitimate Hierophant commissioned by Emperor Julian to restore the rites which had fallen into neglect. A false priest usurped this Hierophant who had predicted the destruction of the sanctuary and the fall of Greece. The sanctuary was overrun by Alaric, king of the Goths, in 396 CE. Alaric brought monks with him who broke up the temple. Greece fell to Alaric, proving the belief that the rites of Eleusis and the Greek state were so intertwined that the destruction of one meant the downfall of the other.

28 Nor Hall, *The Moon and the Virgin*, 1980, p. 59.

29 John Bierhorst (ed.) *In the Trail of the Wind: American Indian Poems and Ritual Orations*, 1971, p. 112.

30 Susan Brownmiller, *Against Our Will: Men, Women, and Rape*, p. 203–4.

31 Adrienne Rich, *Of Woman Born, Motherhood as Experience and Institution*, 1977, p. 194.

32 Kahlil Gibran, *The Prophet*, 1966, p. 20.

33 Monica Sjöö and Barbara Mor, *The Great Cosmic Mother*, 1987, p. 210.

34 Barbara Walker, *The Women's Encyclopedia of Myths and Secrets*, 1983, p. 25.

35 Ibid, p. 25.

36 Ibid, p. 25.

37 Lewis Spence, *The Mysteries of Britain*, 1982, p. 157.

38 Charlene Spretnak, *Lost Goddesses of Early Greece*, 1978, pp. 98–110.

39 Evelyn-White, op. cit., p. 322.

40 Jane Harrison, op. cit., p. 120.

41 Johann Bachofen, op. cit., pp. 179–80, quoting Sophocles, Oedipus at Colonus, p. 337.

42 Virgil, *Georgics*, Vol. 1, 4: p. 475. 1916–1918.

43 Carol Kerenyi, op. cit., p. 78.

44 Charlene Spretnak, op. cit., p. 98.

45 Ibid, p. 108.

46 Marie Louise von Franz, *Papyri Graecae Magicae*, quoted in *The Problem of Evil in Fairy Tales: a collection of essays*, 1967, p. 112.

48 Barbara Black Koltuv, *The Book of Lilith*, 1986, p. 39.

49 Ibid, p. 29.

50 Ibid, p. 39.

51 Ibid, p. 50.

52 Ibid, p. 81.

53 Monique Wittig, *Les Guerilleres*, 1969, p. 89.

CHAPTER 4

1 See Caitlin and John Matthews, *The Western Way: A Practical Guide to the Western Mystery Tradition*, 1985, pp. 23–5.

2 Marija Gimbutas, *The Gods and Goddesses of Old Europe 7000–3000 BC, Myths, Legends and Cult Images*, 1974.

3 See Marija Gimbutas, ibid, and Monica Sjöö and Barbara Mor, *The Great Cosmic Mother: Rediscovering the Religion of the Earth*, 1987.

4 Starhawk, *The Spiral Dance*, 1979, pp. 2–3.

5 Ibid, p. 3.

6 Jeanne Achterberg, *Woman as Healer*, 1990, p. 28.

7 Starhawk, op. cit., p. 4.

8 Robert Graves, *The White Goddess*, 1961, p. 50.

9 Ibid, p. 61.

10 Ibid, p. 61.

11 For example: Robert Graves, op. cit., *The Mabinogion*; Marion Zimmer Bradley, *The Mists of Avalon*, 1983; Caitlin and John Matthews, op. cit.

12 Robert Graves, op. cit., pp. 30–2.

13 Ibid, p. 19.

14 Ibid, p. 20.

15 Ibid, p. 20.

16 Ibid, p. 22.

17 Caitlin and John Matthews, op. cit., p. 34.

18 Ibid, p. 35.

19 Zsuszanna Budapest, *The Holy Book of Women's Mysteries*, *volume I*, 1980, p. 86.

20 Ibid, p. 87.

21 Ibid, p. 88.

22 Robert Graves, op. cit., p. 131.

23 Zsuzsanna Budapest, op. cit., p. 88.
24 Ibid, p. 89.
25 Margaret Murray, *The Witch Cult in Western Europe: A Study in Anthropology*, 1921, p. 49.
26 Barbara Walker, *A Woman's Encyclopedia of Myths and Secrets*, 1987, p. 1082.
27 Simone de Beauvoir, *The Second Sex*, 1972, p. 71.
28 Barbara Walker, op. cit., p. 1082.

CHAPTER 5

1 Reverend Montague Summers, *The History of Witchcraft and Demonology*, 1926, pp. xliv–xlv.
2 Matilda Joslyn Gage, *Women, Church and State* [first edition 1893], 1980, pp. 106–7.
3 Barbara Walker, op. cit., p. 599.
4 Ibid, p. 599.
5 J B Russell, *Witchcraft in the Middle Ages*, 1972, p. 286.
6 Kremner and Spregner, *The Malleus Maleficarum*, translated by the Reverend Montague Summers, 1928. [Second edition 1971.]
7 Edward Peters, *The Magician, the Witch and the Law*, 1978, p. 152.
8 Barbara Walker, op. cit., pp. 61 and 62.
9 Charles Godfrey Leland, *Aradia, or the Gospel of the Witches*, 1899, pp. 104–6.
10 Hugh Trevor-Roper, *The European Witchcraze of the Sixteenth and Seventeenth centuries*, 1969, p. 127.
11 Mary Daly, *Gyn/Ecology: the Metaethics of Radical Feminism*, 1979, p. 184.
12 Christine Larner, *Enemies of God – The Witch-Hunt in Scotland*, 1981, p. 97.
13 Barbara Walker, op. cit., p. 1087.
14 Ibid, p. 447.
15 Ibid, p. 441.
16 Elisabeth Brooke, *Women Healers Through History*, 1993, pp. 83–5.
17 Charles Leland, op. cit., pp. 5–7.
18 Robert Graves, *The White Goddess*, 1961, p. 14. [First edition 1947.]
19 Ibid, p. 488.
20 Ibid, p. 15.
21 Ibid, p. 17.
22 For example, the magical poetry of W B Yeats: Kathleen Raine,

---

230

Yeats, the Tarot and the Golden Dawn, 1968; Robin Skelton, *Spellcraft: A Manual of Verbal Magic*, 1978; Stephen Dunstan, *Tarot Poems*, 1980.

23 Robert Graves, op. cit., p. 479.

24 Ibid, p. 14.

25 Caitlin and John Matthews, *The Western Way*, 1985, p. 132.

26 Ibid, p. 132.

27 Isaac Bonewits, 'Witchcult: Fact or Fancy?', *Gnostica*, Vol. III, no. 4, 1973, p. 5.

CHAPTER 6

1 J G Frazer, *The Golden Bough: A Study in Magic and Religion*, 1957, p. 930.

2 Sibyl Leek, *Moon Signs*, 1977, p. 17.

3 *The precession of the equinoxes*: as the earth moves around the sun, its axis wobbles imperceptibly and a circle is traced in the skies. It takes 26,000 years for the earth to describe this circle. This great round gives us the World Ages, of Pisces and Aquarius etc. The cycle appears to be moving counterclockwise through the zodiac, thus we are at present moving from the age of Pisces into the Age of Aquarius. See Maggie Hyde, *Jung and Astrology*, 1992, Chapter I.

4 Marsilio Ficino, *Opera Omnia*, 1576, p. 537.

5 By traditional astrology, I mean that which was practised and written about by seventeenth-century astrologers such as William Lilly, *Christian Astrology*, 1647. See Derek Appleby, *Horary Astrology, An Introduction to the Astrology of Time*, 1985.

6 See Elisabeth Brooke, 'Case of the Missing Gallstones', Company of Astrologers *Bulletin*, No. 3, 1990, pp. 8–12. 1991, *Mary's Red Flower*, p. 19–22.

7 M Best and F Brightman, *The Book of Secrets of Albertus Magnus*, 1973, p. 72.

8 Elisabeth Brooke, *Herbal Therapy for Women*, 1992, pp. 10–11, and pp. 44–9 for a discussion of the same.

9 Barbara Walker, *Women's Encyclopedia of Myths and Secrets*, 1983, p. 642.

10 Ibid, p. 642.

11 Elisabeth Brooke, op. cit., pp. 44–9.

12 Mary Daly, *Be-Laughing*, Women of Power Magazine, issue eight, Winter 1988, pp. 76–80, recounts Emily Culpepper's experience of taking on the Gorgon aspect when she confronts a man who broke into her house. He blanched and fled.

13 Especially that of Albertus Magnus, William Lilly, Nicholas Cul-

peper, and Marsilio Ficino who recorded women's wisdom and, being men, were to some extent safer from the ravages of the Inquisition.

14 Marsilio Ficino, op. cit., p. 157.

15 Thomas Moore, *The Planets Within*, 1982, pp. 157–9.

16 Marsilio Ficino, op. cit., p. 557.

17 Thomas Moore, op. cit., pp. 162–3.

18 A hetaira was a woman from ancient Greece who chose not to marry but took lovers. She was treated as an honorary man, in that she had access to education, had control over her property, and could mix freely in the world of men. She was usually a foreigner. For an in-depth analysis of the hetaira archetype, see Nor Hall, *The Moon and the Virgin*, 1980, pp. 133–160.

19 Plato, *The Symposium*, 1959, p. 50.

20 Thomas Moore, op. cit., p. 110.

21 Plutarch, quoted by Nor Hall, *The Moon and the Virgin*, Reflections on the Archetypal Feminine, 1980, p. xiii, no reference given.

22 To get a copy of your chart try the chart calculation service of the Company of Astrologers, 6 Queen Square, London WC1 3AR. You need to know your date, time and place of birth. Read Lindsay River and Sally Gillespie, *The Knot of Time: Astrology and Female Experience*, 1987, for the meaning of the planets, signs or houses, or, better still, treat yourself to a consultation from an astrologer. But avoid computer printouts.

23 Zsuszanna Budapest, *The Feminist Book of Light and Shadows*, Vol. I, 1979, p. 75.

24 It is beyond the brief of this book to go into a lengthy discourse about astrology. See Lindsay River and Sally Gillespie, op. cit., for a comprehensive guide to astrological symbolism. And Raphael's *Ephemeris* is published each year, in September for the following year, and details the movements of the planets as well as the exact times of new and full moons.

25 Sibyl Leek, op. cit., p. 148.

26 Organised by the Lucis Trust, 3 Whitehall Court, London, SW1.

CHAPTER 7

1 Traditionally women have menstruated around the new or dark moon, see Penelope Shuttle and Peter Redgrave, *The Wise Wound*, 1980, pp. 156–8. Modern women, however, have other cycles. My friend Mary Swale says that she bleeds at the full moon and ovulates at the dark moon. So for her, 'the full moon is the blood drawn forth, and the dark is the secret coming of the egg.'

2 Glamour is the witch's ability to create illusions, to make spells, to confuse and distort reality.

3 See the Appendix on Correspondences for various incenses and anointing oils.

4 Don't worry if you hate water, can't swim. In guided imagery the psyche finds its way around the physically impossible or unappealing by inventing chair-lifts, barges. flying and other means of transport. The point is your intent should be to move, in whatever way is possible for you.

5 *I Ching or Book of Changes*, translated by Richard Wilhelm, 1965, p. 185.

6 See Elisabeth Brooke, *An Astrological Herbal for Women*, 1995, p. 9.

CHAPTER 8

1 The main sources have been Christina Hole, *English Custom and Usage*, 1941; P H Ditchfield, *Old English Customs*, 1896; Eleanor Hull, *Folklore of the British Isles*, 1928; Charles Hardwick, *Traditions, Superstitions, and Folklore*, 1872; Robert Graves, *The White Goddess*, 1961; and J G Frazer, *The Golden Bough*, 1957.

2 Christina Hole, ibid, p. 10.

3 Eleanor Hull, op. cit., p. 227.

4 R W Chamber, *The Book of Days*, 1863, p. 519.

5 Robert Graves, op. cit., pp. 182–3.

6 Ibid, p. 253.

7 Ibid, p. 253.

8 Ibid, p. 203.

9 Ibid, p. 260.

10 Eleanor Hull, op. cit., p. 241, quoting *Silva Gadelica I*, translated by S H O'Grady, p. 121.

11 Ibid, p. 228.

12 By forgiveness I don't mean the Judeo-Christian turning the other cheek, but allowing for differences in other people and letting go of your part in the quarrel.

13 Christina Hole, op. cit., p. 22.

14 P H Ditchfield, op. cit., p. 29.

15 Robert Graves, op. cit., p. 36.

16 Ibid, p. 260.

17 Lucius Apuleius, *The Golden Ass*, translated by Robert Graves, 1959.

18 Robert Graves, op. cit., p. 184.

19 Christina Hole, op. cit., p. 32.

20 Robert Graves, op. cit, p. 412, quoting 'Carmina Gadelica,' a Gaelic poem.

21 Ibid, p. 199.

22 Robin Skelton and Margaret Blackwood, *Earth, Air, Fire, Water*, 1990, p. 158.

23 Ibid, p. 103.

24 Barbara Walker, *The Women's Encyclopedia of Myths and Secrets*, 1983, p. 267.

25 Robert Graves, op. cit., p. 293.

26 Philip Stubbes, *The Anatomie of Abuses*, 1583. [No page numbers.]

27 Christina Hole, op. cit., p. 6.

28 Eleanor Hull, op. cit., p. 256.

29 Quoted by Christina Hole, op. cit., p. 69. [Not referenced.]

30 Ibid, p. 73.

31 Charles Hardwick, op. cit., pp. 147–8.

32 Ibid, p. 148.

33 Robert Graves, op. cit., p. 301.

CHAPTER 9

1 Andy Smith, 'For All Those Who Were Indian in a Former Life,' *Woman of Power* magazine, No. 19, Winter 1991, pp. 74–6.

2 Alice Bailey, *The Destiny of the Nations*, 1949, pp. 107–36.

3 S L MacGregor Mathers, quoted by Robin Skelton in *Spellcraft: A Manual of Verbal Magic*, 1978.

4 Zsuzsanna Budapest, 'Political Witchcraft,' *Woman of Power* magazine, No. 8, winter 1988, pp. 38–40.

5 Mantram of the New Group of World Servers, The Lucis Trust, 3 Whitehall Court, London SW1.

CHAPTER 10

1 Robin Skelton, *Spellcraft*, 1978, p. 17.

2 Webster's Collegiate Dictionary, seventh edition, 1963, p. 840.

3 Mary Daly and Jane Caputi, *Webster's First New Intergalactic Wickedary of the English Language*, 1988, p. 165.

4 William Pitt-Root, *Striking the Dark Air for Music*, 1973, p. 86.

5 See Chapter 7, Ritual, for the outline of a basic ritual.

CHAPTER 11

1 See Roberto Assagioli, *Psychosynthesis: A Collection of Basic Writings*, 1976, p. 145; also Piero Ferrucci, *What We may Be: The Visions and Techniques of Psychosynthesis*, 1982.

2 'See' in this context means more 'see-feel'. Most people sense rather than see the aura, but gifted and trained people will see details such as dark spots, leaks, etc.

3 C W Leadbeater, *The Chakras*, 1927, p. 4.

4 The Yoga sutras of Patanjali. There are various translations; the one I use is: Alice Bailey, *The Light of the Soul*, 1922.

5 Alice Bailey, *Esoteric Psychology Vols I and II*, 1936–1942.

6 Carlos Castaneda, *The Teachings of Don Juan*, 1970, pp. 180–247; Carlos Castaneda, *Tales of Power*, 1976, p. 118. See also Donald Lee Williams, *Border Crossings: A Psychological Perspective on Carlos Castaneda's Path of Knowledge*, 1981, pp. 84–91 and 100–102.

7 All the chakras correspond to nerve plexuses in the body. Similarly there is a connection between the chakras and hormonal secretions. See Alice Bailey, *The Soul and its Mechanism*, 1930, pp. 30–54.

8 For example, Alice Bailey's work with the Tibetan, op. cit., which she undertook extremely reluctantly.

CHAPTER 12

1 Diane Wolkstein and Samuel Kramer, *Innana Queen of Heaven and Earth*, 1984, p. 53.

2 Elizabeth Haich, *The Wisdom of the Tarot*, 1975, p. 22. See also Eberhard Zangger, *The Flood from Heaven: Deciphering the Legend of Atlantis*, 1992.

3 Court de Gebelin, *Le Monde Primitif*, 1781, quoted by Stephen Hoeller, *The Royal Road*, 1975, p. 1.

4 Frederick Lionel, *The Magical Tarot, Vehicle of Eternal Wisdom*, 1980, p. 7.

5 Eliphas Levi, cited by Stephen Hoeller, op. cit., p. xii.

6 Some say THE MAGICIAN is ruled by Mercury, and THE HIGH PRIESTESS by the Moon.

7 A E Waite moved THE JUSTICE card to XI (11) and STRENGTH to VIII (8) so that the astrology would match and be sequential. Here, JUSTICE is Libra, which comes after STRENGTH, which he gives to Leo in the zodiac. Older packs, however, always put JUSTICE first and I have kept to that order.

8 Elinor Gadon, *The Once and Future Goddess*, 1990, p. 124.

9 See Elisabeth Brooke, *A Woman's Book of Herbs*, 1992, p. 7 for a discussion of the four humours.

10 Sally Gerhart and Susan Rennie, *A Feminist Tarot: a guide to intrapersonal communication*, 1977, p. x.

CHAPTER 13

1 Roberto Assagioli was a pupil of the psychotherapist Carl Jung and also the Tibetan teacher of Alice Bailey. He developed Psychosynthesis, based on their teachings.

2 Robert Graves, *The White Goddess*, 1961, p. 27.

3 Elisabeth Brooke, *A Woman's Book of Herbs*, 1992.

4 Bill Griffiths, *The Nine Herb Charm*, 1981. [No page numbers.]

5 Billie Potts, *Witches Heal*, Lesbian Herbal Self Sufficiency, 1981.

6 Carlos Castaneda, *The Teachings of Don Juan*, 1970.

7 Ibid, pp. 74–8.

8 Carlos Castaneda, *The Second Ring of Power*, 1977, p. 233.

9 Carlos Castaneda, op. cit., 1970, p. 56.

10 Robert Graves, op. cit., pp. 166–188.

11 Elizabeth Brandon-Jones from her proposal for the Witch Garden, the rest of the quotes come from this source unless referenced.

12 Isobel Irvine, *Witch Garden*, Panakaeia Magazine, no. 7, Beltane 1985, p. 19.

13 Marie McGoldrick, *The Herbal Medicine Wheel*, Panakaeia, no. 8, Autumn Equinox 1987, pp. 14–16.

14 Ibid, p. 15.

15 Ibid.

16 Leo Vinci, *Incense: Its Ritual Significance, Use and Preparation*, 1980, p. 14.

BIBLIOGRAPHY

Achterberg, Jeanne, *Woman as Healer*, Rider, London, 1990.

Adler, Margot, *Drawing Down The Moon, Witches, Druids, Goddess-Worshippers, and Other Pagans in America Today*, Revised edition, Beacon Press, Boston, MA, 1986.

Anon., *Meditations on the Tarot*, Amity, New York, 1985.

Apuleius, Lucius, *The Golden Ass*, translated by Robert Graves, Penguin, Harmondsworth, 1950.

Appleby, Derek, *Horary Astrology: An Introduction to the Astrology of Time*, Aquarian Press, Wellingborough, 1985.

Ashcroft-Nowicki, Dolores, *Inner Landscapes*, Aquarian Press, Wellingborough, 1989.

Assagioli, Roberto, *Psychosynthesis: A Collection of Basic Writings*, Penguin, Harmondsworth, 1976.

Bachofen, Johann, J, *Myth, Religion, and Mother Right*, Princeton/Bollingen, New Jersey, 1967.

Bailey, Alice, *The Light of the Soul*, The Lucis Press, London, 1922.

Bailey, Alice, *The Soul and Its Mechanism*, The Lucis Press, London, 1930.

Bailey, Alice, *Esoteric Psychology*, Vols 1–5, The Lucis Press, London, 1936–1942.

Bailey, Alice, *The Destiny of Nations*, The Lucis Press, London, 1949.

Beauvoir, Simone de, *The Second Sex*, Penguin, Harmondsworth, 1972.

Best, M, and Brightman, F, *The Book of Secrets of Albertus Magnus on the Virtues of Herbs, Stones and Certain Beasts*, also *A Book of Marvels of the World*, 1550. [Reprint, Clarendon Press, Oxford, 1973.]

Bierhorst, John (ed), *In the Trail of the Wind: American Indian*

Poems and Ritual Orations, Farrar, Strauss & Giroux, New York, 1971.

Bonewits, P E I, *Real Magic*, Creative Arts Book Company, Berkeley, 1971.

Bonewits, P E I, 'Witchcult: Fact or Fancy?,' *Gnostica*, Vol III, no. 4, 1973.

Bradley, Marion Zimmer, *The Mists of Avalon*, Michael Joseph, London, 1983.

Brooke, Eisabeth, *A Woman's Book of Herbs*, The Women's Press, London, 1992.

Brooke, Elisabeth, *Herbal Therapy for Women*, Thorsens, London, 1992.

Brooke, Elisabeth, *Women Healers Through History*, The Women's Press, London, 1993.

Brownmiller, Susan, *Against Our Will: Men, Women, and Rape*, Simon & Schuster, New York, 1975.

Buckland, Raymond, *The Complete Book of Saxon Witchcraft*, Weiser, New York, 1974.

Budapest, Zsuzsanna E, *The Holy Book of Women's Mysteries*, Part I, Susan B Anthony Coven No. 1, Oakland, 1979.

Budapest, Zsuzsanna E, *The Holy Book of Women's Mysteries*, Part II, Susan B Anthony Coven No. 1, Los Angeles, 1980.

of Knowledge, Penguin, Harmondsworth, 1970.

Castaneda, Carlos, *A Separate Reality*, Penguin, Harmondsworth, 1973.

Castaneda, Carlos, *Tales of Power*, Penguin, Harmondsworth, 1976.

Castaneda, Carlos, *The Second Ring of Power*, Penguin, Harmondsworth, 1979.

Chamber, R W, *The Book of Days*, 2 Vols, Chambers, London, 1863.

Cirlot, J E, *A Dictionary of Symbols*, Routledge & Kegan Paul, 1962.

Cockayne, The Reverend Oswald, *Leechdoms, Wortcunning and Starcraft in Early England*, Longman, London, 1866, Vols, I, II and III.

Cohn, Norman, *Europe's Inner Demons*, Chatto Heinemann, London, 1975.

238

Crowley, Aleister, *The Book of Thoth*, Samuel Weiser, New York, 1972.

Culpeper, Nicholas, *The Ephemeris of 1651*. [Held in the British Library.]

Daly, Mary, *Gyn/Ecology: The Metaethics of Radical Feminism*, The Women's Press, London, 1979.

Daly, Mary with Caputi, Jane, *Webster's First New Intergalactic Wickedary of the English Language*, The Women's Press, London, 1988.

Ditchfield, P H, *Old English Customs*, Geo. Redway, London, 1896.

Douglas, Alfred, *The Tarot*, Penguin, Harmondsworth, 1976.

Dunstan, Stephen, *Tarot Poems*, Bloodaxe Books, Newcastle upon Tyne, 1980.

Dworkin, Andrea, *Woman Hating*, Dutton, New York, 1974.

Ehrenreich, Barbara, and English, Deirdre, *Witches, Midwives & Nurses*, Feminist Press, Old Westbury, New York, 1974.

Evelyn-White, E (translator), *The Homeric Hymns*, Loeb, London, 1920.

Fairfield, Gail, *Choice Centered Tarot*, Choice Centered Astrology and Tarot Publishing, Seattle, 1982.

Ferrucci, Piero, *What We May Be: The Visions and Techniques of Psychosynthesis*, Turnstone Press, Wellingborough, 1982.

Ficino, Marsilio, *Opera Omnia*, 2 Vols, Basel, 1576.

Franz, Marie Louise von, *The Problem of Evil in Fairy Tales: a collection of essays*, C G Jung Institute, Zurich, 1967.

Frazer, J G, *The Golden Bough: A Study in Magic and Religion*, Macmillan, London, 1957.

Frost, Gavin and Frost, Yvonne, *A Witch's Grimoire of Ancient Omens, Portents, Talismans, Amulets and Charms*, Parker, West Nyack, New York, 1979.

Gadon, Elinor, *The Once and Future Goddess*, Aquarian Press, Wellingborough, 1990.

Gage, Matilda Joslyn, *Women, Church and State*, Persephone Press, Watertown, MA, 1980. [First edition 1893.]

Gantz, Jeffrey (translator), *The Mabinogion*, Penguin, London, 1976.

Gardner, Gerald B, *Witchcraft Today*, Citadel Press, New York, 1955.

Gardner, Gerald B, *The Meaning of Witchcraft*, Samuel Weiser, New York, 1959.

Gardner, Richard, *The Tarot Speaks*, Wyndham, London, 1976.

Gardner, Richard, *Evolution through the Tarot*, Samuel Weiser, New York, 1977.

Gerhart, Sally and Rennie, Susan, *A Feminist Tarot: a guide to intrapersonal communication*, Persephone Press, Watertown, MA, 1977.

Gibran, Kahlil, *The Prophet*, Heinemann, London, 1966.

Gimbutas, Marija, *The Gods and Goddesses of Old Europe, 7000–3000 BC, Myths, Legends and Cult Images*, Thames & Hudson, 1974.

Goodison, Lucy, *Moving Heaven and Earth: Sexuality, Spirituality and Social Change*, Pandora, London, 1992.

Gordeon, B L, *Mediaeval and Renaissance Medicine*, Peter Owen, London, 1959.

Gordon, Lesley, *Green Magic*, Ebury Press, London, 1977.

Graves, Robert, *The White Goddess*, Faber and Faber, London, 1961.

Grieve, Maude, *A Modern Herbal*, Peregrine Books, London, 1976.

Griffiths, Bill, *The Nine Herb Charm*, Tern Press (no town given), 1981.

Haich, Elisabeth, *The Wisdom of the Tarot*, Allen & Unwin, London, 1975.

Hall, Nor, *The Moon and The Virgin*, The Women's Press, London, 1980.

Harding, Esther, *Women's Mysteries*, Colophon Books, New York, 1971.

Hardwick, Charles, *Traditions, Superstitions, and Folklore*, A Ireland & Co, Manchester, 1872.

Harrison, Jane, *Epilegomena to the Study of Greek Religion*, Cambridge University Press, Cambridge, 1921.

Harrison, Jane, *Prolegomena to the Study of Greek Religion*, Merlin Press, London, 1961. [First published 1922.]

Harrison, Jane, *Themis: A study of the social origins of Greek religion*, Cambridge University Press, Cambridge, 1927.

Hoeller, Stephen, *The Royal Road, A Manual of Kabbalistic Meditations on the Tarot*, Quest, Wheaton, Illinois, 1975.

240

Hole, Christina, *English Custom and Usage*, Batsford, London, 1941.

Hope, R C, *Holy Wells of England*, Eliot Stock, London, 1893.

Hoyt, Charles Alva, *Witchcraft*, Southern Illinois University Press, Carbondale and Edwardsville, Illinois, 1981.

Hull, Eleanor, *Folklore of the British Isles*, Methuen, London, 1928.

Hyde, Maggie, *Jung and Astrology*, Aquarian, London, 1992.

Innes, Brian, *The Tarot*, Orbis, London, 1977.

Jung, Carl, *Psychological Reflections*, edited by Jolande Jaobi, Harper Torchbooks, New York, 1961.

Jung, C G and Kerenyi, C, *The Science of Mythology: Essays on the Myth of the Divine Child and the Mysteries of Eleusis*, Ark, London, 1985.

Kaplan, Stuart, *The Classical Tarot: its origins, meanings and divinatory use*, Aquarian Press, Wellingborough, 1980.

Kenton, Warren, *The Celestial Mirror*, Thames and Hudson, London, 1974.

Kerenyi, C, *Eleusis*, vol. 4 of *Series Archetypal Images in Greek Religion*, Routledge & Kegan Paul, London, 1967.

Kerenyi, C, *Gods of the Greeks*, translated by Norman Cameron, Penguin, London, 1958.

Koltuv, Barbara Black, *The Book of Lilith*, Nicholas Hays, York Beach, Maine, 1986.

Lao Tzu, *Tao Te Ching*, Translated by D C Lau, Penguin, Harmondsworth, 1963.

Larner, Christina, *Enemies of God: The Witch Hunt in Scotland*, Chatto & Windus, London, 1981.

Leadbeater, C W, *The Chakras*, Theosophical Publishing House, Wheaton, Illinois, 1927.

Leek, Sibyl, *Moon Signs*, W H Allen, London, 1977.

Leland, Charles Godfrey, *Aradia, or Gospel of the Witches*, David Nutt, London, 1899.

Levi, Eliphas, *The Key to the Mysteries*, Translated by A Crowley, Rider and Co, London, 1969.

Lilly, William, *Christian Astrology*, Regulus Publishing (no town given), 1985. [Reprint from 1647 edition.]

Lionel, Frederic, *The Magical Tarot: Vehicle of Eternal Wisdom*, Routledge & Kegan Paul, London, 1980.

Long, George, *The Folklore Calendar*, Philip Allen, London, 1930.

Loomis, R S, *Arthurian Literature in the Middle Ages*, Oxford University Press, Oxford, 1959.

Mariechild, Diane, *Mother Wit: A Feminist Guide to Psychic Development*, The Crossing Press, New York, 1981.

Matthews, Caitlin and Matthews, John, *The Western Way: A Practical Guide to the Western Mystery Tradition*, Arcana, London, 1985.

Matthews, Caitlin and Matthews, John, *Hallowquest*, Aquarian Press, Wellingborough, 1990.

Moonfire, Blue, *The Matriarchal Zodiac*, self-published, London, 1985.

Moore, Thomas, *The Planets Within, Ficino's Astrological Psychology*, Bucknell University Press, Toronto, 1982.

Murray, Margaret, *The Witch Cult in Western Europe: A Study in Anthropology*, Oxford University Press, Oxford, 1921.

Murray, Margaret, *The God of the Witches*, Oxford University Press, Oxford, 1933.

Murray, Margaret, *The Divine King in England*, Oxford University Press, Oxford, 1954.

Neumann, Erich, *The Great Mother, An Analysis of the Archetype*, Princeton Bollinger, Princeton, 1972.

Nichols, Sally, *Jung and The Tarot*, Weiser, New York, 1980.

Noble, Viki, *Motherpeace: A Way to the Goddess through Myth, Art and Tarot*, Harper & Row, San Francisco, 1983.

Ouspensky, P D, *The Symbolism of the Tarot*, Dover, New York, 1976.

Packwood, Marlene, *Witchcraft in the Middle Ages*, London, 1980. [Pamphlet]

Pagels, Elaine, *The Gnostic Gospels*, Penguin, Harmondsworth, 1979.

Papus, *The Tarot of the Bohemians*, translated by A P Morton, Arcanum Books, New York, 1965.

Parvati, Jean, *Hygieia: A Woman's Herbal*, Wildwood House, London, 1979.

Paul, Hayden, *Queen of the Night, Discovering the Astrological Moon*, Element Books, Shaftesbury, 1990.

Pera, Sylvia Brinton, *Descent to the Goddess*, Inner City Books, Toronto, 1932.

242

Peters, Edward, *The Magician, The Witch and the Law*, Harvester Press, Hassocks, Sussex, 1978.

Pitt-Root, William, *Striking the Dark Air for Music*, Atheneum, London, 1973.

Plato, *The Symposium*, Penguin, Harmondsworth, 1965.

Plutarch, *Moralia III*, translated by F C Babbit, Harvard University Press, Cambridge, MA 1968. [15 Vols.]

Pollack, Rachel, *Seventy-Eight Degrees of Wisdom*, Part I, Aquarian Press, Wellingborough, 1980.

Potts, Billie, *A New Women's Tarot*, Elf and Dragon Press, Woodstock, 1977.

Potts, Billie, *Witches Heal*, Lesbian Herbal Self Sufficiency, Hecubas Daughters Inc., Woodstock, 1981.

Raine, Kathleen, *Yeats, the Tarot and the Golden Dawn*, Dolmen Press, Dublin, 1968.

Rakoczi, Basil, *The Painted Caravan*, L J Bouche, The Hague, 1954.

Raphael's *Ephemeris*, published yearly, Foulsham & Co, Slough.

Rich, Adrienne, *Of Woman Born, Motherhood as Experience and Institution*, Virago, London, 1977.

River, Lindsay, and Gillespie, Sally, *The Knot of Time: Astrology and Female Experience*, The Women's Press, London, 1987.

Rohde, Elenor Sinclair, *Old English Herbals*, Minerva Press, London, 1972.

Rudhyar, Dane, *The Lunation Cycle*, Thorsen Aurora Press, New York, 1986.

Russell, Jeffrey Barton, *Witchcraft in the Middle Ages*, Cornell University Press, Ithaca and London, 1972.

Shephard, John, *The Tarot Trumps: The cosmos in miniature*, Aquarian Press, Wellingborough, 1985.

Shuttle, Penelope and Redgrove, Peter, *The Wise Wound: Menstruation and Every Woman*, Penguin, London, 1980.

Sjöö, Monica and Mor, Barbara, *The Great Cosmic Mother: Rediscovering the Religion of the Earth*, Harper & Row, San Francisco, 1987.

Skelton, Robin, *Spellcraft: A Manual of Verbal Magic*, Routledge & Kegan Paul, London, 1978.

Skelton, Robin and Blackwood, Margaret, *Earth, Air, Fire,*

Water: Pre-Christian and Pagan Elements in British Songs, Rhymes and Ballads, Arcana, London, 1990.

Smith, K V, *The Illustrated Earth Garden Herbal*, Nelson, Melbourne, 1978.

Sophocles, *Oedipus at Colonus*, translated by Robert Fitzgerald, Faber and Faber, London, 1951.

Spence, Lewis, *The Mysteries of Britain*, Aquarian Press, London, 1928.

Spretnak, Charlene, *Lost Goddesses of Early Greece, A Collection of pre-Hellenic Mythology*, Moon Books, Berkeley, 1978.

Spretnak, Charlene (ed.), *The Politics of Women's Spirituality, Essays on the Rise of Spiritual Power within the Feminist Movement*, Anchor Press, New York, 1982.

Starhawk, *The Spiral Dance: Rebirth of the Ancient Religion of the Great Goddess*, Harper & Row, San Francisco, 1979.

Starhawk, *Dreaming the Dark, Magic, Sex and Politics*, Beacon Press, Boston, 1982.

Starhawk, *Truth or Dare, Encounters with Power, Authority, and Mystery*, HarperCollins, San Francisco, 1990.

Stone, Merlin, *Ancient Mirrors of Womanhood*, Beacon Press, Boston, 1984.

Strabo, *Geography*, 8 Vols, edited and translated by H L Jones, Loeb Classical Library, London, 1917–1932.

Stuart, Micheline, *The Tarot Path to Self Development*, Routledge & Kegan Paul, London, 1977.

Summers, Reverend Montague, *The History of Witchcraft and Demonology*, Kegan Paul, London, 1926.

Summers, Reverend Montague, *Malleus Malificarum*, Pushkin Press, London, 1948.

Thomson, William, MD, *Healing Plants*, Macmillan, New York, 1980.

Tindall, Gillian, *A Handbook on Witches*, Arthur Barker, London, 1965.

Trevor-Roper, Hugh, *The European Witchcraze of the Sixteenth & Seventeenth Centuries*, Penguin, Harmondsworth, 1969.

Usher, Arland, *The Twenty Two Keys of the Tarot*, Dolmen Press, Dublin, 1976.

Uyldert, Mellie, *The Psychic Garden: Plants and their Esoteric Relationship with Man*, Thorsens, Wellingborough, 1980.

Valiente, Doreen, *The ABC of Witchcraft Past and Present*, St. Martins Press, New York, 1973.

Vinci, Leo, *Incense: Its Ritual Significance, Use and Preparation*, Aquarian Press, Wellingborough, 1980.

Virgil, *Georgics*, translated by H R Fairclough, Loeb, London, 1916–18.

Waite, A E, *Pictorial Key to the Tarot*, University Books, New York, 1959.

Walker, Barbara, *The Women's Encyclopedia of Myths and Secrets*, Harper & Row, San Francisco, 1983.

Walker, Barbara G, *The Secrets of the Tarot: Origins, History, and Symbolism*, Harper & Row, San Francisco, 1984.

Walker, Barbara G, *The Crone: Woman of Age, Wisdom, and Power*, HarperCollins, New York, 1988.

Wang, Robert, *An Introduction to Golden Dawn Tarot*, Aquarian Press, Wellingborough, 1978.

Wilhelm, Richard, *The I Ching or book of changes*, Routledge & Kegan Paul, London, 1965.

Williams, Donald Lee, *Border Crossings: A Psychological Perspective on Carlos Castaneda's Path of Knowledge*, Inner City Books, Toronto, 1981.

Wittig, Monique, *The Guerilleres*, Bard Books, New York, 1969.

Wolkstein, Diane, and Kramer, Samuel, *Innana Queen of Heaven and Earth*, Rider, London, 1984.

Young, Alan, *Spiritual Healing: Miracle or Mirage?*, De Vorss & Co, Marina del Rey, California, 1981.

Zangger, Eberhard, *The Flood from Heaven: Deciphering the Legend of Atlantis*, Pan, London, 1992.

Periodicals

Company of Astrologers Bulletin, 6 Queen Square, London WC1 3AR.

Dog's Mercury, London 1980–1992. (Occasional.)

Gnosis, PO Box 14217, San Francisco, CA 94114.

The Herbal Review, The Herb Society, Boscobel Place, London SW1. (Quarterly.)

Panakaeia, London, 1984. (Occasional.)

*Woman of Power Magazine: A magazine of feminism, spiritu-
    ality, and politics*, PO Box 827, Cambridge, MA.
    (Quarterly.)
Woman of Power Magazine, No. 15, Fall/Winter 1990, 'Faces
    of the Goddess'.
Woman of Power Magazine, No. 19, Winter 1991, 'Ritual and
    Magic'.

Tarot Packs
For beginners, I would recommend the Rider-Waite deck as I
find the symbolism particularly evocative and the cards are
easily available. The Motherpeace deck is delightful and
multicultural, although the cards are to my mind too large to
handle easily. This is another good beginners' deck. The book
is a stimulating, thought-provoking read. Another modern
deck I fell in love with is the Hallowquest deck and the
beautiful book that goes with it, ideal for anyone wanting to
learn more about the Arthurian cycle.

I use the Marseille deck for myself and the Bembo (also
known as the Visconti-Sforza) pack. The Crowley cards are
beautifully painted and are attractive in their own right.

Many booksellers now stock Tarot cards; all of the above
are distributed by US Games Systems.

Index

RELATED BOOKS BY THE CROSSING PRESS

An Astrological Herbal for Women
By Elizabeth Brooke
$12.95 • Paper • 0-89594-740-4

Ariadne's Thread: A Workbook of Goddess Magic
By Shekhinah Mountainwater
$14.95 • Paper • 0-89594-475-8

Casting the Circle: A Woman's Book of Ritual
By Diane Stein
$14.95 • Paper • 0-89594-411-1

*Creating Circles of Power and Magic:
A Woman's Guide to the Sacred Community*
By Caitlin Libera
$12.95 • Paper • 0-89594-712-9

The Dark Goddess: Dancing with the Shadow
By Marcia Starck and Gynne Stern
$10.95 • Paper • 0-89594-603-3

*The Goddess Book of Days:
A Perpetual 366-Day Engagement Calendar*
By Diane Stein
$10.95 • Paper • 0-89594-551-7

*The Goddess Celebrates: An Anthology of Women's
Rituals*
Edited by Diane Stein
$14.95 • Paper • 0-89594-460-X

Lady of Northern Light: A Feminist Guide to the Runes
By Susan Gitlin-Emmer
$12.95 • Paper • 0-89594-629-7